Material cultures

Consumption and space

Series editors

Peter Jackson, *University of Sheffield*
Michelle Lowe, *University of Southampton*
Frank Mort, *University of Portsmouth*

Adopting an inter-disciplinary perspective and combining contemporary and historical analysis, *Consumption and space* aims to develop a dialogue between cultural studies and human geography, opening up areas for serious intellectual debate.

Published

Sean Nixon
Hard looks: masculinities, spectatorship and contemporary consumption

Daniel Miller (editor)
Material cultures: why some things matter

Material cultures
Why some things matter

Edited by

Daniel Miller
University College London

UCL
PRESS

First published in 1998 by UCL Press

UCL Press Limited
Taylor & Francis Group
1 Gunpowder Square
London EC4A 3DE

20180721

The name of University College London (UCL) is a registered
trade mark used by UCL Press with the consent of the owner.

British Library Cataloguing-in-Publication Data
A CIP catalogue record for this book is available from the British Library.

Library of Congress Cataloging-in-Publication Data are available

ISBNs: 1-85728-685-5 HB
         1-85728-686-3 PB

Typeset by Solidus (Bristol) Limited, UK.
Printed by Arrowhead Books Limited, Reading, UK.

To the memory of Beatrice Hart

Contents

Acknowledgements

The introduction makes note of the fact that all the contributors worked together for several years as a team in order to produce this volume. But it does not acknowledge the social context through which this was done. Indeed the most important acknowledgement in this case should perhaps go to the role of alcohol, without which it is doubtful that this volume would have been produced, or at least with the degree of enthusiasm and excitement that I hope comes through in the various chapters. As you might guess, such an acknowledgement begs a story.

The story begins in January 1992. All the contributors to this volume except Sophie Chevalier were registered as students in the Department of Anthropology, University College London, working for their PhDs under my supervision. Since many of them had families and found it difficult to come in for most of the more regular departmental functions, we decided to initiate a monthly evening meeting at which one of us would present a pre-circulated chapter that would be discussed by the others. The first evening set up a routine that has since remained unaltered. We would meet at around 5.00pm at a pub near the department. Here we would sit and drink, gossip and talk about things and persons in a manner that shall certainly not be repeated in print. At some time around 7.05pm (when I tend to get restless since my mental "clock" is telling me I am missing *The Archers* – a radio soap opera) we would move on to a nearby Italian restaurant that had the advantages of being relatively inexpensive, self-service and having large tables with, on a weekday, relatively few people. At this point beer could give way to wine and gossip to discussion of the chapter in question. By this point also, enough alcohol had usually been consumed that the comments that paper-givers received were often of a fairly robust and uninhibited kind, so that we all bear the scars of our particular encounters with the group. This was the public sphere within which the various ideas and papers rewritten as chapters of this book were created.

Sophie Chevalier is the exception here, in that she came as a post-doctoral student after studying with Martine Segalen in Paris. Although based at

Cambridge, she became a regular attender at these evenings for a period of two years and contributed papers to the group along with the others. The drinking group has also included visitors who have come for a year from abroad, Denmark and Israel in the past, Estonia currently. On these grounds acknowledgement must be given to all those who were either participants for at least a year or who are current members of this group but not included in this volume. These are Pauline Garvey, Anat Hecht, Denise Homme, Esther Juhatz, Anu Kannike, Gertrude Ollgaard, Andrew Skuse and Karen Smith. Although I am formally the editor of the collection it is the case that virtually everything has been read by everybody at some stage or other, and to that extent this is the product of a collective rather than any individual.

The book is dedicated to another member of the group – Bea Hart, who brought to us the same enthusiasm that was evident in all that she was involved with. Sadly Bea died while this book was in preparation and the dedication reflects our collective sense of loss.

Notes on contributors

Sophie Chevalier is Lecturer in Anthropology at the University of Besançon. Recent publications include Transmettre son mobilier? Le cas contraste de la France et d'Angleterre, in *Ethnologie Française*.

Alison J. Clarke is Senior Lecturer in the History of Design, University of Brighton. She is presently completing a volume of *Tupperware and post war consumption* for Smithsonian Press. Recent publications include Tupperware: suburbia, sociality and mass consumption, in *Visions of Suburbia* ed. R. Silverstone (London: Routledge).

Justin Finden-Crofts is completing a PhD thesis on the consumption of calypso at the Department of Anthropology, UCL.

Neil Jarman is a research officer at the University of Ulster (Coleraine). Recent publications include *Parade and protest* (with D. Bryan, University of Ulster) and *Parading culture* (Oxford: Berg).

Mark Johnson is Lecturer in Social Anthropology at the University of Hull. He has written several articles on transgendering and consumption in the Philippines, and *Beauty and power: transgendering and cultural transformation in the southern Philippines* (Oxford: Berg).

Daniel Miller is Professor of Anthropology at UCL. Recent publications include *Capitalism: an ethnographic approach* (Oxford: Berg), *Acknowledging consumption* (London: Routledge) and *Worlds apart* (London: Routledge).

Andrea Pellegram is a Planning Manager for a UK statutory authority.

Sigrid Rausing is completing a PhD on current transformations in Estonian identity at the Department of Anthropology, UCL.

Jo Tacchi is a Research Associate at the University of Bristol, studying teenage pregnancy, and completing a thesis on the consumption of radio sound at the Department of Anthropology, UCL.

PART I

Introduction

CHAPTER 1

Why some things matter

Daniel Miller

The title of this chapter is intended to be taken quite precisely. It is as different from the question "Why things matter", as it is from the question "Why some things are important". It is these differences that represent the original contribution of this volume. The question "Why things matter" would have led to the general study of materiality and the foundation of material culture studies in the insistence upon the continued importance of material forms. This was in effect the battle fought against mainstream social sciences in the 1970s and 1980s and the insistence that taxonomies of material forms were often of significance precisely because being disregarded as trivial, they were often a key unchallenged mechanism for social reproduction and ideological dominance.

The development of material culture studies may then be seen as a two-stage process. The first phase came in the insistence that things matter and that to focus upon material worlds does not fetishize them since they are not some separate superstructure to social worlds. The key theories of material culture developed in the 1980s demonstrated that social worlds were as much constituted by materiality as the other way around (e.g. Bourdieu 1977; Appadurai 1986; Miller 1987). This gave rise to a variety of approaches to the issue of materiality varying from material culture as analogous with text (e.g. Tilley 1990, 1991) to applications of social psychological models (Dittmar 1992).

This book represents a second stage in the development of material culture studies inasmuch as the point that things matter can now be argued to have been made. This volume, by contrast, concentrates on something different and equally important. The volume demonstrates what is to be gained by focusing upon the diversity of material worlds which becomes each other's contexts rather than reducing them either to models of the social world or to specific subdisciplinary concerns such as the study of textiles or architecture. It will be argued, by example, throughout this volume that studies of material culture may often provide insights into cultural processes that a more literal "anthropology" has tended to neglect.

A volume called *Material cultures* is obviously situated within what may be easily recognized as a general renaissance in the topic of material culture studies. After several decades in the academic doldrums this has re-emerged as a vanguard area liberating a range of disciplines from museum studies to archaeology. Although there are a large number of volumes and articles which together constitute the evidence for this development in academic interests, there are still relatively few publications that have as their particular concern the nature of material culture or material culture studies. This is in part because the subject does not exist as a given discipline, and it is not part of this volume's agenda to propose or attempt to legitimize any such discipline. As has been argued in the introductory editorial to the new *Journal of Material Culture*, there are many advantages to remaining undisciplined and many disadvantages and constraints imposed by trying to claim disciplinary status.

This freedom from disciplinary foundations and boundaries is used to considerable effect by the contributors to this volume. Together they demonstrate the excitement and rewards of taking an unshackled approach to the topic of material culture. More specifically this is expressed in a freedom from reductionism. Studies of the house do not have to be reduced to housing studies, nor studies of design to design studies. By the same token studies of the transnational identity of commodities do not have to be reduced to kinship, class or gender.

Prior to the very few works that act as precedents to the current volume, most works in material culture are best understood in relation to the issues that they address. In effect they make up relatively discrete bodies of texts formed around particular problematics. An early example was a series of works that centred upon historical archaeology in the USA and that was influenced by structural analysis but applied this to diachronic data (such as the work of Glassie 1975; Deetz 1977). This paralleled the concern for objects that was arising within European historical studies that conjoined macro-surveys of material culture, both at the regional level as advocated by Braudel (1981) and at the temporal level as advocated by Friedman and Rowlands (1977), with the micro-studies of specific context exemplified by Schama's (1987) work on Amsterdam (see also Brewer & Porter 1993). One of the most influential bodies of work has arisen from the discipline of anthropology and has been primarily concerned with the nature of commodities and consumption (Miller 1995a, 1995b). Key works include Douglas and Isherwood (1978), Appadurai (1986) and Bourdieu (1984). Another trend was the analysis of visual materials as pseudo-texts which, through journals such as *Screen*, dominated media studies for more than a decade. One of the most recent examples has emerged from a new self-consciousness within museum studies, and in particular, the focus upon collecting as a more general activity within industrialized societies (Belk 1995; Pearce 1995).

Indeed these few conspicuous examples of literatures that involved taking a stance with respect to material culture studies can easily turn into a flood depending upon how inclusive one is prepared to be. At the centre there is a continuity of tradition within the many European institutions of ethnology (Frykman and Löfgren 1987; Rogan 1992), as well as a continuous production of exemplary studies within more mainstream anthropology and sociology (Forrest 1988; Guss 1989; MacKenzie 1991). But on the margins there are a vast number of studies which range from obvious parallels with much of the work that has been developed through cultural studies (e.g. Grossberg et al. 1992) to some of the concerns within geography on space and place, or within architecture and design on the materiality of buildings. These also include many individual essays that seem to have arisen out of some particular eye for detail on artefacts such as record sleeves (Gilroy 1993) or other minutiae of everyday life (Baker 1986).

Each of these literatures contributes to the sense of vitality within material culture studies as a whole. Some, such as the work of Bourdieu (1977) in *Outline of a theory of practice,* have remained key texts for two decades. But in many cases material culture is better identified as a means rather than an end. Furthermore it was most often a means that emerged pragmatically from other concerns with little self-consciousness about the implications of this particular technology of investigation. There are exceptions, for example, the work of Ian Hodder (1982) and his students within which, although the initial agenda was archaeological interpretation, much of the work did focus on general issues within material culture studies (e.g. Hodder 1982; Moore 1986; Tilley 1990, 1991). One of the reasons that material culture was avoided as the primary focus of attention was that it invited the accusation of fetishism. It was assumed that the ideals of social analysis would be so usurped by the means of artefact analysis that this would prevent rather than enhance the study of cultural life that has been the avowed aim of all those who study material culture, including the contributors to this volume.

This legacy of these academic studies mainly conducted since the mid-1970s is the context for the present work. Our aim is to steer a course which unlike most of the work just reviewed, does indeed take as its immediate focus the study of material culture *per se*. But in using the term "material *culture*" we believe that there are many ways in which the results can be far less fetishistic than many of those works that do not purport to have such an object focus. At the same time the intention is to focus upon the artefactual world without this being founded in any general theory of artefacts or material culture. The next section is intended to indicate how this might be accomplished.

The diversity of material domains

Material culture differs from, for example, linguistics partly in the sheer diversity of its subject matter. In the case of language many of the most interesting things that an academic can address relate to the generality of linguistic phenomena. In material culture, by contrast, although this is also a possible strategy there is a great deal more potential in looking at the diversity of material form than would be the case with linguistics.

Languages consists of relatively few specific domains. These might include the written word, speech and grammar. Each divides up the larger sense of linguistics into domains with their own specificity. These remain relatively restrained and encompassable differences. By comparison, material culture virtually explodes the moment one gives any consideration to the vast corpus of different object worlds that we constantly experience. Within an hour of waking we move from the paraphernalia of interior furnishing through the decisions to be communicated over choices of apparel through the moral anxieties over the ingestion of food stuffs out into the variety of modern transport systems held within vast urban architectural and infrastructural forms. Each of these domains possesses considerable specificity in comparison to the others, and in turn generates considerable internal diversity.

For this reason the current volume attempts no general theory of the object world as an abstract set of relationships to be applied indiscriminately to a plethora of domains. Instead what this book addresses is perhaps rather more useful and exportable to the wide range of people who work with material culture though not necessarily within material culture studies. Unlike language we cannot hope even to enumerate the types and varieties within which the object world might be categorized and we are soon aware that any attempt imposes various arbitrary classifications over what is actually an endless creative and hybrid world. This problem of unordered diversity is perhaps one of the main stumbling blocks in the formation of a material culture studies as against linguistics, but it also offers a huge potential if we try to consider what it might offer academic analytical concerns. The clear imperative then is to turn what at first seems daunting and problematic into the very significance and interest of material culture studies.

To do this, I want to suggest that the generality of materiality, that is any attempt to construct general theories of the material quality of artefacts, commodities, aesthetic forms and so forth, must be complemented by another strategy that looks to the specificity of material domains and the way form itself is employed to become the fabric of cultural worlds. To a degree this has arisen by default. We have already constructed in academia specific journals and academies concerned with the study of food, of clothing, of architecture and so forth. Each of these takes as axiomatic the particular character of their domain. But because these have arisen by default through pragmatic and increasingly commercial concerns, they do not perceive themselves as part of a larger study of material culture and therefore at present do not even much concern themselves with how the specificity of each particular material domain might add up to the larger, as it were, generality of difference.

This, however, is exactly what material culture studies should do. It is of some concern that something so obvious in the potential of material culture at present remains overlooked. One of the disadvantages of the present state of academic study is that the specificity of material forms are most likely to be of interest and concern if they happen to fall within what has already become constituted as an institutional domain such as building studies or food studies. What this book is designed to demonstrate is how much is thereby lost. The topics that this volume covers may flow in and out of such previously constituted disciplines, but the bulk of what is addressed here would probably not find any easy or evident place in any of them, with the possible exception of anthropology. It is precisely because all the contributors take their commitment and orientation from material culture as a more general phenomena that they have emerged with such a fascinating set of diverse topics of enquiry.

So the positive potential of material culture studies is presented in the form of studies that range from musical forms such as calypso through gardens to the use of paper in the office. None of these chapters have to constrain themselves to fall within an institution devoted to furnishing, clothing or the arts. But this is only the first stage of what may be perceived to be the benefits of such an approach. Merely allowing more creative selection of topics of enquiry would itself be important, but it is what one does with the topic and not merely its selection that counts. This leads to the second stage in the development of such studies which is drawn from this same emphasis upon specificity.

The materiality of specific domains

There is a marked difference between the chapters of this volume coming out of material culture studies and the way these same topics might be addressed within some other tradition, and this is simply the degree of attention given to the specific materiality of each topic investigated. Indeed that this should be so follows directly from the first stage of delineating material culture studies. If we focus directly on the materiality of things then we must immediately confront the different forms of object that they represent.

The chapters that follow bring out clearly both this diversity but also what is gained by a focus upon their specificity. Let us take as an example Chapter 2 by Tacchi on radio soundscape. The author has used the very idea of material culture to interpose a key element between the more traditional studies of radio and its audience. This is textured soundscape that is emitted by radio and that is used to form a kind of space within the home. The material presence of a radio that is on is quite different from the little box constituted by a radio that is off. It fills an area with volume and substance and may be experienced as much as an emanation expressive of the associated individual as coming from the box itself. Indeed, using material culture as her foundation, Tacchi is able to make radio more like clothing than media, expressive of highly individualized presencing. At the same time she focuses on the particular qualities that radio has as radio. For example the material presence of sound is opposed to the equally material presence of silence as a form that, in relation to conditions such as loneliness, can have a quite oppressive, almost claustrophobic texture. If, as I suspect, Tacchi is able to evoke the manner in which some people can or indeed must "feel" silence with a poignancy that gives that sense of silence a particular presence for the reader, then the argument for its use as an example of material culture is surely made. Tacchi's findings emerge directly from her sensitivity to what here is being called the specificity of materiality.

Almost exactly the same point can be made with an entirely different medium in the case of Jarman in Chapter 6. It is easy to see what others are likely to make of the banners used in the Orange Order marches in Northern Ireland. These could easily be decontextualized as an item within the discussion of politics or as an icon within a presentation of art within a gallery or museum. By insisting that first we address the materiality of the banners, Jarman manages to contribute more to both the political and the aesthetic understanding of these forms than a more direct expropriation would have done in either case. First, Jarman draws attention to what the banners are made from and argues for the centrality of such textiles to the recent social and economic history of the area, which is precisely what makes them of such significance to political debate. In this and in his more general work on the topic, it is again a focus on the precise details of what is being portrayed and how it is being portrayed that prevents the banners being superficially recontextualized as art or craft objects and forces us to engage at a more profound level with the form and aesthetics of the banners as against some other expressive form such as murals or the phenomenon of marching itself.

A third case may be made from my own study of Coca-Cola in Chapter 8. Once again the literature on this topic is voluminous. But in almost all cases Coca-Cola is flung around as some generic symbol that stands for almost anything people want to fill it with. I argue that its presence is rather like that which Quinn (1994) has argued for the European use of the swastika, a kind of meta-symbol that is dangerously separated off from the world as a symbol of symbols or in this case commodity that stands for all commoditization. My argument is intended to directly confront this kind of free-floating symbol and bring it back down to its most basic artefactual quality as glass bottle containing a sweet fizzy drink. It is only then as material culture that we can address the actual context in which Coke becomes a quite specific element in the objectification of Trinidad as a whole and being Trinidadian as an identity divided between various component parts.

It is as unlikely that Jarman's chapter would have been written from a school of studies of textile than Tacchi's would come out of conventional media studies, or mine from studies of business. What we may regard as unique to our approach is that we remain focused upon the object that is being investigated but within a tradition that prevents any simple fetishization of material form. Indeed we feel it is precisely those studies that quickly move the focus from object to society in their fear of fetishism and their apparent embarrassment at being, as it were, caught gazing at mere objects, that retain the negative consequences of the term "fetishism". It is for them that Coke is merely a material symbol, banners stand in a simple moment of representation or radio becomes mere text to be analyzed. In such analysis the myriad diversity of artefacts can easily become reduced to generic forms such as "text", "art" or "semiotic". In such approaches it is not only the objects that remain fetishized but also, as Latour (1993) has argued with respect to the fetishism within debates about science, it is the idea of "society" as a kind of thing-like context to which all such materials should be properly reduced that becomes equally a moment of fetishism. Here, by contrast, through dwelling upon the more mundane sensual and material qualities of the object, we are able to unpick the more subtle connections with cultural lives and values that are objectified through these forms, in part, because of the particular qualities they possess. In a similar fashion, the effect of Pellegram focusing directly upon paper in the office is not to fetishize paper, but on the contrary, to reveal what a material, which is so mundane as to be taken for granted, is actually doing in social terms.

By adopting an approach constituted by the term "material culture studies", each individual study resists the more immediate contextualization in the realm of that particular form. The study of gardening by Chevalier in Chapter 3 is not contextualized by a general literature on gardens or even by a comparative anthropology of gardens. By taking the garden as material culture, it is first assessed in relation to other material domains. In this case the English garden is situated in relation to the English lounge and its equivalent in France is argued to be not the French garden but the French kitchen, since Chevalier argues that the English passion for the transformations of natural forms enacted in the garden are most clearly comparable with the passions with which the French confront the skills of cuisine. By avoiding the immediate locating of gardens in gardening, the idiomatic potential of the work on the garden can be located and used for a wider academic analysis. The same applies to the chapters by Clarke, Finden-Crofts, Rausing and Johnson, where the contextualization is more immediately social life. In these chapters the objects of concern, be they television, gold jewellery, aid from Sweden, calypsos or catalogues of goods for sale, are not focused upon so directly but the importance of their specific materiality emerges through studies that show how the images of society people live through are constituted through these domains.

Material matters

As already noted, the point that material things matter and can be theorized as such may now be regarded as having been made and there is little point in reiterating it here. There was, however, a major fault with the body of work that established this theorizing of cultural forms, much of which came out of various versions of formal, structural and semiotic analysis associated with writers such as Barthes, Baudrillard, Douglas and Lévi-Strauss (see Riggins 1994 for a more recent example of how this tradition has developed). In formal analysis the major technique was to reveal the homologies between distinctions drawn in one sphere with those of another. So, for example, a dimension already regarded as important such as class or gender could be shown to be reproduced in part through a host of material taxonomies as in clothing, building or systems for the classification of time, which may not at first have appeared to be based upon the same structural order but through analysis were revealed to be part of what Bourdieu called the same "habitus".

The problem with such analysis is that it could apply to almost any area of cultural life, or material form, and although it pointed to the significance of domains of difference in general it did not specify, or single out, any particular artefacts as being of special significance. Since the roots of this analysis lay in the structuralist concern with order in general, the items used in manifesting that order were in some sense arbitrary. Furthermore, such analysis tended to a kind of social reductionism that rarely challenged the foundational social distinctions that are taken as axiomatic goals of analysis. That is, studies that map material culture onto gender or class are hardly likely to do other than reiterate the ideas of gender and class that they start with.

Since then one development has been the rise of more sophisticated theories of material culture which, by using concepts such as that of objectification, refused any such reductionism or privileging of something called "society". In my work on Trinidad I have tried to show how kinship and ethnicity could be taken equally with home decoration or the media as forms though which certain value systems have been transformed over many decades (Miller 1994: 257–90).

Here, however, the concern is rather to move from the general question of the importance of material forms to the specific analysis of particular artefacts or artefactual domains. The emphasis on selectivity demands a criterion for prioritization and this is why the distinct element of the question "Why things matter?" rests ultimately upon the last word of my title, that is "matter". I would argue that the term "matter" tends to point in a rather different direction from terms such as "importance" or "significance". These alternative terms tend to imply a criterion derived solely from analytical enquiry, as in the idea that "I demonstrate an important relationship between social dimension A and artefact form B". The term "matter", by contrast, tends to a more diffused, almost sentimental association that is more likely to lead us to the concerns of those being studied than those doing the studying. It puts the burden of mattering clearly on evidence of concern to those being discussed.

We have to recognize how easy it is to be wrong about what matters. Geertz (1980) reports a case where the Dutch, having conquered the Celebes in Indonesia, were trying to establish the exact boundaries between two principalities that had often fought each other in the past, and were surprised that, given this degree of fighting, the princes still seemed unclear as to where the boundaries lay. One of the princes replied, "we had much better reasons to fight with one another than these shabby hills". In other words it is quite problematic merely to assume another group's criteria for mattering (Geertz 1980: 25). Similarly in my current ethnographic work on shopping in north London, I could argue that a choice matters to a housewife because it reflects the love she bears her partner, but this would be open to the critique that it should matter because it obscures the amount of work and exploitation involved in such an act of caring, even from the woman who is doing the shopping.

The issue of mattering not only leads to a concern with the consequence of things for those associated with them but also fits well with a move from a primary emphasis with producing things to a concern with consuming things. All of those writing in this volume have relinquished a simpler Marxist ontology that insisted a priori that the species being is constituted in the act of production, to an appreciation that the key moment in which people construct themselves or are constructed by others is increasingly through relations with cultural forms in the arena of consumption. This is in recognition of a historical shift from production to consumption and a legacy of the neglect of consumption as people remained wedded to theories devised in another time (Miller 1995a).

The idea of "mattering" is, however, by no means a simple or straightforward criterion. It is certainly not reducible to an open question to an informant "does this matter?" and being led by the answer. Sometimes, of course, this is the source of our concern. For example, an outsider might claim that it should not matter that a particular group in Northern Ireland is able to march down a particular street in Londonderry, but underlying Jarman's Chapter 6 is the clear evidence of the many people to whom it clearly matters a great deal. Similarly the starting point of Finden-Crofts' Chapter 7 is that while calypso at one level should not be of any great regard, being merely a form of popular song, many people in Trinidad insist that such songs matter to the degree that they can bring down governments or pronounce on the current state of almost any important issue in the island.

This in and of itself would lead to the fairly simple criterion that "if it matters to them, it should matter for us". This certainly removes us from the tradition of formal and structural analysis, which took no regard at all as to whether something mattered. Lévi-Strauss (1982) famously pronounced of the "hau", as analyzed by Mauss, that it was of little consequence whether the native thought the ideas mattered. Yet this new criterion is in many ways as problematic as that which it negates, since it leaves the question of what matters entirely to the declared judgement of those being studied. As such it would fit current fashions in anthropology and some other social sciences particularly well. Books such as *Anthropology as cultural critique* (Marcus & Fischer 1986), which were the harbinger of a massive shift from structural analysis to a kind of postmodern redefinition of academic responsibility, have led to some academics going to the other extreme and claiming that the only thing that matters is what those being studied identify as mattering. To attempt to refuse these "voices of experience" is said to impose an unwarranted authority by academic fiat, which cannot be morally justified.

In the more extreme forms of this approach, the role of the academic becomes merely to give voice in establishment and educational contexts to those who could not give a criterion for mattering because they themselves were not deemed to matter. It also returns us to the most old-fashioned form of positivism which forbade the philosopher to go beyond that which was immediately observable (or in this case sayable), since that alone represented the key goal of "experience", the term most often used to mask the positivistic grounding of this work.

This would be clearly disastrous for a study of material culture, whose subject is almost always mute and where the importance of the object world is often precisely that artefacts were often most effective in social reproduction when they were assumed to be merely trivial and not to matter. The epistemological foundation of material culture must remain realist rather than positivist, with a clear latitude for the critique of ideology. For this purpose material culture must find some channel between on the one hand mere reportage of the voice of experience, and on the other hand the merely formalistic application of schema of analysis. We must have our own criteria for determining why some things matter.

The solution to this dilemma is, however, not particularly hard to find. Another characteristic of the present volume is that every chapter is the result of ethnographic study. Ethnography tends to lead to a much deeper involvement in people's lives than just what they say about themselves. Ethnography used in material culture also tends to emphasize careful observations of what people actually do and in particular do with things. As such we are constantly faced with the everyday discrepancies between what people say matters to them and what they actually give their attention to. Pellegram starts her Chapter 5 with a consensus that paper should not matter. The Estonians described by Rausing in Chapter 9 are trying to pretend to themselves that Swedish aid does not matter, since they feel degraded by being the recipients of charity. The Trinidadians described by Finden-Crofts in Chapter 7 are quite ambivalent whether calypso should be allowed to affect directly a field that is formally supposed to matter a great deal more, that is politics.

The kind of material culture analysis presented in this volume has therefore its own criterion of mattering, one that emerges largely through ethnographic enquiry. It is one which insists that it does indeed emphasize those objects that can demonstrably be seen to matter to people, even where those same people do not make any claim. Language is as often taken to be merely a form of legitimation. In my recent ethnography I found several cases of elderly informants who in public claimed to support corner shops and bemoan the rise of huge supermarkets, and in private praised large supermarkets and declared themselves happy for corner shops to disappear.

Clarke, with whom I conducted joint fieldwork on provisioning in a north London street, documents in Chapter 4 the increasing use of *Argos* as a catalogue that allowed people to browse for goods at home rather than through shop windows. One advantage of this is that one has greater leisure to establish mattering as a criterion for spending money as opposed to the impulse purchasing that may arise from more traditional window shopping. *Loot*, which is used to advertise second-hand goods, by contrast, leads to the direct exploitation of uncertainly creating the condition for a more game-like interaction where people, who feel they have the requisite skill, can take advantages of this lack of clarity as to how much things might be worth.

The logic of mattering is equally well exposed in the climax to Chapter 5 by Pellegram. Here there is in a sense a double discrepancy to the question of mattering. On the one hand this is a particularly fine example of the ethnographer putting into focus a substance – paper – which is disregarded as in itself trivial, even though through observation of, for example, the concern with the place it is stored, it can certainly be shown to matter. Beyond this, however, is a marvellous instance in which the transformation of mattering takes place quite explicitly at the scene of the action. All paper that becomes part of the archiving of information is assumed not only to matter but also to be essential. Bureaucrats who failed to give full regard to the importance of duplicating and storing such paper would be unlikely to retain their job. Yet after this virtual fetishism of paper as archive over a considerable amount of time, the management constructs a new ritual in which people are free suddenly to remove vast amounts of the same paper that up to that point mattered so much and declare it sufficiently insignificant that it can be thrown away, in an orgy of de-archiving.

By the time we reach the chapters by Rausing and Johnson, the issues of mattering achieves a poignancy that allows us to contemplate directly the kind of sentimentality that the concept of mattering evokes as a term. The problem for both Estonians in the post-Soviet world and Filipina women is that the criteria of what could or should matter have themselves become extremely fragile; as a result people are left with an uncomfortable ambivalence in directing their own actions, since for them (as for the ethnographer) mattering is designated as much by what they choose to do as what they say. There is a humiliation for Estonians in not knowing whether they should consider Western or Eastern goods as high or low quality. For the Filipina women studied by Johnson in Chapter 9, everything that has led up to a certain point has insisted that what should matter is gold. Yet there is clearly some force that has led to a moment in which when they go to work in the Middle East, the Hungry Bunny burger has become an object of such significance that its consumption is deemed essential, even though the net result is that a woman returns without the gold expected of her. Johnson's task is precisely to define those radical oppositions between tradition and the modern that have become objectified in women's values and positions and that reveal mattering to be itself pulled apart in highly opposed aspirations.

Ambivalence and tension are central also to Rausing's account in Chapter 9 of the relationships to the new, Western objects on a remote collective farm in Estonia. There, the distinction between the old/Soviet and the new/ Western goods tends to be unstated and inarticulated, despite the dramatic process of appropriation complemented by the recontextualization of Soviet forms. The reason for this is that too explicit an articulation of the foreign-ness of the Western would threaten to expose Estonian ethnicity as something Eastern, rather than support their claim to be already "naturally" Western. Humphrey (1995) has shown how this kind of transience of mattering has been taken to its extreme in Moscow, where the sheer level of uncertainty has made it virtually impossible to know what one should or should not care about.

The question of mattering is then precisely the point at which the chapters in this volume move from the general concern with the materiality of each specific domain of artefacts that they have chosen to study to the criteria that allow us to choose particular articulations between persons and objects as significant. This is the shift that allows the subtlety and nuance of ethnographic enquiry to deepen more formalistic analysis. At this stage Tacchi moves from the importance of radio sound to the considerable differences between individuals in their regard for such sound depending upon the current state of their social life. Similarly Rausing demonstrates the strategies developed by an individual Estonian to keep the sympathy of different audiences by dressing herself differently according to each context.

Consumption and space

Having opened out this wider potential for the study of subject–object relations, it would be hard to say where the boundaries of such a study might be. Once we ask which things matter to whom and why, we are immediately faced with an endless proliferation of criteria of mattering. Obviously only certain of these can be addressed either in this introduction or in the chapters themselves. For present purposes I shall focus on a single dimension that acts as a common thread though the volume and thereby defines it against other potential uses of these ideas. It not only acts to describe what all the chapters have in common but also is a key dimension of difference that organizes them into distinct sections. This dimension of space links a concern with the most private domestic arena to the most public and global sphere. The volume accomplishes this in three stages: the first three chapters reflect on the private sphere, the second three on the public sphere, while the final three help bridge the relationship between the two spheres.

The chapters by Tacchi and Chevalier are both concerned with the way people take forms from the public sphere and use them to construct a balance between privacy and sociality. Tacchi's Chapter 2 reflects the considerable difficulty of bringing the potential of ethnographic enquiry into the topic of privacy and loneliness. Using comparative ethnography, she is able to evoke the sense in which both sound and silence can become a richly textured presence, part of an almost sensual intimacy for the individual. As such she is able to reveal sound as a highly material aspect of culture. At the same time radio becomes a key instrument by which the private domain is more or less exposed to another kind of space – one that can stretch from the more immediate space-time of a local chat show through to the vast space-time of global pop classics. As such, tuning into the radio becomes a kind of tuning in to sociality in the larger world in order to make the highly private and immediate domestic sphere that much more livable, but within the safety of one's own domestic arena.

Chevalier in Chapter 3 also deals with the minutiae by which people bring a global form, in this case nature, into what may be called literally the "domesticated" sphere. She notes its implications for both intra-household relations and also positioning the home within the neighbourhood. But to Tacchi's ethnographic sensitivity she is able to add a historical aspect, since the differences between the French and the British articulation between gardens and homes makes sense only in terms of longstanding differences in the way the temporality of the family itself is constructed as a project of inheritance. Yet in turn the significance of these different historical trajectories is made manifest only through the detailed account of both her informants' views on the garden and Chevalier's detailed observations of precisely what is done to both home and garden.

With Clarke in Chapter 4 we move to a still more complex understanding of what is presently constituted as the domestic. In many ways this reflects the kind of new thinking about space that is evident in Morley's (1992) discussion of the television usually situated within the living room of a private home but that is at the same time the primary contact with the globe. One of the major impacts of the *Argos* catalogue is that it returns much of shopping choice to the home itself, and thus has a major impact on groups such as children, where shoppers would wish to consult their children but know full well the dreadful consequences of actually having children with them during the act of shopping. *Loot,* by contrast, appears to be a comparatively local journal based in London, but it is best used by people with highly cosmopolitan knowledge, including picking up on the connotations of which particular part of London their exchange partner is living in, and then often travelling a great deal further than would be likely in more conventional shopping. So the local is best appropriated by those with the most global forms of knowledge.

The next three chapters are in some ways in marked contrast to the first three, which reflects the often radical disjuncture in contemporary societies between the domestic sphere and the public sphere. As will be evident in the details of the chapters themselves, this becomes of considerable significance in examining the question of why certain things matter. The difference is essentially between what people do within the privacy of their own homes and the implications of display within an open social context. Again the three chapters provide an interesting sequence with respect to this difference. They move from a chapter where mattering is largely hidden and has to be excavated by the ethnographer, through calypso where there is a public discourse that retains some uncertainty as to whether such things should matter, through to the situation in Northern Ireland where banners are explicit symbols, sometimes literally to die for.

In all three cases there is a carefully analyzed relationship between the medium and the message. Pellegram's Chapter 5 contrasts the relative intimacy of the yellow Post-it® Notes and the way that formal paper is used to express the seriousness of the organization as a whole to the outside world. Finden-Crofts shows in Chapter 7 that with calypso the singers compete to be the key medium for the expression of that particular year's style, whether it is the party spirit of the Donkey Dance or the spirit of political critique. In Jarman's case in Chapter 6 the banner takes its specific place against the qualities of alternative media such as murals or the parades themselves as a mobile form in which the symbol of a group can (as it were) mark its territoriality.

Another common theme for material culture in the public sphere relates to the pragmatic advantages of plurality in form. Jarman concludes on this theme, and sees it not only as a means for using history without the formalism of historical narrative but also as a means by which banners can confront their different contexts, for example, both facing inwards to the community who produce them and outwards as an expression of that community to others. The situation is similar for Finden-Crofts, though here this plurality exists within the specific frame of that year's carnival, where a large number of new calypsos compete to become (as it were) the key banners paraded for public debate in that particular year. We would expect and indeed find that the bureaucratic context for Pellegram's investigation imposes a more rule-like order upon the relationship between difference and context, though even here there is relative flexibility if one moves between the two modes she describes of overt and latent message.

Being part of the public sphere sets its own constraints not found in the first three chapters. The topic of mattering is brought out into the open, though in quite different ways. Where the Trinidadians are quite ambivalent about the importance of calypso, Pellegram's office workers are as consensual about the unimportance of paper as the Northern Irish are consensual about the importance of banners. By juxtaposing the three chapters, one can see how consensus about mattering can become a rather problematic form of closure as against the open debate that is evident in Trinidad.

The final three chapters may be seen as in some ways addressing the disjuncture between the chapters that deal with domestic and those that deal with the public sphere. This is because their subject matter is largely that of global–local identity. In a sense they bring out the meta-level at which the previous chapters are connected, since in many ways the local is objectified in the construction of a domestic sphere which achieves its sense of privacy precisely through defining itself against another sphere experienced as public or increasingly as global. In all three cases the primary concern is with the way this articulation is expressed in consumption, but perhaps unusually for consumption studies, they are all explicitly concerned with the implications that follow from the source of these goods, for example, in production for Miller and in gifts from abroad for Rausing and in actually going abroad for Johnson.

In all three cases consumption is also highlighted as the instrument that both expresses and resolves dual aspects of identity. Miller in Chapter 8 shows how the red sweet drink (as opposed to Coke) becomes the form by which African Trinidadians can complete their own identity as Trinidadian through ingesting a symbol of the other ethnic group – the Indian. Rausing in Chapter 9 shows how Estonians struggle to construct a sense of being naturally "Western" in order to divest themselves of what might otherwise erupt as an ambivalence between a desire to incorporate elements of the West while retaining what otherwise would have to be acknowledged as "Eastern" aspects of their identity. Johnson in Chapter 10 shows how women struggle to retain their sense of being female while incorporating something of the freedom and access to externality that was previously largely associated with males.

The degree to which a generic notion of the "West" or more specifically "America" has become the specific instrument of globality is striking in all these chapters. Estonians, Trinidadians and Filipinas all seek to lay claim to what may be regarded as the modernity and style of Coca-Cola or Marlboro cigarettes, but in all three cases they have developed mechanisms for disaggregating the qualities symbolized by Western goods into those that they are able or desire to accept as against those qualities that they see as evil or at least inauthentic to themselves. Indeed in comparison with the general discourse of local–global articulation, this emphasis upon material culture seems to offer important insights into the ability of groups to use the variable objectifications available in a range of commodities to create a much more subtle and discriminatory process of incorporation and rejection than that allowed for in simple models of Americanization or globalization.

The subtitle for this part, "World Wide West", has then a serious import. All three chapters demonstrate the complexity of the question as to where "the West" is located, even prior to the use of the Internet. Rausing notes that 53 per cent of the people in her otherwise rather marginal village had been abroad. The material effect of working abroad for Filipinos is evident in Johnson's chapter, with the added poignancy that it is women, commonly emblematic of the domestic, who are primarily involved in this circular migration. At the most extreme, my surveys in Trinidad found that the majority of families were transnational at the nuclear level. Yet the impact of this is, if anything, more acute through the presence of local signs of the West, which threaten the integrity of that which would otherwise be the unambiguous symbol of the local. As Rausing puts it, it is the local West that is at issue here. Indeed it is striking that much of this debate is informed by encounters with equally aggressive candidates for global status – Soviet socialism in the case of Estonia and Islam in the case of the southern Philippines.

Johnson suggests that the tension set up by a concept of "Western" style simultaneously takes two entirely opposed forms. On the one hand, style can be taken as the "tradition" of the West, which in turn can be incorporated locally as simply a new version of tradition, as in an extra ceremony within a wedding. At the same time the West can represent a much more radical form of individualized freedom from structures that would repudiate both kinds of socialized tradition, the older form and the new. The dilemma for many women is that their new experience as migrant workers allows them to objectify either of these forms of Westernization, but one tends to be at the expense of the other.

This part exemplifies the advantages of this volume over other approaches to the same issue. There are a plethora of books published on "local–global" relations and articulations. Many of these tend to constant repetition about global homogenization or heterogeneity using symbols such as Coke and hamburgers reduced down to clichés and dramatic juxtapositions of Western goods in exotic contexts. By contrast, Johnson and Rausing provide a nuanced sense of just how these encounters are experienced and how what have been represented as grand clashes of meta-symbols become the mundane reality of everyday life.

Conclusion

These final chapters bring us in many ways full circle back to the opening chapter by Tacchi. She also focused on how material culture is used to objectify the presence of a space-time that evokes a global world of possibility held against a highly constrained set of domestic obligations and responsibilities. As such this reinforces the larger point that material culture is often the concrete means by which the contradictions held within general concepts such as the domestic or the global are in practice resolved in every-day life. Throughout these chapters it is clear that one of the key struggles of modern life is to retain both a sense of authentic locality, often as narrow as the private sphere, and yet also lay claims to a cosmopolitanism that at some level may evoke rights to global status.

This achievement cannot be reduced to either method or theory *per se.* There is certainly an ethnographic orientation to fieldwork, but there are also historical sections in many of the chapters and most particularly in Jarman's chapter. Material culture studies is not then constituted by ethnography, but remains eclectic in its methods. Approaches from history, archaeology, geography, design and literature are all equally acceptable contributions. Similarly while these chapters are theoretically informed, they do not reduce their material to overly abstract theoretical models such as formalism or a structuralism derived from linguistic analogy, which treat objects as signs but do not account for the degree to which they matter to people. At the same time the concept of mattering used here is a wide one that does not reduce down to merely what people say about things. There are many instances where clearly things matter to people even when in speech they deride them as trivial and inconsequential.

The possibility of material culture studies lies not in method, but rather in an acknowledgement of the nature of culture, as understood by theorists such as Simmel (e.g. 1968). We as academics can strive for under-standing and empathy through the study of what people do with objects, because that is the way the people that we study create a world of practice. As Simmel argued, human values do not exist other than through their objectification in cultural forms. The specific form taken has an intrinsic tendency to fetishize and be understood merely as form and no longer as the embodiment of ourselves. This is what he saw as the tragic potential inherent in culture. But it is not only academics, but also all social agents, who strive to avoid such a fate and bring back cultural forms of all kinds into the task of humanities self-construction.

Material culture studies can thereby proclaim itself as one tradition that does not fall apart into the antimonies that Latour (1993) has drawn attention to between a reification of science that is in general opposed in anthropology, and a reification of society which in some ways material culture studies is often better placed to critique than mainsteam anthropology. Instead the following chapters reveal such studies as a highly effective means to enquire into the fundamental questions of what it is to be human within the diversity of culture.

References

Appadurai, A. (ed.) 1986. *The social life of things: commodities in cultural perspective.* Cambridge: Cambridge University Press.

Baker, N. 1986. *The mezzanine.* London: Granta.

Belk, R. 1995. *Collecting in a consumer culture.* London: Routledge.

Bourdieu, P. 1977. *Outline of a theory of practice.* Cambridge: Cambridge University Press.

Bourdieu, P. 1984. *Distinction: a social critique of the judgement of taste.* London: Routledge & Kegan Paul.

Braudel, F. 1981. *The structures of everyday life.* London: Collins.

Brewer, J. & R. Porter (eds) 1993. *Consumption and the world of goods.* London: Routledge.

Deetz, J. 1977. *In small things forgotten.* New York: Doubleday.

Dittmar, H. 1992. *The social psychology of material possessions.* Hemel Hempstead: Harvester Wheatsheaf.

Douglas, M. & B. Isherwood 1978. *The world of goods.* London: Allen Lane.

Forrest, J. 1988. *Lord I'm coming home.* Ithaca NY: Cornell University Press.

Friedman, J. & M. Rowlands (eds) 1977. *The evolution of social systems.* London: Duckworth.

Frykman, J. & O. Löfgren 1987. *Culture builders.* New Brunswick, NJ: Rutgers University Press.

Geertz, C. 1980. *Negara.* Princeton, NJ: Princeton University Press.

Gilroy, P. 1993. *Small acts.* London: Serpent's Tail.

Glassie, H. 1975. *Folk housing in middle Virginia.* Knoxville: University of Tennessee Press.

Grossberg, L., C. Nelson & P. Treichler 1992. *Cultural studies.* London: Routledge.

Guss, D. 1989. *To weave and to sing.* Berkeley: University of California Press.

Hodder, I. 1982. *Symbols in action.* Cambridge: Cambridge University Press.

Humphrey, C. 1995. Consumers in moscow. In *Worlds apart: modernity through the prism of the local,* D. Miller (ed.), London: Routledge.

Latour, B. 1993. *We have never been modern.* New York: Harvester Wheatsheaf.

Lévi-Strauss, C. 1982. *The way of the masks.* Seattle: University of Washington Press.

MacKenzie, M. A. 1991. *Androgynous objects: string bags and gender in central New Guinea.* London: Harwood Academic.

Marcus, G. & M. Fischer 1986. *Anthropology as cultural critique.* Chicago: University of Chicago Press.

Miller, D. 1987. *Material culture and mass consumption.* Oxford: Blackwell.

Miller, D. 1994. *Modernity: an ethnographic approach.* Oxford: Berg.

Miller, D. (ed.) 1995a. *Acknowledging consumption.* London: Routledge.

Miller, D. 1995b. Consumption and commodities. *Annual Review of Anthropology* **24**, 141–61.

Moore, H. 1986. *Space, text and gender.* Cambridge: Cambridge University Press.

Morley, D. 1992. *Television, audiences and cultural studies.* London: Routledge.

Pearce, S. 1995. *On collecting.* London: Routledge.

Quinn, M. 1994. *The swastika.* London: Routledge.

Riggins, S. (ed.) 1994. *The socialness of things: essays on the socio-semiotics of objects.* Berlin: Mouton de Gruyter.

Rogan, B. 1992. Artefacts: source material or research objects in contemporary ethnology. *Ethnologia Scandanavia* **22**, 105–18.

Schama, S. 1987. *The embarrassment of riches: an interpretation of Dutch culture in the Golden Age.* London: Fontana.

Simmel, G. 1968. *The conflict in modern culture, and other essays.* New York: Teachers College Press.

Tilley, C. (ed.) 1990. *Reading material culture.* Oxford: Blackwell.

Tilley, C. 1991. *Material culture and text: the art of ambiguity.* London: Routledge.

PART II
The domestic sphere

CHAPTER 2

Radio texture: between self and others[1]

Jo Tacchi

In 1967, Needham was struggling with the "problem" of where, in the categorical processes of anthropology, to place what he saw as the clear link between percussion and transition, i.e. the use of drumming or other percussive sounds in the ritual contexts of *rites de passage*. Trying out a few approaches, which included an attempt to define both percussion and transition in broad terms, he found it difficult to assimilate two apparently distinctive, yet conjunctive "primary, elementary, and fundamental features: 1) the affective impact of percussion, 2) the logical structure of category-change" (Needham 1967: 612). The problem was that empirically, he saw the connection, yet theoretically, they resided in "disparate modes of apprehension"; the emotional and the rational (ibid.). Needham was asking why the noise of percussion was so widely used to communicate with spiritual powers, with the "other world". Needham found it difficult, in the face of a lack of analytical terms and ideas around sound within anthropology, not only to frame his problem, but also to analyze it in more depth.

When thinking about a framework for analysis of a study of radio sound in the home, there is a distinction to be made between the mundane context of domestic media consumption, and the ritualized use of percussive sounds in *rites de passage*. Here, the focus is on the everyday use of sound, and how sound acts to create an environment for domestic living. Radio sound can be seen to fill "empty" space and "empty" time with a familiar routine, so familiar that it is unremarkable. In this way, radio sound is a presence in domestic time and space, which can be viewed as setting a pattern for domestic living, but a pattern that is naturalized to the extent that, as in Needham's focus on percussive sound and rituals, there are few academic pegs from which to hang it. Additionally, it can be seen to provide a frame, not only for social interactions in Goffman's sense, but also for avoiding, or making up for, a lack of social interactions.

Like Needham, I too am faced with elementary features that can be viewed as residing in "disparate modes of apprehension" – the emotional or affective qualities of, and reactions to, radio sound, and the rational and logical business of everyday life. Their empirically observed connection is expressed theoretically, in terms of radio sound providing a texture in which everyday life can take place. Radio is not an essential component for everyday living, but it is one that many use on a regular basis.[2] My starting point is the idea that radio sound creates a textured "soundscape" in the home, within which people move around and live their daily lives.[3] Rather than connecting with other worlds in a supernatural sense, these sounds, on both a social and a personal level, can be seen to connect with other places and other times. Linked with memories and with feelings, either experienced or imagined, they can evoke different states of mind and moods. From the perspective of material culture studies, the soundscapes themselves can be seen to have no intrinsic value or meaning; these are established and re-established continually in each domestic arena, through each individual instance of use.

Miller suggested that "the very physicality of the object which makes it appear so immediate, sensual and assimilable belies its actual nature" (1987: 3). Material culture "is one of the most resistant forms of cultural expression in terms of our attempts to comprehend it" (ibid.). One of the problems with material culture is that its meaning is not experienced linguistically, and therefore any attempt to explain its significance which relies on language as a communicative medium, is bound to fall short of full explanation. Radio as a medium is immediate, intimate and direct. Translating this quality of radio into language, people often speak of it as a "friend", as "company". Such clichéd expressions of the relationship between listeners and radio are used by both producers of radio sound and consumers, because of the experiential nature of listening, which is difficult to define in words. Something that is experiential and a part of everyday life does not normally require explanation. Radio is not a friend in the way that a person whom we are close to is a friend, and it is not the same as the physical company of another person; these terms are used as metaphors to express a particular (and usually unexpressed) relationship with a medium that we are not normally asked to talk or even think about. Thinking of radio sound as textured allows the possibility of considering how it operates, and how people operate within it. As a researcher, it allows me momentarily to "fix" something that is dynamic and flowing. Yet this is true also of objects and artefacts more generally. As already mentioned, their meanings are not static, as one might assume from their concrete physicality. To think about sound as material culture is not intended to translate it artificially into something it is not. Rather, I would suggest that radio sound is experienced as a part of the material culture of the home, and that it contributes greatly to the creation of domestic environments.

Radio sound can be used as a filler of space and of time. It can act as a referencer of memories and feelings, of other places and other times. It can serve to ground someone in the present. It can help to establish and maintain identities, and it is often used as a marker of time. It moves through time; it is a time-based medium. While listening to the radio is predominantly an individual occupation, and radio is seen by both consumers and producers as an intimate medium, I would contend that in this context of the domestic environment, which it helps to create and maintain, it serves a social role.

In this chapter, I shall concentrate on the role that radio in the home plays in the establishment and maintenance of relationships, between the self and others. These relationships may be imagined or real, a distinction that underpins the main supposition of this chapter. Radio can be used in this *pseudo* social way to create a self that could, or would like to be, social. This makes listening to the radio a social activity, in that it can act to reinforce sociality and sense of social self, and at the same time has the potential to fill perceived gaps in one's social life. Radio sound can be used to create a non-public social space, making it a safe environment in which to work on one's sociality. Radio sound, as part of the material culture of the home, is viewed as a texture. The use of radio adds to the sound texture of the domestic environment. Unlike the "solid" material culture of the home itself and the objects within it, or the more "fluid" aspects of the material culture of everyday life, such as clothing, radio sound can be seen to add a dimension of sociability to the lives of individual listeners in their homes. Degrees of sociability will be examined here, beginning with the sometimes feared, sometimes desired, silent environment, moving on to the use of radio as a background texture, in some instances creating a rhythm by which to live, to a consideration of foregrounded radio sound, and its potential creation of an image of a desired society, which is closer to, but essentially and importantly different from, real face-to-face social exchange. I shall demonstrate that it is nevertheless part of "real" sociality.

In order to paint a coherent picture of the gradation between silence at one end of a scale of sociability, and face-to-face interaction at the other, based on my fieldwork data,[4] some generalizations have been made. I have case studies that would dispute some of my findings, but looking at my data in broad terms, there are clear patterns emerging, that lead to the arguments put forward in this chapter.

Silence

When talking about *silence,* many informants displayed an appreciation of the difficulties of definition. For some, silence appeared to mean absence of speech or music, although for some it meant complete absence of sounds. Absolute silence was recognized as being either "very rare" or "not possible". The more generally accepted definition of silence, as used in everyday speech, was seen as a lack of intrusive or obvious noise, perhaps better described as "quiet". When I use the word "silence" here, I am thinking of a state that is not necessarily to do with sound at all. That is, silence is seen here as one end of a scale of sociality. *Social* silence indicates a lack of social interaction, but not necessarily a lack of all noise. Working in the realm of philosophy, Dauenhauer (1980) notes that, while silence occurs most obviously in conjunction with sound, it is "a rich and complex phenomenon" which, with minimal investigation, can clearly be seen to occur, also without the context of sound. Dauenhauer sees silence as necessary in many, if not all, forms of human communication and performance. Sign language, for example, would not be an effective language without the presence of silence, in this case not dependent on the presence of contrastive sound, but a contrastive communication or language that does not involve sound at all. Silence here means a break or pause in communication, which highlights or enhances what is being communicated.

Dauenhauer also cites the performing arts, and activities such as silent reading or viewing works of art, to make his point that silence itself is an active performance (1980: 3–4). Not only is it an active performance, but also it involves *conscious* activity. Therefore, according to Dauenhauer, "the occurrence or non-occurrence of passively or spontaneously encountered noise, of itself, can neither prevent nor produce silence" (1980: 4). My research supports the notion that silence can be actively created, and actively avoided. The question of levels of consciousness, however, poses certain problems. Given the already-mentioned immediate and experiential nature of material culture, in this case radio sound and silence, it is difficult to be precise about levels of consciousness employed. With the viewing of art works in a gallery or museum, one can perhaps be more accurate. The site with which I am concerned, however, is the home, where radio sound (and silence) is interwoven into the larger fabric of everyday life, to the extent that it is often hardly thought about consciously at all.[5] It is often routinized, and naturalized, so that conscious consideration is not necessary. It is very firmly a part of everyday life, and as such, works on both conscious and unconscious levels. *Electric Radioland*, a report on research among radio listeners, prepared for the Radio Advertising Bureau, demonstrates how listeners find it very hard to describe the ways in which they listen to the radio, and what "makes their ears prick up", and concludes that this is because it is "a behaviour which is only semi-conscious (and often unconscious)" (Navigator 1993: 11).

Dauenhauer calls any type of active human performance an utterance, an utterance being any part of any form of language which, when placed with other utterances, forms a discourse. My use of the term "silence" sees each occurrence, or instance of use, employed or experienced on whatever level of consciousness, in the larger context of the sociality of the individual. This in turn is constitutive of social relations, and of the self. Silence can be an activity, and a *condition*, using the notion of *social silence*, as employed in this chapter. A lack of, or low level of, noise for some of my informants was seen as sometimes offering a positive state, where reflection and relaxation could take place. In some of these cases I would argue that silence is used to allow contemplation of sociality. It can be a necessary part of defining sociality for those who have a very demanding job and/or lifestyle. That part of their lives that involves high degrees of sociability is seen more clearly when observed from a situation of non-sociability and without definition and contrast, sociability may be hard to appreciate. Alternatively, a high volume of radio sound was sometimes used by informants to block out distractions, thus creating a form of social or anti-social silence. Sue, for example, listens to a music radio station, and told me how she sometimes "blasts" the radio, that is, she plays it at a very high volume level, "it clears things . . . to clear your mind of what's bothering you and put something else in there . . . I find it very therapeutic".

For other informants, who see their lives as lacking in sociability, silence can offer a reminder of their undesired social situation, and so it is to be avoided (see Gullestad 1992). Some informants will leave their radios on whether or not they are listening, or even present in the home at the time, and some leave it on through the night while sleeping. It is used by some to distract them from their feelings of loneliness and from other unhappy thoughts or worries, yet is not necessarily consciously listened to. In this way, it is an utterance in Dauenhauer's terms, which is primarily used to prevent silence, with silence being the focus of attention and impetus for action, rather than the radio sound itself.

Thus, social silence can be both a positive and a negative thing. Some informants longed for, or at least welcomed it, others feared it. For some, silence could be experienced in both ways, depending on context and timing, or had been at different times in their personal histories. Some of the most negative thoughts on silence were expressed in relation to the evenings and night-times, when the rest of the world is apparently sleeping. For some, the availability of silent times that hold this capacity to highlight other aspects of their lives was to be feared, because of their unease, or discontent with, the quality of their social lives, or their feelings of isolation or loneliness:

Researcher: Do you ever like silence?
Deborah: Not really, I used to but not now, it is because I'm by myself I know that, whereas before I used to read a lot more, now I watch telly and the radio a lot more because it is company . . .
Researcher: How long have you been on your own?
Deborah: Two years.
Researcher: Before that you wouldn't have listened to radio in bed?
Deborah: No, I'd have read a book, it is the silence, that's why I stick the radio on . . . it is company, the reason I do like talk shows rather than listening to Radio 1 [contemporary popular music] is that it is someone talking rather than music, that's why I like it when I go up to bed, because I

suppose it is a way then of knowing that someone else is around.

Deborah is a 27-year-old divorcée with two young children. She has what she described to me as a virtually non-existent social life. When she is not caring for her children or doing housework, she will be at work (part-time) in a supermarket, or attending college, where she goes twice a week to try and improve her job prospects. If an individual like Deborah is not happy with her social life, silence would surely emphasize this. Silence as a commentary on sociality can therefore exist in the elements of one's life: in the sounds, for example, that remind us of our mundane and perhaps lonely existence. These will be very individual connections – for some, the ticking of a clock, or the sound of church bells. Silence can reside in certain sounds, or circumstances. In these situations, radio can, and for many of my informants, does, cover up such silences. It creates an alternative activity or a distraction, an alternative textured soundscape with which to surround oneself. In doing so, it can be seen in some instances to create an alternative form of silence, one that is more acceptable because it silences the troubling silence, and takes the edge off the contrast between different aspects of sociality. In such a case it may be that the sound of the radio is not listened to for itself; instead, it can be listened to as a reminder that there is a world of sociability out there, creating a link with it that does not actually require risk-taking, as face-to-face social interaction often does.

A background texture

Although the *content* of the radio transmission may not always be heard, it does not necessarily follow that the content is therefore irrelevant. With the growth in commercial radio there are many new stations to listen to, offering different styles of music and speech, delivered in different ways. There are now nine national, three local, one regional, and at least two pirate stations at any one time available to listeners in the Bristol area.[6] For the purposes of this chapter, I take radio sound as a generic group, in order to investigate the qualities that radio sound possesses in more general terms, which nevertheless allows me to address some of the most basic questions about radio sound and its use in the home.

One of the ways in which almost all of my informants talked about radio use was as a "background" to activities in the home. When Anne is at home on her own she says she would feel that there was something missing if there was no sound from the radio or the television.

> I tend to have it as background around the house, I've got music in virtually all rooms, so, it's always on . . . I'm not necessarily listening to it as such, but it's on.

Anne is a 32-year-old charity co-ordinator who lives alone and finds that having the radio on at home helps her to relax.

> I see it as something to relax to, even the debates, I just, it's nice to hear it going on and have a smile, but I wouldn't turn it up loudly, I don't, probably I don't necessarily wanna hear it but I just know it's there.

The radio itself is seen by Anne as the creator of an environment that means relaxation. She will listen to stations as different as Radio 1, local pirate stations or local BBC. As a very busy person she sees the radio as an aid to taking "time out" from her hectic life, yet the stations she will most often listen to in order to relax relate very directly to her working and social environment. Anne is a Black woman working in a job that involves her with many local Black families' lives, in a very direct and intimate way. The pirate stations that she tunes to when wanting to relax are seen by her and many others as the sounds of the Black community. So when Anne listens to these stations she does so to keep "in touch" but at the same time she takes "time out".

> I'm a person who likes my own company and I'm very grateful when there's very little going on, because this job keeps us really busy you know . . . so I do look forward to time at home just to chill out, and that's the radio and TV . . . like I said, on Friday it's like, Yea! this is the weekend, put the radio on, puts you in the mood, I mean, if they're playing decent music, yea – it's just a bonus I tell you.

Joe is 29, married with a 10-year-old daughter. He will sometimes listen to the radio with his family, but it is rarely the focus of attention, more often it provides a background so that

> We'd chat through some of the less important bits . . . it would be shhh for the news slots, there might be a bit of informal stuff in between, a bit of music, so we'd talk over that, but just listen out for the more formal bits.

This would be when they are listening to *Asian Hour* on the local BBC station, otherwise they will be listening to one of two local pirate stations that play mainly music. Like Anne, Joe is African Caribbean and he likes to keep in touch with the wider Black community. One of the ways he does so is through his listening to Black stations (these are "pirate" stations which Joe prefers to call "community" stations). With these stations the volume is often turned up quite loud, but Joe still explains it as providing a background to what he is doing:

31

if I'm using it as a background, doing something else, it will be right up, I wouldn't use radio as a background to a conversation or anything like that, or writing a report or letter . . . but cleaning windows and things like that, and then cooking . . . turn the volume up . . . it's to create an atmosphere really, you know, the sort of dance hall atmosphere. It sounds crazy to create it while you're cooking but it's a bit of nostalgia really, you know, because we don't get out as often as we used to . . . so it's like, sometimes you create as near to a dance hall atmosphere as you can, it just reminds you of when you used to go out dead regular.

Both Anne and Joe have very full social lives. Radio for them is often used as a way of "switching off" from social aspects of their lives, while retaining a link. They, like many others, use radio as a background of unfocused sound, that provides them with an environment that is nevertheless social and thus reassuring, but demands nothing of them. As the site of their sociality, the social world is very important to them and it is reassuring to know that it is continuing, but they need some silence, or break from it, in order to better define and appreciate their sociality.

Two studies that come out of the tradition of ethnomusicology have a particular relevance to the notion of sound as texture, and point to ways in which we can think about the materiality of sound. Waterman (1990) looked at the relationship between music, identity and power in a modernizing African society, specifically at *juju* musical style as performed among the Yoruba in contemporary Nigeria. He concentrates mainly on performance of this popular musical style in the context of the national environment, seeing the diverse range of stylistic systems as an opportunity for individuals to place themselves on a map of shifting identity patterns in an urban setting that is culturally heterogeneous and densely populated. Feld (1990) looked at sound as a symbolic system among the Kaluli of Bosavi, Papua New Guinea; specifically at what he sees as the most important myth among the Kaluli, the boy who became a *muni* bird, and its role as mediator between ritualized performance of weeping, poetics and song, and culturally specific personal emotions. Feld comments that the way in which the Kaluli use these sounds in ceremonies relates to their larger cosmic world (their origin myth) and to culturally specific personal emotions, which in turn are related to their conceptions of death and sadness.

Feld concludes from his ethnography that the human ability to organize and think about things – in other words, the classificatory process – is "complexly symbolic" (1990: 218). It is a creative process that depends on the pragmatic needs of any situation, but is broadly defined in social ways, and is deeply felt on an individual basis. Looking at Western cultures in their heterogeneity is clearly a different exercise from the study of a particular myth in Bosavi, yet any generalizations that one would want to draw from

Feld's work can be tested for their applicability to the current research. The point I wish to make here is that the use of radio sound in the home in Bristol does seem to have some analogous links with Feld's research, in that it is clear that personal uses and preferences of radio sound are structured both on an individualistic, and a social, level. Feld's analysis of the social, ceremonial use of sound is related directly to everyday sounds, which in fact are seen to ground the ritualized uses of sound, that is, everyday understandings of sounds affect the production and use of sound in a social context. The wider world is not shut out when we listen to the radio in the home; in fact it has a very direct channel into this most private sphere. The important thing to try to understand is how it is woven into that private existence. Looking at sociality and the use of radio sound, we can begin to understand the weave of domestic life and links between self and others.

Waterman focuses on the historical and contemporary performance of *juju*, a popular music style, and one of many in Nigeria. According to Waterman, musical style may articulate and define communal values in a rapidly transforming, heterogeneous society (1990: 8). *Juju* is one of many musical styles that are popular, and the very naming of such a style is seen as a declaration of "cultural consolidation". The choice of radio stations could be seen in a similar way – the classic gold stations, for example, which offer popular music predominantly from the 1950s, 1960s and 1970s, is a choice that is related to taste and position in society. One of my informants seemed to use a classic gold station because of the era it recreated for him:

> of course, when I grew up all that was sort of starting to die out, the traditional family you know, the neighbourhood feel, and all get-togethers and parties at each other's house, I mean that was starting to go in the '70s and '80s, well as I say it's practically non-existent today I think . . . it used to be a close knit society and, they [his parents] said to me a couple of years ago, "you would have really loved it in the '60s because it was in each other's houses, always having parties" so it really was a lovely time. So I mean that's probably why, I mean I love get-togethers and things like that you see so perhaps in my mind I'm wishing I was in the '60s.

The interesting thing about Paul is that he is aged only 29, and so the past that he looks to as a "lovely time" is an imagined past. He is thereby creating a certain nostalgic soundscape that evokes an idealized past that he was too young to experience. Such stations perhaps offer the opportunity for nostalgia and a syncretism of past and present, analogous to Waterman's exploration of the syncretism of tradition and change in modern Nigerian musical style. This is a particular characteristic in Nigeria, where rapid change and heterogeneity are firmly rooted in tradition among the Yoruba. For Paul, the textured soundscape created by his choice of radio sound provides an environment in which he feels comfortable, and links him with what, for him, is an imagined society, part of which he feels he has experienced through the tales of his parents, and through past experiences such as his stints as a Red Coat during summer months. This work at a holiday camp is, for Paul, analogous to the 1960s, because of the particular form of sociability it re-creates. He wants to live in such a social environment, and radio sound in his flat, where he lives alone, helps him to imagine this. His ideal social life is made real through his re-creation of it as a backdrop to his domestic life, and elements of his imagined and experienced past are brought into play in his present.

Waterman shows how it is the people in a heterogeneous setting, rather than the musical style, or the culture, that accept or reject new ideas and practices (1990: 9). Equally, it is the listener who, as the radio sound enters the "moral economy of the household" (Silverstone & Hirsch 1992), accepts or rejects ideas and practices from the radio. Gretta, when I first met her in 1995, also listened to classic gold radio, and had done for some time, although, as I pointed out to her, at the age of 37, she is quite young to call the music of the 1950s and 1960s, which she particularly liked, of her "era":

> No, when I was growing up it was all the Jacksons and the Osmonds, all that sort of stuff, but as I got older this was the sort of music that I could relate more to . . . I like all the old stuff. . . . it's just the people who introduce it as well, they're good, but I can't say I'd ever go to another station again, I don't think I'd ever go back to Radio 1, it's just not my music at all.

Three months later, Gretta had changed her station. She had started to listen to a different ILR (Independent Local Radio) station that played con-temporary pop music alongside pop music from the 1970s and 1980s. Later, her listening habits were to change again. These changes were directly related to relationship changes in her life. Gretta has been divorced for almost two years, and she has two sons, aged 12 and 19, the elder living away from home when I first met her. She lives in a top (fourth) floor council flat and receives Income Support. She sometimes works part-time as a catering assistant.

Over the previous year, Gretta had developed four different relationships with men, and each time her listening had changed with her changing emotional situation. The interpretation or reception of radio is not predictable, but individual, so that the same radio output would not necessarily create the same, or even similar, soundscapes for different people, or in different contexts, or at different times. Within the home, as Gretta demonstrates, other factors come into play, such as changing relationships and work patterns. For Gretta, radio's importance and presence in her life has fluctuated along with her emotions. It has, at different times, provided a link to an outside world, which she has felt somewhat excluded from when she has been alone. At other times, it has provided a link with someone she has been romantically involved with, so that on more than one occasion, she has changed her station to one that her current boyfriend listened to. Nevertheless, her preference for what radio stations would define as classic gold music has always remained important to her, and this is the sound that has dominated her listening choices, and to which she has always returned.

Gretta demonstrates how radio sound can be used to provide a changing backdrop to social relationships. Radio sound can also reinforce a routine; it can provide a rhythm to prepare oneself for social life. Bob, a 46-year-old financial adviser, switches Radio 4 on as he gets ready for work, as he puts on his suit and tie. It is a preparation for the day, which keeps him in touch with what's going on in the world, and puts him in the right frame of mind. He will surround himself with the sound of the radio, so that both of the sets in his house can be on at the same time; he will:

> turn it on first thing in the morning in the bedroom and listen to it, if I'm moving around the house then I've often got both sets on [the other set is in the kitchen] quite loud so I can hear it all over the house.

When he returns home after work, it is put on again, always on Radio 4. This is his routine that he says has not changed for many years, and he predicts that it will remain the same in the future. It is a part of his life. It keeps him in touch with a world that interests him and helps him to define who he is in such a world.

Foregrounded sound: a moving soundscape

A soundscape is not a static, two-dimensional thing. Waterman writes of a "densely textured soundscape" created by "Juju music, with voices, guitars, and talking drum amplified at high decibel levels . . . which conditions the behaviour of participants in Yoruba neo-traditional life cycle celebrations" (1990: 214). He sees the possibilities of investigating music not simply in its context – the usual ethnomusicologists' approach – but as a context "for human perception and action"(ibid.). Thus, the concept of a textured soundscape produces a means of looking at the effect of sound on the actors involved, and on their effect on that sound.

The choice of the type of radio output – music, speech and combinations of both – seems to depend in part on what activities the listener is engaged in, what state of mind or mood the listener is in or wants to achieve and what level of backgrounding or foregrounding is required: in other words what sort of textured soundscape. Feld found that sound was used as an

35

expressive means for articulating shared feelings and emotions, and he uncovered a pattern linking activities, myths, feelings, gender and expressive performance. This pattern pointed to "linkages between sounds, both human and natural, and sentiments, social ethos and emotion" (1990: 14). While Feld's emphasis is on the symbolism of sound in a ritual context, in a postscript he concentrates on his informants' reactions to his findings and relates how his informants felt that he should have paid more attention to more mundane daily sounds:

> the ones that tell the weather, season of year, time of day. They asked why I told so much about birds but so little about frogs, insects, different animals. They asked why I had told about the *muni* bird myth, and not told many others. They asked why I had not told about how all sounds in the forest are mama, "reflections" of what is unseen. (Feld 1990: 264)

Taken in isolation, his analysis of certain uses of sounds were seen by his informants as providing only a part of a much wider picture. This led Feld to look again at sound in the ritualized context, relating it more to "the kind of practical and feelingful everyday interaction with environmental sound" (1990: 265) in everyday life. His informants had made it clear to him that "every sound was a 'voice in the forest' " (ibid.) and that he should pay attention to them all. He found that everyday sounds serve to ground the ceremonial performances. To look at radio sound as texture in the domestic sphere, requires an understanding of the ways in which a soundscape can operate to link the social and the private. Within the texture of a domestic soundscape, listeners can work on their sociality, keeping the outside world firmly in the background, or bringing it closer and surrounding oneself with it. The domestic universe, with its particular soundscape, can thereby provide some sort of validation, company, stimulation or simply a background texture in which to embed, or against which to relate, oneself. This could be seen as an exercise in "grounding" the listener.

Radio sound, and sound in general, has the capacity to become foregrounded or backgrounded. To look at a soundscape as some sort of two-dimensional entity, would be to miss the ways in which different sounds appear to integrate to create it. Waterman makes the point that sound is, in itself, textured. Both Feld and Waterman see the soundscape as consisting of interacting and overlapping sounds. Feld names this constantly changing soundscape a spatio-acoustic mosaic, a term that offers a perception of the depth and motion of soundscapes.

To look at it more closely, this mosaic has potential for developing an understanding of the use of radio sound, because it allows for the ways in which sounds can be brought forward or pushed back, depending both on their particular form, and on the uses the listener has in mind, or credits them with: "all sounds are dense, multilayered, overlapping, alternating, and interlocking" (Feld 1990: 265), discrete sounds do not appear in nature. The Kaluli have a concept for this which they call *dulugu ganalau* or "lift-up-over-sounding". This is the most general term used to describe the natural sonic form of the forest, and explains Feld's conception of the Kaluli soundscape as a mosaic:

> The constantly changing figure and ground of this spatio-acoustic mosaic is a "lift-up-over-sounding" texture without gaps, pauses or breaks. The essence of "lift-up-over-sounding" is part relations that are simultaneously in-synchrony while out-of-phase. The overall feeling is of synchronous togetherness, of consistently cohesive part coordination in sonic motion and participatory experience. Yet the parts are also out-of-phase, that is, at distinctly different and shifting points of the same cycle or phrase structure at any moment, with each of the parts continually changing in degree of displacement from a hypothetical unison. (Feld 1990: 265–6)

Feld makes the point that this is the case, both in the ritualized, ceremonial context, and in the context of the everyday, natural soundscape. The idea that sounds and textures "lift-up-over" one another, is an interesting way of looking at radio listening. Stockfelt (1994) talks about our ability to "disharken" sounds that we see as "normal in the situation", but irrelevant to what we are listening to or doing, so that in a concert hall we disregard, or disharken, the sound of our neighbour's rumbling stomach. Poysko (1994) writes about radios in cowsheds in Finland, where the sounds of cowsheds in recent years have been transformed by mechanization. In their use of radio in the cowsheds, it "is as though the workers resume possession of the acoustic space by covering it with their own music" (Poysko 1994: 85). The noises they are covering are mechanical: "music in a cowshed is a form of soundscaping, and its function is to humanise and personalise" (ibid: 88). *Electric Radioland* reports that "Radio is ... being used primarily as a backdrop: therefore it follows that whatever the primary activity is, it may intrude further onto the radio station and then drop out again" (Navigator 1993: 10). Written for the Radio Advertising Bureau, this report is aimed at advertisers, and seeks to explore ways in which their messages can better be heard. It sees radio as a good medium for advertisers (as opposed to TV) because it sees listeners as "zoning, not zapping". This means that listeners will mentally switch off, or zone out from, what they are not interested in, rather than physically switch stations, as a TV viewer would more likely do. Later on, they would zone back in again. This ties in closely with the ways in which my informants talked about their listening. While radio sound provides a background to activities, it also has the capacity to suddenly become the central activity in itself.

Ear contact

For the Kaluli, weeping and song are about confirming shared emotional states. They are "expressive codes" that reference "items and events to a lived world of actual people, places, actions, and behaviors. At the same time they reference the same items and events to abstract qualities and values, precisely described by the Kaluli notion of *hega* or 'underneath' " (Feld 1990: 222). This concept of "underneath" is most readily translated into English as "meaning". These referencing systems, as Feld describes them, where the real world and the abstract world are brought into play, are able to create a "momentary social and personal 'inside' sensation in which the weeper or singer can be seen, heard, or felt to be a bird" (ibid.). To stretch an analogy, we might consider what referencing systems come into play when we listen to the radio: what role does such an activity play in our conception, and perception, of what is public and private? What effect does it have on our personal identities, and on our creation of our social selves? Does radio allow a momentary "inside" sensation that the listener is a part of something else, perhaps outside of the home, or encompassing it, and does radio sound possess an abstract quality that might somehow get "underneath"?

One of my informants talked to me about his choice of radio listening, which has been fairly consistent throughout his adult life, in terms of the "type" of radio he listens to. He is aged 57, and works for a local utility company. His preference is Radio 4, which he will listen to up until around six o'clock in the evening as often as he can. Other times, he might listen to Radio 3, but this is "only a standby, it's not something I would listen to regularly, it would only be a standby if there was something I wasn't terribly interested in on Radio 4". While he likes radio that stimulates, interests and educates, he prefers Radio 4 to Radio 3 because although he enjoys the music on Radio 3 "the speech tends to get a little bit above my head". According to Roy you have to "have a certain feeling for it", and although he cannot account for his history of choice in radio listening, he knows what he has a feeling for, and what he does not have a feeling for.

Trisha, who is 37, and works part-time as a care assistant, has five radios in her three-bedroom house. She lives with her husband, an engineer (previously a professional sportsman), and three teenage sons. When I first met her, she was a very dedicated listener of an ILR station that plays chart music from the 1970s, 1980s and 1990s.

> I usually have the music on wherever I am in the house . . . sometimes I have it on in the kitchen and in here [lounge] because I like to hear music loud you see, that's me personally, not that I would disturb the neighbours, not to that extent, but I actually do like it quite loud, so if I sometimes have it on in the kitchen and in here it sounds wonderful. . . . If there's a particular record on that I really like I will come back in

and turn it on really loud, because I like to hear, I love the bass of the music coming through you know, so if there's a particular record I like, I'll do it then.

For Trisha, music is an important part of her life. Her husband and three sons are all very interested in sport, and do not share her interest in music, or radio. She feels isolated in her family, and listens to radio when she is on her own at home. This is usually for around seven hours a day. She has a very large collection of CDs, and buys books about pop music, which she uses to research competitions set by the station, and to reinforce her extensive knowledge of popular music. She sees herself as "passionate" about music, and about radio. Her passion is not shared by her immediate family or by her friends:

> I don't really mix with anybody who's particularly interested in music, oh, apart from my brother, I mean if my brother was here now we'd be talking shop ... people are aware where I work that I'm really into music and radio so they'll say to me sometimes, for instance, "there's this record on at the moment and I don't know what it is" and they sing it to me, and I say "Oh, that's ..." but I don't actually mix with anybody that actually has the same interests.

Trisha will listen to her own music collection on CD sometimes, usually when she is having an "off day", as it can lift her out of a mild depression, in a way that radio cannot:

> I just look through my selection and I would know what was the appropriate one to put on, and I play a song and I know I'll feel a lot better after that ... You rely on it don't you [music], I couldn't be without it I know that.

Researcher: So what is it about radio that makes you want to listen to that rather than play your own music all the time?
Trisha: I like some of the slots, particularly that Gary Vincent has in his show, for instance the 10 at 10 which is at the start of his show ... this is 10 songs with a connecting theme in some way and Gary Vincent devised a slot in his show whereby we get the opportunity to send in our suggestions so that's played approximately 10 o'clock till about 20 to 11 it takes about that time, and I really look forward to that every day ... sometimes I'll set my alarm, shows how silly I am, I'll set my alarm after I've been on nights for my radio alarm to come on at 10 for me to listen to it and I'll lie in bed dozing and listening to it and go back to sleep after, because I really do like it.

For Trisha, radio was important because she felt she was sharing her passion with other people. She joined a listener panel, organized by the station, and enjoyed the quarterly meetings, and her involvement in the station. She felt "very privileged to be chosen to go on it". She was unsure, however, about how the others at the meeting saw her. She worried that she may have been viewed by them as "over the top", with her enthusiasm and interest. This meant that she often wanted to make suggestions to the station, but did not through lack of confidence.

> I think I can present as being a little bit over the top and I think sometimes I need to stand back a bit . . . a bit too enthusiastic. And I think you can frighten some people off and sometimes I wonder and question whether that's probably how I presented myself, but I mean it's genuine . . . I don't know if there's anybody who's as over the top as I am.

In her home, she was faced with a similar situation, where she felt that if only she could win a top prize (£1,000), she could justify her involvement with radio to her husband. When alone, she was able to indulge her interest in a way that was not possible when the rest of her family were there. The children preferred to watch television when they got home from school, and her husband would ask her to turn the radio down when he was at home:

> My husband doesn't actually like listening to the radio very loud, if I've got it on ever, so if he ever comes in sometimes and I've got it on the first thing he will say is "could you please turn that down" it's not acceptable to him hearing wise, but to me it doesn't seem particularly loud . . . so there's a conflict sometimes between us . . .
> . . . it causes conflict between our relationship sometimes because I mean, he's into cricket and football and my sons are as well and so I'm on my own regarding my music, I suppose that's why I've taken it on board as being a friend as well because I sometimes feel isolated, I feel I'm up against it really with them being so much into sport and everything, it actually has caused conflict sometimes. As I said before, the noise level sometimes when my husband comes in is unacceptable to him and so sometimes he'll say to me "could you please turn that down Trisha" and inevitably I end up switching it off.

Music plays a central part in Trisha's life, and music radio enabled her to think that she was not alone in this, despite her family isolation. When she saw other people wearing station sweatshirts, she felt relieved and excited that she was not the only one who was proud to walk around with her favourite station's logo displayed on her chest.

40

Trisha is unusual among radio listeners in that she was very actively involved in radio, either through phoning-in for competitions and attending listener panel meetings, or through other events organized by the station. She is unusual in the way in which she engaged with the station, in a face-to-face way, moving beyond using the radio to create a background, to making eye contact, or "ear contact", thus forming a "real" relationship with it. Her case, however, emphasizes the problems that can emerge when the "feeling" for radio, and the particular soundscape created by it in an individual domestic environment, is taken outside of the home, and tested against other interpretations of radio relationships.

Trisha was aware that the station representatives who attended the listener panel meetings did not understand her involvement with and passion for radio, and felt a need to explain this to them, but did not know how to do this. She had invested a lot in the station, which had helped her to define her sense of self, and practise her interest in music, but to the station, she was just another listener, and worse than that, she was seen by them, she felt, as "over the top". She felt that her input during meetings was criticized by the station staff, that they did not appreciate her abilities and knowledge of music: "I really feel deep down that I've got something I could offer [the station]", but her qualities were not recognized. She found herself in a situation where she was looking for ways of improving her relationship with the station, but not finding them. Nevertheless, she was happy to attend the meetings, as this kept the possibility of being recognized for who she was, and developing the relationship on that basis, alive.

After about two years of membership, the listener panel was disbanded by the station, and for Trisha, this marked the breakdown of a real relationship. Trisha had sensed the end of the relationship at the last meeting, although the members of the panel were not told at that time that it was to be the last meeting. She told me how she had "picked up vibes", and knew something was wrong, and had "come home really upset". She felt personally let down by the station.

In a way, Trisha could be seen, metaphorically, to have been having an affair with the radio. It provided her with an escape from the oppression of her family, and her feelings of isolation, but did not contain the risk of a "real" affair. As an affair, it was accompanied by guilt, so that she was continually trying to justify her "passion". It also involved collusion with others who shared her "passion". In the safety of her domestic environment, all was well, but as the relationship moved outside of the home, and entered the realm of face-to-face social relationships, it became fraught with problems, causing her to question her own self-image. While initially, her relationship with the station had acted to reinforce her commitment to it at home, gradually it challenged it. Eventually, she became like a jilted lover, and was left feeling upset, insecure and misunderstood. When I last talked to Trisha, she was trying out other stations in an attempt to find one that was right for her. Although the sound of her previous station had not changed, her relationship to it had.

This interpretation, however, could be oversimplistic and superficial. In the music radio industry, there has been a long-standing notion of a stereotypical female listener, who invites the male presenter into her home, as "romantic visitors descending on a bored housewife" (Baehr & Ryan 1984: 8). Yet, there has been no research to investigate this perceived relationship on a deeper level. The fact that the target audience of Trisha's preferred station is female, and in their thirties, because this is the most prominent section of their audience as shown by ratings, does not make the stereotypical image of the housewife, fantasizing about the male presenter, true. The relationship, if Trisha's case is used as an example, is much more than this. Trisha fits the station's profile of the target listener, but they do not really know who she is.

Trisha was not "having an affair" with an individual male presenter, or with the station as a whole. She was "having an affair" with her self, in relation to a world that can, and does, exist in the soundscape that she was able to create when alone at home. Her father, whom she remembers with affection and sadness, died when she was a young girl. He was a trumpet player, and it is to him that she attributes her interest in and love for music. She is not a musician and cannot play an instrument, and she regrets this. If her father had lived, he would, she thinks, have taught her this. The soundscape she creates on a daily basis, has, as a major contributor, a radio station that tells her, and all of its listeners, through their station rhetoric, that it cares about music and about its listeners. It tells them how it listens to them, and gives them only what they want to hear. It respects the music it plays, not allowing presenters to talk over records. This particular station is very predictable in its sound – it is therefore very reliable. Its tight format means that Trisha can be sure that it will sound the way she expects it to sound, at all times. It therefore contributes, in a very reliable way, to the domestic environment that she creates in everyday life.

On the surface, radio can appear to be an unremarkable thing, yet once it is viewed in the complex environment of everyday lives, it can be seen to act in many different and meaningful ways. There are qualities of radio sound that seem to touch people in a very immediate and intimate way. Perhaps the feeling that Roy describes works in a similar way to the abstract quality described by the Kaluli as "underneath", in the way in which it (momentarily or not) creates a social and personal "inside" sensation. Trisha demonstrates how radio sound can act in the home, to create relationships between self and others that are not the same as face-to-face relationships, but that are nevertheless important in the constitution of a self that is, or would like to be, social. The way in which her construction of self was threatened, when she took her experience of radio sound outside the home, and found that others failed to see her relationship with radio in the way that she did, demonstrates the way in which the home as context provides a safe and manageable environment, for explorations of relationships between self and others that is personal and unique.

What the examples used in this chapter have in common is the use of radio sound to conceptualize social relationships. That is, it is used to contribute to an individual's sociality. For example, it can be used to create silence (social silence) when there is too much sound (social activity), or it can be used to create sound when there is too much silence. Equally, it can act as a reminder of social life outside of the home, when one is too busy, or unable, to take part in it. And as Trisha demonstrates, it can, on a very personal and intimate level, provide a form of sociality that allows for the creation of an alternative environment for living from her perceived, domestic oppression. It is one that draws on many referencing systems, as Feld proposes, referencing a lived world and abstract qualities and values. Trisha is able to create a personal reality that reflects on, and affects, notions of her own sociality.

The research I have undertaken, in order to explore the ways in which radio sound is used in the home, provides many avenues for exploration. This chapter aims to recognize the ways in which radio sound in the home adds to the textured environment (or material culture) within which every-day lives are lived, and social selves are created, re-created and modified. Thus, upon entering the home, radio sound becomes both material and social – it is social in its materiality. Looking again at the example of Trisha, who uses radio to create a sociality that is different from face-to-face social relationships, we can see that it is, nonetheless, real. What she is engaged in is not a vicarious pursuit. The relationships established between self and others are significant, and complementary, in a larger scheme of sociality, and they are present within real lives, not merely imagined. These relation-ships may exist in part in Trisha's imagination, but they have a very direct impact on her as a person, a wife, a mother. They are made material, tactile even, through her creation of her own textured, domestic soundscape. To paraphrase the words of another informant, radio stimulates the imagin-ation, and imagination gives substance to sound. And sound can be seen to give substance, in its materiality, to relations between self and others.

Notes

1. This chapter arises from PhD research funded by the ESRC.
2. RAJAR (Radio Joint Audience Research Limited) figures show that each week 86 per cent of UK adults aged 15 and over listened to radio between January and April 1995, with an average listening per week for those adults of 21 hours (RAJAR/RSL, Quarter 1/95).
3. The term "soundscape" is fairly commonly used in discussions of music and more general sounds. Its definition (although not its invention) as the sonic

environment consisting of both natural and human-made sounds is generally attributed to R. Murray Schafer (1980).

4. The fieldwork for this study is ongoing at the time of writing and is being carried out in and around Bristol using qualitative research methods. Bristol is a city in the south-west of England with a population at the last Census (1991) of approximately 506,000 (Greater Bristol). An Independent Local Radio station based in Bristol serves an adult population of 1,231,000. I have lived in Bristol since 1988. A pilot study followed by the main fieldwork involving 55 informants took place between 1993 and1995. I have used several methods of obtaining data including informal questionnaires, follow-up interviews, diary keeping, sound mapping of the home and participant observation. In addition I have looked at the radio industry, both commercial and BBC, in particular at how they research audiences and assess audience need. The methodology employed and the problems encountered will be described elsewhere.

5. See Silverstone (1989, 1994) on the use of theories on everyday life and domestic television consumption; Morley (1986, 1992) on the need to contextualize television consumption in the home; Silverstone & Hirsch (1992) on the consumption of information and communication technologies in the home.

6. Pirate radio is the name widely used to describe stations operating without a licence. I shall discuss such stations and their listeners elsewhere.

References

Baehr, H. & M. Ryan 1984. *Shut up and listen! Women and local radio: a view from the inside*. London: Comedia.

Dauenhauer, B.P. 1980. *Silence: the phenomenon and its ontological significance*. Bloomington: Indiana University Press.

Feld, S. 1990. *Sound and sentiment: birds, weeping, poetics and song in Kaluli expression*, 2nd edn. Philadelphia: University of Pennsylvania Press.

Gullestad, M. 1992. *The art of social relations: essays on culture, social action and everyday life in modern Norway*. Oslo: Scandinavian University Press.

Miller, D. 1987. *Material culture and mass consumption*. Oxford: Blackwell.

Morley, D. 1986. *Family television: cultural power and domestic leisure*. London: Comedia.

Morley, D. 1992. *Television, audiences and cultural studies*. London: Routledge.

Navigator 1993. *Electric Radioland: report on research among radio listeners*. Prepared for the Radio Advertising Bureau.

Needham, R. 1967. Percussion and transition. *Man* **3** (2).

Poysko, M. 1994. The blessed noise and little moo: aspects of soundscape in cowsheds. In *Soundscapes: essays on vroom and moo*, H. Jarviluoma (ed.). Tampere, Finland: Tampere University.

RAJAR/RSL 1995. Quarterly summaries of radio listening. Quarter 1/95.

Schafer, R.M. 1980. *The tuning of the world*. Toronto: McClelland & Steward.

Silverstone, R. 1989. Let us then return to the murmuring of everyday practices: a note on Michel de Certeau, television and everyday life. *Theory, Culture and Society* **6** (1), 77–94.

Silverstone, R. 1994. *Television and everyday life*. London: Routledge.

Silverstone, R. & E. Hirsch 1992. *Consuming technologies: media and information in domestic spaces*. London: Routledge.

Stockfelt, O. 1994. Cars, buildings and soundscapes. In *Soundscapes: essays on vroom and moo*, H. Jarviluoma (ed.). Tampere, Finland: Tampere University.

Waterman, C.A. 1990. *Juju: a social history and ethnography of an African popular music*. Chicago: University of Chicago Press.

CHAPTER 3

From woollen carpet to grass carpet: bridging house and garden in an English suburb

Sophie Chevalier

Although I did not intend to study it, in the context of a comparative study – in Britain and France – which focused on material culture in the domestic space, I was led to an interest in a specific aspect of British space firmly located within domesticity: the garden.

The key analytical notion within this research is "appropriation": one can understand this term as the construction of an inalienable environment through the use of mass-produced objects (Miller 1987, 1988; Putnam & Newton 1990; Chevalier 1993, 1994, 1995). In the study of material culture, one can distinguish two different traditions, the French and the English. In their approach, French anthropologists focus on technology (Mauss 1950; Leroi-Gourhan 1965; Haudricourt 1987) and they are quite disconcerted by mass-produced objects in opposition to their English colleagues who have not inherited this long tradition. Researchers (e.g. Tardieu 1976), who are interested in the domestic space, study traditional material culture which is now on display at the Musée des Arts et Traditions Populaires in Paris. Nevertheless, there are French sociologists, such as Baudrillard (1968, 1970, 1972) and Bourdieu (1979, 1980) who carry out researches on mass consumption in the sociology of ways of life. There are now some approaches in common between the two countries such as the sociology of techniques (Latour 1991, 1994 for France). But consumer practices have been reconsidered first in English-speaking anthropology (Csikszentmihalyi and Rochberg-Halton 1981; Appadurai 1986; Miller 1987). My own research is associated with this approach which has only recently become established in France.

Jersey Farm's gardens

In this chapter, I would like to examine how people, as creative appropriators, succeed in creating their own interior décor through objects. The result of this construction is a system, fluid but stable enough for observation. The garden is part of this system: the first stage is to consider the relationships between the inside space and the closed outside space, the garden. But this space differs from the interior because of its interface with "nature", and not only with artefacts. In gardening, the actors integrate "nature" in their everyday domestic practices and appropriate it. What have these practices in common with those of the construction of the domestic décor? What are the differences? The aim is to compare the appropriation of the domestic interior with the garden and its natural elements. More abstractly, I intend to consider the garden as mediator linked to the natural, social and cultural environment. Successively the garden will be considered as place, practice and idea.

Then, I would like to go further in my argument by comparing France and Britain, gardening and cooking. Cooking bridges the outside world and the inside one: something "natural" is transformed with the help of artefacts. Inside the house, two spaces are related: the kitchen, where "nature" is transformed, and the dining room, where it is consumed, including its physiological dimension. As I shall show in the description of the Probsts' lounge, the objects displayed in the dining area are usually in affinity with the use of this space (as plates hung on the wall). The number of artefacts – electric appliances – used in cooking is often related to the degree of experience in appropriating raw material. The kitchen work is a space of exchange: the circulation of information as recipes, proficiency, and products such as jam or preserves. Socialization during childhood plays a role in adult skills. But experience is also important to acquire competencies. Some people are labelled "experts" by their family circle or friends, and can give good advice about cooking.

The kitchen or dining area mediates sociability as does the garden: the first space is an internal mediator, inside the family, and the second an external mediator. The organization of the furniture stresses the mediation of cooked food: chairs around the table which oblige people to see each other without the intervention of other artefacts (as the fireplace which mediates the English lounge). As with gardening skills, so also cooking skills are part of household's self-presentation. As with gardening, cooking transforms "nature", and through this appropriation mediations are built, of a temporal, spatial and social nature. In conclusion, I would like to focus on the use of land in these two countries, a comparison based on the difference of time-scale.

This chapter is based on my British data – interviews, observations and the media – collected during my survey and focused on gardens and gardening. The gardens to which my research relates belong to a group of informants I met when I investigated interior décor. Since May 1994, I have been doing a survey in the north of St Albans near London, in an estate called Jersey Farm, built since the mid-1970s. The houses are different sizes; because of this, people can and do move home within this estate according to the stage of their life-cycle. Being home owners, residents are also able to build extensions, to transform and extend their environment. The residents are mainly white-collar workers, and some are retired factory workers. I met the members of thirty households from this area and with ten of them, I conducted a series of interviews and made observations on gardening.

Every resident – except one young woman who lives in a flat – has a private garden divided into two areas, the front and the back garden whose social role is different.[1] As with the size of the house, the size of the garden varies, but generally it is related to the length of the house. Having a big garden offers the possibility of extending one's house. The choice is not only to incorporate a part of "nature", but also to diminish and transform it into domestic space. People choose their garden size in relation to their life-cycle, the number of household members, and the possibility of "invest-ment" (in time and money) in gardening. A widow would like a smaller garden, which is less tiring to take care of: "I had a garden, too big really . . . I was much more active three years ago; I have to find someone to pay to cut the grass." By contrast, a couple with children have big gardens where they install a slide or swing, and where children can play unsupervised.

The front garden acts as the presentation of the household, an identity marker in the absence of any other sign, such as the name on the door. Somebody who visits a French household learns a great deal by reading the letterboxes on the doors: name; composition of the household; familial situation (divorce; cohabitation; stepchildren; etc.).[2] In Jersey Farm, thanks to the front garden, the visitor could also collect some information, but in this case on the social integration of the residents through the similarity of their garden with those of their neighbours.[3] The neighbour of Mr and Mrs Spring transformed her front garden into a "Japanese" style: she replaced the lawn with gravel and put in small bushes and a Japanese lamp. By comparison, they thought that their own front garden "looked really silly". They have started to modify it to match the neighbouring front garden. Mrs Walcot is planning to improve her front garden: she would like to have an "original" garden. The residents' association organizes a competition for "the most beautiful front garden": this presentation is a part of the ideology of "village life" where once everybody knew everybody, and where all other signs of identity are redundant.

The "back garden", more or less protected from outside views by fences, is a private/public space as is the lounge, in opposition to the front garden, which is a public/private space. Only a few authorized persons can enter the back garden. This space expresses the individual and familial identity of the owner through a sense of being "at home". It belongs to a private dimension, but friends and neighbours will be readily invited to enter. A few householders have built an intermediate space between the inside and outside, a "conservatory". They rarely use it according to its original intention, but rather as an extension of the lounge or as a playroom for their children. As in Jersey Farm families, Halle (1993: 23ff) shows that in New York households

49

with young children, the private gardens tend to become "child-dominated" play areas. The greatest space is devoted to items such as swing sets.

The garden as place: the symmetry with the lounge

If the garden is a spatial continuation of the house, I would argue that the disposition of the garden presents analogies with the lounge, another private/public space.

It is easy to observe that all these interiors have some pieces of furniture in common, as "standard". Every living room has similarities with others that need to be examined. But beyond these similarities, one also observes some differences that reflect aspects of the resident's identity. In themselves, the Jersey Farm objects are "nothing special", because they are mass-produced artefacts. It is the relationships among the elements that create the specificities of every room and express the identity of its owner, despite the fact that some of the features are present in all the households. In each case, one always observes a systematic whole with the same basic elements,[4] the "three-piece suite" placed traditionally near the fireplace (and television). People strongly stress the importance of having a focal point in their room. The fireplace is an ideal focal point; if not, the television serves a similar purpose. People may add other furniture, decorative objects and wall decorations around the basic elements, following certain affinities that reflect the household's identity.

All the gardens studied have a similar spatial organization. Because of the architectural disposition of the houses, all gardens form rectangles that run a few metres from the back of the houses, from small patios that stretch along the back façades. The gardens are enclosed all around by fences of one and a half metres high, more or less protecting people from outside view, but not from noise and fumes. The beds are displayed along the fences, with the intention of enclosing the space by plants, with the lawn in the centre.

These gardens have similarities in their content too: sheds where tools and the lawn mower are stored, and they are always "gardens of delight" (Thomas 1983), not vegetable or fruit gardens. Plants are flowers and shrubs, above all evergreens. Thomas shows the expansion in flower-gardening in the eighteenth and nineteenth centuries; since the Elizabethan period the mere vegetable or herb garden was opposed to the "garden of delight". This is related to the emergence of the "non-utilitarian attitude to the natural world" and the delight in nature for its own sake as an end (Thomas 1983: 223ff; McFarlane 1987: 77ff). In fact, the vegetable garden as a productive space for the household declined and gave way to an area for leisure (even if vegetables were also grown there), as it is observed in other countries such as France and the USA. In France, this movement seems quite recent, after the Second World War (Dubost 1984); some people still cultivate vegetables for pleasure or for ecological purposes. In urban and suburban USA, Halle dated this decline to the early 1900s (Halle 1993: 236).

On this basis, people can add other elements through which they express their household's identity: the creation of central beds, a rock garden, a trellis, a compost heap, the choice and the array of flowers, one or two trees, a few vegetables and cooking herbs. In spring, the lawn is full of flowering bulbs, especially daffodils. People also display lots of artefacts: pieces of furniture (such as chairs and tables, benches); ceramic decorations and decorative objects such as mushrooms, tortoises and squirrels, hang on the fences to amplify this natural space (see McCracken 1988: 121 for this redundancy). Birds have their own houses, sometimes of a very sophisticated form in which residents put seeds for food during winter time. All these things are "in excess of" what nature will provide here; they are explicit messages of a desire to be "natural" by providing models of things that are often in fact unacceptable in their natural state.

If we compare the similarities that exist between the interior décor and the garden, we observe an obvious symmetry between them. In the centre of these two spaces, the woollen carpet of the lounge echoes the grass carpet of the garden. In their discourses and practices, Jersey Farm residents stress these items. The choice of the carpet is important because it has to match the other elements such as curtains or the sofa pattern. Informants describe as a "nightmare" being constrained to live with carpets they did not choose. The lawn requires great care: mowing, watering, putting on fertilizer, herbicides and pesticides. During my visit to the garden, they comment on the state of their lawn, apologizing in case it is not like a "woollen or velvety carpet". Jenkins (1994) in her book on American lawn mania describes this interest as a national obsession, born in the late nineteenth century and developed during the twentieth century related to the development of the lawn-care industry. She also (1994: 122) shows how in the USA advertising for lawn articles, in which women were the target since the Second World War, included "images of flowers and household items such as carpets and vacuum cleaners". In fact, the lawn mowers are explicitly compared to vacuum cleaners, as the lawn is to a carpet. Around the "carpets", people display their basic furniture, the wallpaper and curtains in the lounge, the shed and flower beds in the garden.[5] Then they add more personal items, creating their own affinities: decorative objects such as souvenirs, photographs in the lounge and selected plants and artefacts in the garden.

In pushing forward this strong symmetry, I would like to consider the existence of a "bridge" between the lounge and the garden. In this bridging, the view plays an important role. Mukerji shows that in the European history of gardens the "house and garden were continuous sites for cultural accumulation and display, with parterres in the transitional position, bridging house and garden. Gardens were extensions of the house in architecture as well as decoration" (1990: 657). Some informants are aware of that; for example Mrs Walcot describes her garden as "the continuation of

my lounge". In fact, it is the "view" that creates the bridge between the two spaces. The spatial organization of the lounge is such that the furniture is arranged to have the best view of the garden, and to create the illusion of being outside: "From the lounge, it's like being in the garden!" (Mrs Kinson) or "If I can sit here I can see the garden, what I like is to stand up next to the window, very often birds come up close. I am just pleased to see it" (Mr Layland). Historically it is also testified: "these gardens were meant to be viewed from the house" (Mukerji 1990: 663). The boundary between the garden and the "nature" is formed by the "ha-ha", a ditch with a wall on its inner side below ground level. It is not interrupting the view from within, being visible only from a close proximity.

In the garden and in the interior décor, the "view" plays an important role as a basis upon which people create affinities among the different elements. One could argue that the reification of the natural dimension of the garden occurs through this process of distance; however, touch and smell are also important in the appropriation of this space and they are sometimes used as criteria in classifying plants. In their discourses, people are often embarrassed when commenting upon and describing their gardens, especially in naming flowers and plants. Except for a few well-known types of flowers such as carnations, roses, honeysuckle, daffodils and conifers, they use their own descriptive terms, such as "rabbit's ears" for a shrub with leaves similar to this animal's ears or the "plant-with-yellow-flowers". Their description is based on the view, and sometimes on the touch (smooth or downy leaves), but they do not refer to botanical taxonomy. Thomas (1983) shows that since the late eighteenth century, and the introduction of Linneus's classification, and especially the introduction of a new Latin terminology, the gulf widened further between popular and learned ways of looking at the natural world and led to a progressive decline in the popular use of the latter. This new nomenclature is based on observable characteristics of the plants, in other words on what is seen. By contrast, the old "popular taxonomy was based on utilitarian considerations and crucial to these practices was the ancient assumption that man and nature were locked into one interacting world" (Thomas 1983: 78). Indeed, this classification is based on the visual, a new approach described by Foucault (1966) who shows that since the seventeenth century the visual predominates as a distinctive criterion in elaborating taxonomies.

However, this bridge is created not only by the view, but also through the practices that lead to reciprocal "colonization".

The garden as practice: gardening as colonization

The above description and analysis suggest that there is some "interpenetration" between the outside and inside: "nature" enters into the lounge in reified form, and artefacts, such as furniture, participate in the appropriation of the garden, by denaturalizing it. I would like to examine the appropriation of the garden by the practices associated with this space (gardening) taking into account those of the lounge. The process of appropriation could be described as a reciprocal "colonization".

I shall take two lounges and gardens as examples, those of Mr and Mrs Kinson and those of Mr and Mrs Layland. Those households constitute two opposite cases as I shall illustrate.

Mr and Mrs Kinson are married with two teenage daughters both living with them. Mr Kinson works as consultant in a computing company in Coventry. Mrs Kinson is a housewife; a few days a week she carries out voluntary work as a dinner lady in a school. Both are natives of St Albans; they are 40 years old. They live in a detached house that was already extended into two sides to form a lounge and dining room (Fig. 3.1). They bought their furniture only after moving into the house. In the dining room area they have placed a dining table and chairs, a sideboard, a display cabinet and a chest of drawers. These two last pieces of furniture were inherited by Mr Kinson: "we prefer old furniture, but it is not easy to get. So we tried to buy other furniture to match it". But with those pieces they felt that the room did not look right and so they decided to buy a piano to fill a gap on one side of the wall. The colour of the piano was chosen so as to match everything else in the room. On the other side, there is a three-piece suite,

Furniture			*Decorative objects*
1. Three-piece suite	7. Table	I.	Chinese figurines
2. Two bean bags	8. Piano	II.	Old family photographs
3. Television set	9. Table; chairs	III.	Photographs of Mrs Kinson's family
4. Fireplace	10. Sideboard	IV.	Clock ("service gift")
5. Plant stands	11. Chest of drawers	V.	Photographs of both families
6. Coffee table	12. Display cabinet	VI.	Family photographs
		VII.	Washbowl
		VIII.	French clock
		IX.	Porcelains

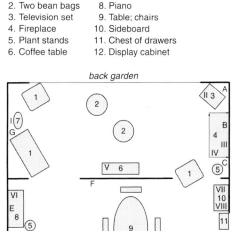

back garden

Wall decoration

Wallpaper grey/white
A. Old photograph of a wheelwright
B. Photograph of the grandfather
C. Photograph of Mrs Kinson's grandparents
D. Reproduction of a landscape
E. School photographs of the daughters
F. Mirror
G. Reproduction of a landscape

– Pink ceiling light; lamps on 4, 7 and 10
– Pot plants on 4 and 5
– Blue carpet; two rugs; cushions; net curtains and floral print curtains

Figure 3.1 Mr and Mrs Kinson: lounge and dining room

two little tables and the television next to the "false" fireplace. They can turn around the furniture to be close to the fire, "like traditional British". They therefore "chose not to have the television as a focal point". Decorative objects are displayed on all pieces of furniture: a few of these are inherited, such as the sideboard or the chest of drawers by Mr Kinson, and the little Chinese figurines by Mrs Kinson from her grandmother. A very important part of the decorative objects is family photographs, not only school portraits which one observes in every lounge in Jersey Farm, but also reproductions of old photographs from the two previous generations. The photographs are displayed on the mantelpiece and on the television.

It is important for this household to own a detached house, even though they are not really interested in gardening: "I could imagine living in a flat, because before we got married, we hadn't got a garden, it didn't bother me . . . I don't mind. My husband likes the garden, but he doesn't do a lot of gardening!" (Mrs Kinson). The garden was created by the previous owners (Fig. 3.2): "It was an established garden before we moved here, there were plants and shrubs already in here. We added a few things, the conifer trees. . . . Sometimes I buy some flowers, I add some plants and herbs. All things my mum gives me" (Mrs Kinson). Nevertheless, they displayed a table with chairs, some small sculptures in stone such as a mushroom, three tortoises and a gnome given by Mr Kinson's aunt: "He came from her garden, so he is really, really old. . . . We don't really like him, but she gave him to us when

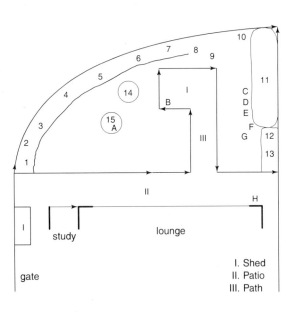

1. Conifer
2. Daisies
3. Honeysuckle
4. Snapdragons
5. Pink flowers
6. Honeysuckle
7. Roses
8. Hydrangeas
9. Yellow flowers
10. Silver birch
11. Shrub (hedge)
12. Magnolia
13. Bright yellow flowers
14. Apple tree (cooking apples)
15. Apple tree (eating apples)

A. Bird house
B. Mushrooms (in stone)
C. Two bird houses
D. Squirrel (in stone)
E. Gnome
F. Bottle and shells
G. Three tortoises
H. Dog
I. Table and chairs

I. Shed
II. Patio
III. Path

Figure 3.2 Mr and Mrs Kinson: back garden

she moved" (Mrs Kinson). They hung a plastic squirrel on one of the apple trees and a bird house on the other tree. As in their lounge, they displayed items in the garden related to their kinship (some plants and sculptures). The two apple trees were already here and they have no other kind of vegetables or herbs. Mrs Kinson gardens when she has time: "I used to go out every six weeks. During the summer, I do it often. My husband cuts the lawn." When she was a child: "We didn't have a garden. . . . We lived above a shop with a big back yard, but there were some offices at the bottom of it, so cars came in and parked there. No grass, just concrete". Nevertheless, her grandparents had an allotment where she used to help. In summer, they sometimes eat outside and invite people; but they dislike barbecued food.

Mr Layland worked in British Aerospace (on the aircraft side) and his wife also worked sporadically in a factory. Both are 65 years old, retired factory workers. Their daughter is married, but their son has been made redundant and is living with them. Mr Layland is a native of London, his wife is from St Albans. They moved from a flat situated 500 metres away to their present three-bedroomed house on the estate. They consider this site as their last house, they do not intend to move again in their retirement. The lounge (Fig. 3.3) is divided into two areas: one is the dining room; the other is the lounge. When they moved in, they changed the colour of the carpet and they bought a new three-piece suite to match. They gave away the old settee that they had bought when they got married, and bought a coffee table and a lady's bureau that she always wanted, but never had space for. They also bought an electric

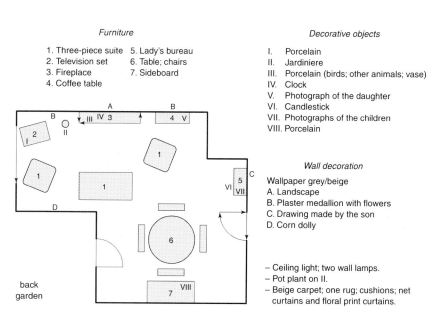

Furniture

1. Three-piece suite 5. Lady's bureau
2. Television set   6. Table; chairs
3. Fireplace   7. Sideboard
4. Coffee table

Decorative objects

I.   Porcelain
II.   Jardiniere
III. Porcelain (birds; other animals; vase)
IV.   Clock
V.   Photograph of the daughter
VI.   Candlestick
VII. Photographs of the children
VIII. Porcelain

Wall decoration

Wallpaper grey/beige
A. Landscape
B. Plaster medallion with flowers
C. Drawing made by the son
D. Corn dolly

– Ceiling light; two wall lamps.
– Pot plant on II.
– Beige carpet; one rug; cushions; net curtains and floral print curtains.

Figure 3.3 Mr and Mrs Layland: lounge and dining room

fireplace, because they wanted to have a "central point" in the lounge and have arranged their three-piece suite around it. They move the coffee table at "tea time", in front of the fireplace and the television. They have displayed a great number of pieces of porcelain on the mantelpiece, porcelains of animals, birds, "all naturalistic things"; many of them are gifts or holiday souvenirs. The dining table and chairs were bought for their flat, but this area is rarely used.

Their garden is the first they have had, and they decided to transform it completely as they did with their lounge: "There was only a shed in the garden, but it was completely run down. There was a fishpond . . . he had lovely ideas. . . . But we are too old. . . . In fact, it was a mess. . . . Lovely bushes, but all run down" (Mr Layland). They filled in the fishpond, built a rock garden, a low wall around the patio and a few steps, put up a new shed (Fig. 3.4). They appropriated the space by transforming it and by gardening. Mr Layland organized a compost heap and a butt for the rainwater. It is a "pleasure garden": there are no vegetables or fruits, but only a few herbs, such as parsley and peppermint. They try to match the colours of the flowers: "It is

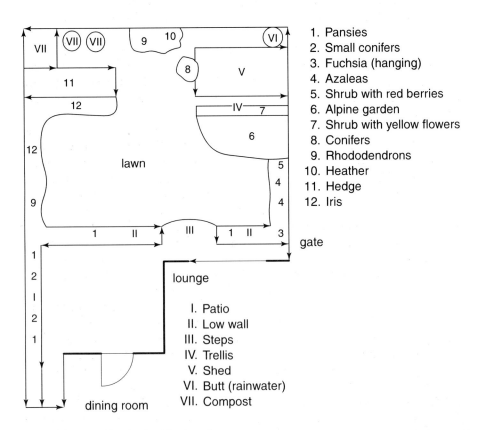

1. Pansies
2. Small conifers
3. Fuchsia (hanging)
4. Azaleas
5. Shrub with red berries
6. Alpine garden
7. Shrub with yellow flowers
8. Conifers
9. Rhododendrons
10. Heather
11. Hedge
12. Iris

I. Patio
II. Low wall
III. Steps
IV. Trellis
V. Shed
VI. Butt (rainwater)
VII. Compost

Figure 3.4 Mr and Mrs Layland: back garden

difficult, some things I don't like. I am not very keen on red, I like yellow roses, or white roses. . . . I like soft colours. We've got iris, I like iris . . . I don't want anything too huge, too big, the garden is quite small, I want reasonably sized plants" (Mrs Kinson). The results of their work do not match their hopes; they tried new experiments that are not always successful: "We try, we cut wrongly, we try again" (Mr Layland). His wife remembers: "I had an uncle who had some ground in Hampshire, it is a lovely county, and he had everything, vegetables, tomatoes, everything, really. . . . He had a greenhouse, he literally lived in his garden". They like to watch TV programmes on gardening and they have books on gardens. They visit garden centres and National Trust gardens. Both are very keen on gardening: it is a common project, as is their lounge. Except for gardening, they do not use their garden:

> We don't like to sit outside and eat. . . . I don't like to eat food outside to be honest, I don't like the insects, the flies . . . I prefer to sit inside, comfortably. We are not sun-lovers actually! We sit inside with the door open. It is more comfortable that way. People have barbecues, I hate barbecues, the smell. . . . It is awful, oh dear! (Mrs Layland)

These cases illustrate two different and opposite possibilities of "bridging" the lounge and the garden, as a process of appropriation. The Kinsons seem quite diffident in dealing with their garden: they leave it more or less as they found it when they moved in, and they "colonized" it with furniture and artefacts to appropriate it. In fact, they use these items to extend their lounge into the garden. By contrast, the Laylands bring "natural" themes or designs into their lounge: they "colonized" it with such items as a collection of birds in porcelain, a picture of a landscape, indoor plants, etc. The Kinsons do not like gardening but do like socializing in the garden (eating outside and barbecues). While the Laylands love gardening, they do not like eating outside, or socializing in their garden, but they like to socialize over fences, exchanging gossip, advice and plants.[6]

These two examples are cases of different colonization: first, the garden is "colonized" by the lounge, and secondly, the garden "colonizes" the lounge. However, more commonly the colonization is reciprocal and quite balanced; people invest both in home decoration and in gardening. People create their own affinities between these different items. The relationships are based on the colours of the flowers, on the aspect of the leaves (for example, smooth or downy leaves), on the size of the plants. But affinities can be built around elements that act as supports for reminiscences: plants given by kin or friends, seeds or plants bought during holidays or inherited garden artefacts. They furnish their garden and display some artefacts. The gardens of Jersey Farm, as with lounges, have similarities with other – "standard" elements – but also some differences and characteristics that reflect aspects of the residents' identities. Natural designs are fashionable for home decoration. They choose a flowery pattern for the curtains and as upholstery for the three-piece suite. They display indoor plants, decorative objects that refer to nature. Their wall decoration is usually related to the local environment with pictures of landscapes. Halle shows that in the USA landscape pictures, especially depopulated landscapes, are very popular among all social classes (Halle 1994: 59ff). In Jersey Farm, these landscapes are often historical landscapes with monuments such as churches or castles. Nevertheless, by comparison with French interior decoration, the natural designs and the references to nature are much more important in Britain.

Lounge and garden are "bridged" through practices, not only by the symmetry of their organization. Unilateral or reciprocal colonization creates this bridge. But also it is created by the mediating function that may be played by both sites.

Gardens as mediator: bridging people

Gardens in Jersey Farm are strongly related to sociability, even if the private aspect of this space is apparently at variance with this claim. A young woman who lives in a flat describes her situation:

> It is a problem with a flat, you don't have your own garden, you are really restricted where you can sit. A day like today, there is nowhere you can sit. . . . With the washing too: you have to dry it inside. No pets, no washing, no flowers. . . . In summer, people speak to each other, for example, when they wash their car; but in winter, when you come home from work, it is dark, cold outside. . . . When you don't have a garden, you don't really see people, it is strange. It is not like living in a house, where you see your neighbours, quite friendly. . . . In fact, I cannot really have a social life here because I haven't a garden ! (Miss Clulow)

The fact that the garden is enclosed and private is not an obstacle: "I have no problems really, because that fence goes to the public path. . . . If you are in your garden, people pass, usually somebody stops and have a chat; even children" (Mrs Engel).

Beyond, but linked to the gardening itself, gardens are spaces of circulation: plants, seeds, services, advice, knowledge (competencies and experiences), values, people. As with decorative objects, people exchange gifts of plants (cuttings), seeds or fruits and vegetables. This giving of gifts is not related to ritual occasions such as weddings or Christmas. Mrs Engel:

> My friend's mother gave me some tomato plants. People give me seeds too. My uncle gave me from Leicestershire some "lilies of the valley", mint, small plants. Lot of plants were given to me by friends. Since my

friend moved out, I have given her some plants, indoor plants I made some cuttings, the lemon trees on the window. . . . It is a good way of meeting people too; my neighbours two doors away, they moved in at Easter, they gave me some plants.

These exchanges happen among kin, friends and neighbourhood networks. Unlike the exchange of decorative objects, they take place among neighbours. Usually these gifts are associated with advice. The exchange of services is another important side of circulation connected with the garden. These services could be not only to water plants and sprinkle lawns, but also to clip hedges or roses.[7]

Nevertheless, these exchanges are part not only of the gift economy, but also of the market economy. First, a gift exchange can draw upon the resources of the commodity economy (Cheal 1988: 166). Plants and seeds are commodities: people buy them in garden centres (there are several of these close to Jersey Farm) and in the open market in St Albans. Garden furniture and decorative objects can be bought in the same shops as plants, or in big retail shops such as John Lewis. Some residents pay gardeners to do heavy duties (to clip trees or hedges for example). Prices are a continuous source of complaint within the residents' discourses, preventing them from buying all the plants or tools for gardening they would like. At the least, everybody has a personal lawn mower and some small tools to clip or dig.

Some people are considered "experts" in gardening: neighbours and family come to them for advice. They have particular competencies and knowledge about gardening. Mrs Engel: "My friend, she is very good at gardening. Neighbours, next door, their son and daughter-in-law come every weekend to help her, and I ask their advice". Mrs Lawing is the "expert" of her neighbourhood: people come to ask her advice, about cuttings or about how to take care of their garden when they go on holidays. She is very proud of her role and is always ready to help, even though during the previous summer holidays she had eight gardens to take care of. She had a garden when she was a child and a large one during her first marriage (with many vegetables and a herb garden). She complains about the small size of her present garden where only some carrots, beans and apples are growing.

Gardening is related to competence and experience: people inexperienced in gardening have to carry out experiments. Mrs Engel: "Sometimes I get seeds with instructions on the back. I just put them in and hope for the best! I have to try and learn, I am sure I make mistakes. But it is just good fun!" Everybody is socialized in home decoration in their childhood home; by contrast not everybody is socialized into gardening, especially because the Jersey Farm residents are often the first generation to own their own house with a garden. This learning is often an implicit one and related to kinship: spending time helping their grandfather and so on. The value of the garden is based on labour, including the time devoted to gardening. The comments on neighbours' gardens are always linked to the time or effort expended. A neglected garden is a source of possible pollution for others: overhanging branches, slugs and weeds.[8] It is also a source of potential conflict between neighbours.

I argue that the garden is the primary way that neighbourhood relationships may be created and maintained, even if people can meet each other in other places in the area (pub, shops, car parks, etc.). Mrs Kinson:

> We have barbecues in summertime, people come from across the road. . . . We know a lot of people around here. People meet more often during the summer. . . . They do so, because it is dark early in winter, people would go home. I like summer when it is very light, I just go outside, do anything, everybody does the same. In winter time people stay at home.

In fact, this space, relative to its importance in the discourse, is often underused except by people with children or to invite neighbours or friends for barbecues outside during summer. The garden as a mediator of sociability is linked to the idea of the little community through the constant circulation of elements, or the village where co-operative exchange is based on labour. If I compare the mediation role of the lounge and the garden, again one observes a kind of symmetry. The organization of the furniture – the three-piece suite – around the fireplace mediates relationships. The lounge seems to be an internal mediator, inside the family, and the garden an external mediator between non-kin who nevertheless share the same "space". The garden is a means by which the neighbourhood is created and defined. They have symmetrical functions in terms of sociability.

Sources of inspiration in gardening and home decorating

The symmetry between gardening and home decorating is quite obvious at the national level, especially in the media. They provide the source of inspiration for Jersey Farm residents. There is an important body of literature on the historical construction of the idea of the garden (see especially Williams 1973; Thomas 1983), related to ideas of landscape and nature. But I will not deal directly with this, only its modern "descendant" as observed in the media. All my informants watch or listen to programmes or read articles on gardening. Households without children and retired people visit public and historical gardens, flower shows and garden centres too. This leisure activity becomes more and more important as they get older.

The media coverage on the "garden" is considerable and long established, compared to programmes about home decoration. On television, all the channels present programmes on gardening at peak time, focusing on specific topics. Related to these series, the BBC publishes a monthly magazine called

Gardeners' World in which the readers could recognize the same stars (Pippa Greenwood, the late Geoff Hamilton, for example) that are on the television or radio.[9] Radio also has public forums, where people can ask questions, for instance *Gardening Forum* on Classic FM or *Gardeners' Question Time* on Radio 4 (which was broadcast for the first time in 1947 from the North of England). Local television and radio stations have their own programmes. Most newspapers have articles on gardening, especially the Sunday newspapers. Books provide technical information on plants or on practices which people look at for answers for specific questions.

Usually the media mix technical advice with presentations of different actual gardens. The style is very pedagogical ("do not try to cram into an average town backyard all the components of a country garden"). The proposed gardening techniques often involve some a priori competencies and knowledge, as do the answers given to listeners by the gardeners on the radio. Colours and smells of flowers are taken into account, and the audience is very sensitive to such details: " My television is black and white, it is not the same. . . . After Christmas I will rent a colour television, I watch, but at the moment it is not the same!" (Mrs Engel). People are encouraged to match colours and types of flowers. There is a typology of gardens – cottage gardens, wild gardens, exotic gardens – and there are many references made to the past ("native honeysuckle", "old roses") or to historical gardens. The names of the plants are given in botanical terms (in Latin), displayed as subtitles on the television screen, although most people do not remember this learned terminology.

The media are a source of inspiration for Mr and Mrs Waldock, who pick up tips: "I saw on television, you get a lemonade bottle, you cut it like a tube, and you put it around your young plant to protect it. I do that with trees". But their interest is more for pleasure than to try and transform their own gardens into "perfect gardens": the comments reveal a social distance. These gardens are not for them, they are too expensive, they do not fit with their small plot. Anyway, they watch these programmes as some kind of "national following", a redefinition of identity. Even if they do not have time to watch it they know the programme timetables.

The media coverage of cooking in France is less important than that of gardening in Britain. However, there are very popular programmes on French television with "stars".[10] People can find recipes in specialist or women's magazines (as the well-known "fiches cuisine" of *Elle* magazine) – which do not always contain gardening advice – and books. These books and television programmes often involve prior knowledge and compe-tencies, combined with specific terminology. They use typology to distinguish "nouvelle cuisine" from "cuisine bourgeoise" and so on. Distinctions are made between national and regional tradition, and foreign cooking. One main part of this literature is the writing of culinary critics in newspapers or guides. Parallel to guides of the "best gardens", guides of the "best restaurants" (with stars or chef's hats) help people organize their leisure. The purpose of holiday trips can be testing restaurants, especially when people become older. During their day out, they try to pick up some ideas from the food they eat for their own practices, as my British informants do by visiting gardens.

In Britain, the public and historical gardens visited, the flower shows attended (the Chelsea Flower Show is a national event) are pleasant for leisure, but may not be a real source of inspiration. In fact, the garden centres are the best places to pick up ideas and to choose plants, as are the furniture retail shops for choosing pieces of furniture. They sell flowers, plants and tools, provide advice and help (a nursery for plants when you go on holidays) and restaurants for welcome breaks. Customers are at the same time both visitors and consumers:

> It is just nice to have a look and at the same time to learn. You get something, so we can plan something for our garden. And you see plants you have never seen before. . . . You are just learning all the time. We enjoy it. It is never ending, we see such lovely things. But it is expensive. (Mrs Layland).

This elderly couple visit gardens during their holidays or on day excursions, unlike younger households.[11]

British gardens are defined as part of a cultural identity and national heritage: the "guardians of the tradition" define the models, diffused by the media, and every innovation is submitted to "experts" for approval. In their gardens, through their practices, people endlessly reaffirm their cultural identity in everyday life. However, commoditization of gardening (and landscapes) introduces a vast range of vegetal products, tools and so on, which encourage people to consume "nature" through their gardens and spread this movement to countries not traditionally keen on gardening.[12]

Even if home decoration has not quite the same status as part of national identity as gardens, it also plays an important role in everyday life. The media present different programmes on home decoration or about objects, for instance the *Antiques Road Show*, a very popular public forum. In addition, some drama series introduce antique objects into the story, *Lovejoy* for example in which the detective is an antique dealer. Often magazines give advice on gardening and on home decorating in the same issue. As with their gardens, people are encouraged to match the colours and patterns of curtains, with the upholstery and carpet. During the weekend, people like to browse in home decoration shops, showrooms or to visit the Ideal Home Exhibition, even if they do not propose to buy an item of furniture or an object. For all the Jersey Farm residents, the ideal garden and home decoration are always embodied in the Victorian cottage as "the dreams of retirement to a honeysuckle cottage" (MacFarlane 1987: 77).

This section shows clearly that home and garden are bridged at all levels: in the symmetry of their spatial organization, in their role as mediator for social interactions, and in national social life through the media. A successful appropriation of the natural environment creates links or "bridges" between these two spaces.

Does "land" bridge people through generations?

It is well known that the history of the relationship to nature and the history of gardens are quite different in France and Britain. My purpose is here not to detail all these differences, but to show that they still exist in British and French suburbia, through everyday life practices.

Thomas (1983: 295ff) and MacFarlane (1987: 94ff) describe the ambivalence that makes British society one of the first capitalist ones – the most exploitative and simultaneously the most protective towards nature. This appears very early in England (for Thomas this development occurred between 1500 and 1800). In the nineteenth century, England was the "most urbanised country in the world, yet one where the yearning for the countryside and rural values was the most developed" (MacFarlane 1987: 77). And "as agriculture became more rational, orderly and intensive, so people yearned for the opposite" (MacFarlane 1987: 81). For Thomas (1983: 244ff), this "ancient pastoral ideal has survived into the modern industrial world", for example "in the vague desire of so many people to end their days in a country cottage" which I already quoted as an ideal for Jersey Farm's residents. However, for the same historical reasons, only a small class were ever owners of the land. There was no peasantry owning land through generations, but the quick and early – in comparison with other European countries – transformations of social structure led to the disappearance of small ownerships to the advantage of the upper class (Williams 1973).[13] These peculiar relationships to land result from different historical transformations (earlier urbanization and industrialization; capitalist agriculture), which "survive" in the actual residential projects of people, as I shall show below.

The group I wish to compare with the Jersey Farm inhabitants are the residents of a group of 60 council-flat households, in a suburban Parisian collection of tower-blocks located in west Paris (Les Fontenelles) where I conducted my French fieldwork. They were built in the early 1970s. The initial settlement was meant to rehouse people who were evicted by the construction of La Défense. The estate consists of flats in six high-rise, high-density council tower-blocks; all are similar with constrained spaces that cannot be modified. It is not possible to construct extensions or other modifications to the building. The residents have to adapt to the flat and to use furniture and decorative objects for personalizing it. The inhabitants are all factory workers and blue-collar workers; it is ethnically a mixed population (French and immigrants).

One of the main forms of exchange or circulation of objects is transmission, which has a specific function of reflecting kinship, sometimes including the extended family. It also gives the status of inalienability to the objects involved in this kind of circulation. Usually these objects are memorabilia, especially if they are previously inherited or if they are part of a person's proposed inheritance. Some people invest a lot of money to constitute or keep furniture-capital (some pieces of furniture they would like to give to their children); some of them try to build up an inheritance, by buying antique objects or collect objects from among their kin. Few succeed in creating furniture as capital without previous ancestral transmission. Inherited objects are powerful items and are constraining in the construction of a domestic décor.

To illustrate my argument, I would like to introduce a French family, Mr and Mrs Probst. The Probsts are married with two children, one of whom still lives at home. They are 55 years old. Mr Probst is an office worker in a big company and Mrs Probst is a housewife. Both are natives of the Paris suburb. They bought all their furniture in 1956, so it is homogeneous in style. Later they added a nest of tables and two black leather sofas. Decorative objects are displayed on all pieces of furniture. The room is divided into two spaces: the lounge and dining room (Fig. 3.5). The dining area contains ancient and delicate objects of value; they are in functional

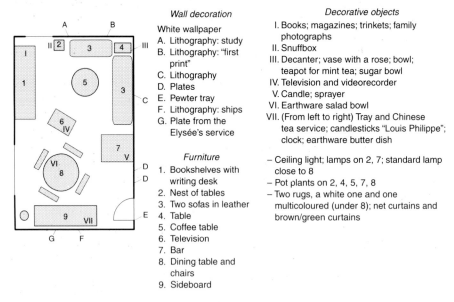

Wall decoration

White wallpaper
A. Lithography: study
B. Lithography: "first print"
C. Lithography
D. Plates
E. Pewter tray
F. Lithography: ships
G. Plate from the Elysée's service

Furniture

1. Bookshelves with writing desk
2. Nest of tables
3. Two sofas in leather
4. Table
5. Coffee table
6. Television
7. Bar
8. Dining table and chairs
9. Sideboard

Decorative objects

I. Books; magazines; trinkets; family photographs
II. Snuffbox
III. Decanter; vase with a rose; bowl; teapot for mint tea; sugar bowl
IV. Television and videorecorder
V. Candle; sprayer
VI. Earthware salad bowl
VII. (From left to right) Tray and Chinese tea service; candlesticks "Louis Philippe"; clock; earthware butter dish

– Ceiling light; lamps on 2, 7; standard lamp close to 8
– Pot plants on 2, 4, 5, 7, 8
– Two rugs, a white one and one multicoloured (under 8); net curtains and brown/green curtains

Figure 3.5 Mr and Mrs Probst: lounge and dining room

affinity with the use of the space (plates/dining room). For example, there is a plate that apparently comes from the Elysée's service, made in Limoges.[14] The objects on the sideboard were inherited by Mrs Probst through her maternal kin. The other side of the room is "modern" with leather sofas and abstract prints that are professional gifts from her husband's customers. Many photographs are displayed on the bookcase.

Like the Probsts, people often dream of building their interior décor around such objects. They try to highlight them, to find objects and pieces of furniture that match with or exist in reminiscent affinities with them. They handle these objects respectfully even though they may not be liked, that is may not suit their taste. For the French as for the English, there is a strong link between the décor and the house itself. They appropriate their house or flat to transform it into a "home". When they move in, they renew the carpet and the wallpaper. In Jersey Farm, people extend their house and refurbish the kitchen. The furniture and the decoration allow them to personalize their space. On arriving in a new house, some renew all the furniture as in the case of Mr and Mrs Layland. This process transforms the house into a home. They are conscious of the harmony between the architecture of the house or building and the style of their furniture.

The décor itself cannot be transmitted: only the set of elements and the affinities among them are worthy of consideration as a reminiscent whole. It expresses the couple who built it up; it contains at the same time a symbolic and material dimension. For example, if the couple dies, the décor in order to be transmitted requires a process of de-symbolization to transform the "home" into a house with its contents. One must disrupt the affinities among the elements, linked to each other in a characteristic combination. Only the material dimension of the domestic décor can survive. So the diverse elements can be transmitted, each one is now attributed to a specific symbolic dimension for the heirs as inherited objects.

The residents of Jersey Farm focus on the single residence that they own. Throughout their life-cycle, they try to move to bigger houses, if possible a detached house with a bigger garden. These stages express the trajectory of the couple, but do not relate to a project of transmission to the next generation. Once the children become adults, they do not belong in this space. This house and its transformation into home symbolizes the couple, their alliance. It is a transient elaboration, of their financial and emotional investments which they do not wish to transmit to their children. The "home" is a common project of a couple and will disappear with it (Finch 1994: 427). Mr and Mrs Spring (50 years old) bought a big detached house in 1980 which they extended with a second lounge and a patio. They are waiting for their daughters to leave this house, when they will sell it. Mrs Spring inherited a bungalow: she decided to sell it and not to give it to one of her daughters: "They have to do things their own way. . . . We did the same, they have to make their own mistakes!". Mrs Spring's house is a result of the couple's project; it is related to the couple and cannot be taken over by somebody else (Finch 1994: 425). As I have already shown, the Laylands renewed all the furniture of the lounge and thoroughly transformed their garden.

There is no sense of "materializing" the lineage in space. Being a home owner does not change this perspective. Even after a process of de-symbolization which transforms the "home" into a house, people do not plan to transmit the house itself. Nevertheless, evidence of the lineage is not absent in Britain from the interior décor. Most of the decorative objects are formal photographs, either school portraits in cardboard frames or wedding photographs (Halle 1993). They are displayed on the television, on the mantelpiece or hung on the walls. The genealogical depth is two generations. These representations are often the only "material" clue of descent which are part of the transient construction. The main house, as home, is the embodiment of the couple, its anchorage is in time and space, as long as their alliance remains. The "home" is the common project of a couple, not of a family. Moreover, the domestic interior is always presented as a result of the couple's effort, even if in practice only the female partner has taken charge of the decoration.[15]

The French – across all social groups – have a double residential project: the first one that serves as their main house and the second as a home in which they anchor their descent in space. They intend to keep or to buy a second residence, but not necessarily to live there. This purchase is not necessarily related to an identity dimension (the place of the family's origin, for example). The aim is the symbolic anchorage of the lineage in a materialized space, a home that they solely own or they own as jointly held property. The content and the décor of the second home is inalienable and for this reason nobody would move furniture to their main residence. For example, nobody would move the sideboard from Brittany to a suburban flat, not only because this piece of furniture is too big to enter the flat, but also for symbolic reasons, this piece of furniture is attached to the family house. Weiner (1985: 210), referring to Mauss (1990) in *The Gift*, described these objects as "*immeuble*" because they are inalienable wealth that could not be detached from their origins. On this point, one could also compare the French case with the Maori one re-examined by Weiner. These bones and the stones of the Maori are believed to "anchor" a lineage to a particular locality, physically securing its identity and ancestral rights (Weiner 1985: 211). But in addition, in the French case, people can use the commodities market to create as many "bones" as they would like to have to anchor their lineage.

The forms of transmission are submitted not only to a logic of practical efficiency, but also to a cultural intentionality. So, in France, the trans-mission of the familial identity is embodied in material culture – objects and houses – including the idea of lineage. The objects and houses tend towards being inalienable and circulate slowly outside of the sphere of market commodities. For the English, lineage is not necessarily embodied in material culture; except for a few objects, the transmission is "de-materialized".[16]

In terms of timescale, one could argue that in France the land is related to long-term relationships. The French relate land to "ancestral" land (real or not) which is echoed in "ancestral" objects. Two authors (Barou & Prado 1995) who examined the differences in British and French representations of land reach similar conclusions: for the French, land is a space of reminiscence for people. They argue that this aspect could be related to the long-term practice of acquisition and inheritance of land in France, especially throughout the nineteenth and the twentieth centuries.

In France, the idea of owning land is pertinent for a much wider section of population than in Britain. For historical and cultural reasons, the British do not have a direct relation to landownership or inheritance, since only a small class was ever owners of the land. Their relationship to the land is thus created in their garden: they appropriate the land through their own practice and skill. But it has to be renewed with each generation. Most young people have little interest in gardening: this is something that comes with age and through which a project related to the house becomes extended. So this relationship to the land – through the garden – is a short-term project, related to a couple, in contrast to the French generational use of land.

Conclusion: about passions

Gardening can be considered as an appropriation of nature through everyday practices in the constitution of the domestic sphere. In France, the area of transformation is not the land but takes place in the kitchen through cooking. This activity is a short-term everyday practice, like gardening, within the domestic sphere. Nature is appropriated by transformation: in France and in Britain, the externalities of temporalities and mediations are different. The difference between the kitchen and the garden follows the differences between lineage and couple. Lineage is embodied in the use of land in France, by contrast to the short-term use of land by British couples. The French express couple-relations and affections through cooking, the British through gardening (as a continuation of home decorating).

Both have a strong affective dimension: cooking is sheer passion and is of concern to all levels of French society, from the couple to the national community, as gardening is sheer passion and attachment in Britain. Mr Layland expresses its passion: "I like everything, even cutting the lawn . . . I quite enjoy; to me, it is so relaxing, after gardening I feel good . . . I just enjoy, digging. . . . Just enjoy".

Acknowledgements

I would like to thank the residents of Les Fontenelles and Jersey Farm who welcomed me during both these surveys, and the Museum of St Albans (especially Harriet Purkis and Matthew Wheeler). Many thanks to Professor Marilyn Strathern for welcoming me in her department for two years. I wish to acknowledge grant support from the Swiss National Research Fund. For their helpful comments on various stages of my research and drafts of this chapter I want to thank Prof. Alan MacFarlane, Prof. Daniel Miller, Prof. Martine Segalen, Marie Howes, Deema Kaneff and Prof. Tim Putnam. I am also grateful to Polly and Giles Courtice, Alain Hirsch, Sylvie Muller and Muriel Tapie-Grime.

Notes

1. In the mid-1980s, 85 per cent of British households had a garden (Hoyle 1991).
2. For example: "Mr Dupont and Mrs Martin" indicates cohabitation; "Mr and Mrs Martin, Simon and Anne Dupont" indicates a couple in which the wife has two children from a previous marriage, and so on, so even at the first meeting, the French informants are not as anonymous as the British.
3. But a fussy French caretaker can convince the residents to have standardized letterboxes, all similar to each other.
4. Furniture and objects are related to each other by affinities that combine the elements created by the actors. The first affinity between items of furniture is found in every Jersey Farm living room, irrespective of its size, and installed on the carpet. The basic furniture is the "three-piece suite". These affinities or relationships are built and based on certain specific aspects of objects – I call them *echoes* – because they are not necessarily morphological, related to the form of the object, in opposition to the sign. See Chevalier (1993, 1994, 1995, 1996, 1997).
5. The bedding system began in the 1830s with the increasing number of plants arriving from all around the world (Hoyle 1991).
6. It is a favourite topic for comedians to imitate the gossip and advice that neighbours engage in over the garden fence.
7. In the council estate buildings in France where I carried out the survey, there are also exchange of services with respect to indoor plants (as well as the exchange of cuttings, plants and advice).
8. I observed the same process in run-down suburban areas: inhabitants consider that a dirty environment (the entry-hall of the building or the lift, for example) as a potential source of pollution of their interior, so they may clean up their entry-floor, even if there is a cleaner to do it.
9. The *Gardeners' World* television programme has about 5 million viewers.
10. A very popular programme called *La Cuisine des mousquetaires* is broadcast at midday on national television (FR3) with a cook Maïté, who is becoming a popular star and has acted in a film.
11. One observes in France a new interest for visiting gardens as a leisure activity,

linked to the idea of patrimony: landscapes, gardens and plants have become a national heritage and quite a popular craze. A French anthropologist who is working on this topic called her book *Vert Patrimoine* or "Green heritage" (Dubost 1994). Since 1992, there has been a flower show in France called "Festival de Chaumont-sur-Loire" which is becoming very popular. This event was reported in the *Guardian* (12 August 1995) in an article entitled "Revolution blooms in the back garden".

12. For the introduction of exotic plants see Hoyle (1991) on the link between the development of the botany and colonization.

13. Owner-occupiers held about 20 per cent of the land at the beginning of the nineteenth century; by the end of the century, it was only 12 per cent. In 1873, half of the country was owned by some 7,000 people, in a rural population of around 10 million (Williams 1973: 190ff).

14. Elysée is the house of the French president; every new president receives a porcelain service made in Limoges, the well-known factory in France.

15. The duties in the garden are usually shared between the couple; but if it is the woman only who is in charge of the housework she generally does the gardening too, except cutting the lawn. Cf. Goody (1993: 315): "In suburban gardens, the allocation, or assumption, of tasks, as between house and work, inside and outside, flowers and vegetables, is less fixed than before, especially in the domain of vegetables".

16. Again, one explanation could lie in their different historical roots. Some authors speak about English individualism (MacFarlane 1978) and the fact that people rely less on the help given by the family (Finch 1994). Another element is the power to bequeath freely in English law in opposition to the legal reserve for children in continental law. Nevertheless, the most interesting fact is that the difference remains in suburban lower-middle classes, and may be observed in mass-produced objects.

References

Appadurai, A. (ed.) 1986. *The social life of things: commodities in cultural perspective*. Cambridge: Cambridge University Press.
Barou. J. & P. Prado 1995. *Les Anglais dans nos campagnes*. Paris: L'Harmattan.
Baudrillard, J. 1968. *Le Système des objets*. Paris: Gallimard.
Baudrillard, J. 1970. *La Société de consommation*. Paris: Denoël.
Baudrillard, J. 1972. *Pour une critique de l'économie politique du signe*. Paris: Gallimard.
Beck, U. 1986. *Risk society*. London: Sage.
Bourdieu, P. 1979. *La Distinction: critique sociale du jugement*. Paris: Ed. de Minuit.
Bourdieu, P. 1980. *Le Sens pratique*. Paris: Ed. de Minuit.
Cheal, D.J. 1988. *The gift economy*. London: Routledge.
Chevalier, S. 1993. Nous, on n'a rien de spécial. ... In Chez soi. Objets et décors: des créations familiales? M. Segalen & B. Le Wita (eds). *Autrement* 137, 86–101.
Chevalier, S. 1994. Au-delà d'une apparente banalité et d'un standard: des décors particuliers. *Archives suisses des traditions populaires* 2, 165–85.

Chevalier, S. 1995. The anthropology of an apparent banality: a comparative study. *Cambridge Anthropology* **19** (3).

Chevalier, S. 1996. Transmettre son mobilier? La cas contrasté de la France et de l'Angleterre. *Ethnologie Française* **XXVI** (1).

Chevalier, S. 1997. L'idéologie culinaire en Angleterre ou comment séparer le blanc de jaune. *Ethnologie Française* **XXVII** (1) 73–9.

Ciskszentmihalyi, M. and E. Rochberg-Halton 1981. *The meaning of things: domestic symbols and the self.* Cambridge: Cambridge University Press.

Dickens, P. 1992. *Society and nature: towards a green social theory.* London: Harvester.

Dubost, F. 1984. *Côté jardin.* Paris: Scarabée.

Dubost, F. 1994. *Vert Patrimoine: la constitution d'un nouveau domaine patrimonial.* Paris: MSH.

Elias, N. 1973. *La Civilisation des moeurs.* Paris: Calmann-Lévy.

Elias, N. 1974. *La Société de cour.* Paris: Calmann-Lévy.

Finch, J. 1994. Inheritance, death and the concept of the home. *Sociology* **28** (2), 417–33.

Foucault, M. 1966. *Les Mots et les choses.* Paris: Gallimard-NRF.

Francis, M. and R.T. Hester 1990. *The meaning of gardens: idea, place and action.* Cambridge, MA: MIT Press.

Giard, L. & P. Mayol 1980. *L'Invention du quotidien: habiter, cuisiner.* Paris: UGE.

Goody, J. 1982. *Cooking, cuisine and class.* Cambridge: Cambridge University Press.

Goody, J. 1993. *The culture of flowers.* Cambridge: Cambridge University Press.

Halle, D. 1993. *Inside culture: art and class in the American home.* Chicago: University of Chicago Press.

Haudricourt, A.-G. 1987. *La Technologie science humaine.* Paris: MSH.

Hay, R. & P.M. Synge. 1975. *The colour dictionary of garden plants.* London: Bloomsbury.

Hirsch, E. 1992. The long term and the short term of domestic consumption: an ethnographic case study. In *Consuming technologies: media and information in domestic spaces*, R. Silverstone and E. Hirsch (eds). London: Berg.

Hoyle, M. 1991. *The story of gardening.* London: Journeyman.

Jenkins, V.S. 1994. *The lawn: a history of an American obsession.* Washington, DC: Smithsonian Institution.

Latour, B. 1991. *Nous n'avons jamais été modernes: essai d'anthropologie symétrique.* Paris: La Découverte.

Latour, B. 1994. Une sociologie sans objet? Remarques sur l'interobjectivité. *Sociologie du travail* **4**, 587–607.

Leroi-Gourhan, A. 1965. *Le Geste et la parole.* Paris: Albin-Michel.

Leroi-Gourhan, A. 1973. *Evolution et technique.* Paris: Albin-Michel.

Lévi-Strauss, C. 1968. *L'Origine des manières de table.* Paris: Plon.

Lowenthal, D. and E. Penning-Rowsell (eds) 1986. *Landscape: meanings and values.* London: Allen & Unwin.

MacCormack, C. and M. Strathern 1980. *Nature, culture and gender.* Cambridge: Cambridge University Press.

McCracken, G. 1988. *Culture and consumption.* Bloomington: Indiana University Press.

MacFarlane, A. 1978. *The origins of English individualism.* Oxford: Blackwell.

MacFarlane, A. 1987. *The culture of capitalism.* Oxford: Blackwell.

Mauss, M. 1950. *Sociologie et anthropologie*. Paris: PUF.

Mauss, M. 1990. *The gift: form and reason for exchange in archaic societies*. New York/London: Norton.

Mennel, S. 1985. *All manners of food: eating and taste in England and France from the Middle Ages to the present*. Oxford: Blackwell.

Miller, D. 1987. *Material culture and mass consumption*. Oxford: Blackwell.

Miller, D. 1988. Appropriating the state on the council estate. *Man* **23**, 353–72.

Mingay, G.E. 1994. *Land and society in England, 1750–1980*. London: Longman.

Mukerji, C. 1990. Reading and writing with nature: social claims and the French formal garden. *Theory and Society* **19**, 651–79.

Pevsner, N. 1956. *The Englishness of English art*. Harmondsworth: Penguin.

Putnam, T. and C. Newton (eds) 1990. *Households' choices*. London: Middlesex Polytechnic and Futures Publications.

Pynson, P. 1987. *La France à table, 1960–1986*. Paris: La Découverte.

Schama, S. 1995. *Landscape and memory*. London: HarperCollins.

Stoppard, T. 1993. *Arcadia*. London: Faber & Faber.

Strathern, M. 1992. *After nature: English kinship in the late twentieth century*. Cambridge: Cambridge University Press.

Tardieu, S. 1976. *Le Mobilier rural traditionnel français*. Paris: Aubier-Flammarion.

Thacker, C. 1979. *The history of gardens*. Berkeley: University of California.

Thomas, K. 1983. *Man and the natural world*. London: Allen & Unwin.

Weiner, A. 1985. Inalienable wealth. *American Ethnologist* **XII** (2), 210–27.

Williams, R. 1973. *The country and the city*. London: Chatto & Windus.

CHAPTER 4

Window shopping at home: classifieds, catalogues and new consumer skills

Alison J. Clarke

> Nothing, perhaps, more directly depends on early learning, especially the learning which takes place without any express intention to teach, than the dispositions and knowledge that are invested in clothing, furnishing and cooking or more precisely, in the way clothes, furniture and food are bought. (Bourdieu 1984: 78)

Material culture, its acquisition and appropriation, is integral to the construction and negotiation of social worlds and identities. The myriad decisions and complexities of household provisioning embody consumption as an arena of power in which social relations and knowledge are constantly rehearsed, rearranged and challenged.

In accordance with seminal works on the relationship between people, objects and consumption in modern societies (Douglas and Isherwood 1978; Bourdieu 1984; Miller 1986) this study posits the acquisition of commodities and goods as the very basis of households in industrial (or capitalist) societies. As Carrier, in his discussion of gifts and commodities in contemporary industrial societies, observes, "a household exists in part because its members appropriate the commodities that are circulated and consumed within it" (Carrier 1995: 16).

This ethnographic study highlights the household as a crucial site of power and information. Focusing on two modes of informal acquisition, *Loot*, a localized classified paper, and *Argos*, a catalogue linked to a nationwide bulk distribution outlet, the study explores the development of consumptive skills. In conjunction with a range of other modes of acquisition, *Loot* and *Argos* highlight the dynamic of class, style and knowledge in consumptive activity.

Although *Loot* deals with non-standardized, second-hand goods or objects with "histories" (Appadurai 1986) and *Argos* deals with alienable, mass-produced commodities, formal analysis of these two text-based mediums suggests a shared aesthetic appeal to social groups precluded from expensive high street shopping. Both *Argos* and *Loot* originated as non-formal modes of acquisition, offering cut-price goods and maximum choice through non-retail direct distribution. Neither source allows first-hand physical assessment of the goods offered for sale, or the intermediate sales advice of a third party.

While these methods of acquisition are motivated in part by utility and economics, this chapter frames such notions and consequent choices as culturally bound actions. The concomitance of commerce and sociality is played out through the everyday concepts of authenticity, newness, thrift, and excess. Household issues ranging from romantic love and gendered divisions of labour to parental anxiety become manifest in chosen patterns of consumption.

While practices of consumption effectively illuminate social categories such as gender, class, ethnicity and age, exploration of the specifics of appropriation and material culture reveals the means by which these externally defined roles are understood and contested. Why is an impoverished family compelled to pay the maximum, high street price for a child's bed, available "brand new" for half the price in a local classified paper (Caplovitz 1967)? Why would a household with soiled furniture and no bathroom be the home to fifty designer suits and a copy of *Debrett's ettiquette and modern manners*?

Ultimately this ethnography reveals that provisioning is not only a question of obtaining goods, but also the application of particular schemes of knowledge and style to particular genres of information about goods. Poverty and wealth, as both Douglas and Isherwood (1979) and Bourdieu (1984) have pointed out, are based on a complex articulation between forms of knowledge and forms of possession. In this ethnographic encounter we see the experiential detail through which this articulation becomes manifest.

Shopping in "the street"

A street in north London forms the basis of this ethnographic enquiry into consumption. As a joint project, shared with Daniel Miller, the enquiry involves ethnographic study of the informal and formal aspects of acquisition. While Miller deals with the formal shopping habits of informants (accompanied supermarket visits, etc.) this portion of the research deals with ostensibly home-based and informal modes of acquisition.

The street, comprising private owner-occupied, rented and state-subsidized housing, forms the basis of this ethnography of consumption and social identity. A number of predominantly middle-class streets extending from the main street of our study have been included in the findings. The first phase of the research has included 76 households. The street proper is positioned between two major shopping areas, Wood Green Shopping City and Brent Cross Shopping Centre, which provide residents with the possibility of identifying with two distinct, formal shopping areas. The shopping facilities of central London, including the prestigious West End, are also easily accessible using public or private transport.

From the array of informal provisioning used by the street's house-holders (including stolen goods, Tupperware parties, Colour-Me-Beautiful sessions, jumble and rummage sales, clothing catalogues, cigarette coupons, door-to-door sales, etc.) *Loot* and *Argos*, in particular, defied simplistic definitions in terms of class, ethnic and gender patterns of usage.

Exchange and Mart, a well-known and established classified paper, acts as the significant precursor to *Loot*. *Exchange and Mart* offers new and used goods at bargain prices through the eradication of formal retail distribution expenses. Its users describe it as a hard-edged, no-nonsense form of acquisition particularly useful for buying and selling used vehicles. It appeared to offer similar, but more convenient and assessable facets of a house clearance or car auction. Like the *Argos* catalogue, overheads of space, distribution and sales staff are visibly absent from *Exchange and Mart*'s classified pages. From their inception, both *Argos* and *Exchange and Mart* offered simple and accessible means of saving money on substantial household purchases and were aimed at a lower income population.

In recent years *Argos* has altered its customer profile. Its showrooms have expanded from cheaper inner-city sites to high street locations and *Argos* catalogues are now delivered, as a matter of course, to extensively middle-class areas. Similarly *Loot*, which unlike its competitors offers free advertising, has altered rapidly from a weekly to a daily publication considerably overshadowing the established role of *Exchange and Mart*.

Forms of acquisition, like commodities, carry with them ideological discourse. As Rutz and Orlove (1989: 6) state, "consumption has an ideological character, in that it appeals to shared understanding and thus it allows for disagreement".

Mainstream mail order catalogues, for example, bear the stigma of restricted, credit bound consumption. As a mode of purchase historically aligned, in British culture, to hire purchase and working-class credit functions, the mail order catalogue is bound to culturally and socially poignant meanings. Its overtly mass, non-personalized, and visually based appeal have associated it with the alienation of modern commodity purchase (Carrier 1995). Unsurprisingly then, for informants it was this specific mode of purchase that provoked a familiar, socially and morally grounded debate regarding saving, spending, quality and value.

Mention of mail order catalogues warranted strong reactions from many, predominantly middle-class, informants, who disassociated themselves from the foolhardy practice of buying "long-distance". They frequently aligned this hazardous form of purchase with the quality and aesthetic of the goods themselves, to quote one such example: "cheapy nasty girlie catalogues . . . with tacky underwear and leotards and things, oh no I'd never use them".

Others removed themselves from the economic imperative suggested by catalogue use. Credit schemes and over-inflated prices seemed to have direct bearing on the goods themselves: "those Littlewoods things . . . I'd never have those . . . I think it's a social thing . . . a class thing because, I mean you can buy in instalments and I used to have a cleaner who used to get all her Christmas presents through a catalogue".

Many informants, although keen catalogue users themselves, depicted tawdry images of overdependent catalogue users; to quote one such opinion: "I've met women who have furnished their entire homes top to bottom straight from just one catalogue!"

While for some shoppers Christmas presents, intimate apparel and home furnishings demanded less distanced and more proactive forms of acquisition, many informants relied entirely on catalogue purchases as a necessary budgeting measure. Far from taking advantage of the effortless leisure of mail order purchase, these consumers, economically precluded from formal shopping, used catalogues as a buffer against the risk and uncertainty of the market place and prided themselves on their discerning purchasing abilities.

Evidently, all modes of acquisition and their material culture carry with them culturally constituted meanings. In this sense *Loot* and *Argos*, in contrast to more established forms of acquisition, are being actively appropriated and redefined through new consumer knowledges and skills. The prominence of these genres across class, gender, age and ethnic households allows insight into the incorporation of recently formulated and historically specific modes of acquisition.

Loot

Loot is a London-based free-advertising paper sold daily at the price of £1.30. It describes itself as "London's Notice Board" and according to many informants successfully operates in this fashion; many browse regularly with little or no intention of buying but merely to "get a feel about what's out there". In this sense it acts as a virtual market place where the excitement (and frustration) of rummaging and browsing are translated into the reading of obscure four-line prose:

For Sale: Video Editor vanguard, 3 in 1 unit, AV,

dubbing edit with picture enhancer,

as new, £50. Gary 0181 [phone number] eves or

0171 [phone number] days Hammersmith

While *Loot* purports to offer "Everything for everyone, everyday" (as its sales pitch reads) many readers spoke of "frequenting" particular areas of the paper, deliberately imposing self-limitations in a sea of purchasing opportunities. Some informants referred to *Loot* in purely instrumental terms, confining their use to specific circumstance such as accommodation seeking or occasional car sales. Most, however, used *Loot* regularly and less strategically.

Many male informants used the paper as a staple read, browsing the section on cars even when they were not actively concerned with buying or selling a vehicle. For others, *Loot* functioned as a vital source of information for swapping in "car conversations", and informants talked of enjoying vehicle descriptions and the sense of keeping "in touch" through *Loot*.

While a small number of male informants read comparable classified papers such as *Exchange and Mart*, *Loot* was perceived as a more localized, community orientated publication – even though both papers shared the functional task of selling cars. Notably *Loot*, as a free-to-advertise publication, surpassed its commercial position and enhanced its value as a means of sale and purchase.

Acting as a form of non-corporate commercial exchange, *Loot* seemingly offers a type of democracy to otherwise marginalized shoppers, giving access to thousands of daily bargains. It is considered by many as an essential urban shopping guide, blurring the productive and consumptive aspects of household provisioning. A typical statement (from Barry, a long-term unemployed civil servant) proffers *Loot* as the most obvious and logical mode of enquiry into any proposed purchase: "he [a friend] was looking for a computer and I said, 'surely you've checked out *Loot*', you don't know what you're doing till you've looked in there".

Recent developments, including a *Loot* property sales service, Internet link, and sister papers in the north-west and Midlands, reveal the growing significance of *Loot*'s appeal to informal economic activity. Originally a weekly publication, it now circulates each weekday using corresponding colours (blue, pink, gold, red, green) to emphasize its daily currency. Some *Loot* readers, newsagents pointed out, were becoming confused by the expansion and daily colour coding of the paper and lamented its new, unwieldy size.

"Whether you are collecting antiques, selling your property or looking for romance . . ." (as the promotional plea reads) *Loot* offers a diverse, informal consumption space. The paper is organized into ten separate sections, related to the goods and services of everyday life, beginning with introductory instructions on how to use the publication. Once initiated, the reader can peruse sections that include household goods, homes and family, cars, jobs, personal, computers, hi-fis, holidays and health and fitness. Private advertisers can advertise anything freely and are promised publication in the next day's issue provided they meet the appropriate deadline. The free advertisement appears once and charges are made if the advertiser requires a repeat advertisement for consecutive days. An individual can place up to three free advertisements for different items in each issue of *Loot*.

Columns and columns of private advertisements are interspersed with occasional trade advertisements. It is, however, ostensibly a forum for non-commercial, individualized exchange. While there remains a constant risk that divisions between commercial and private sales might blur, informants stressed the personalization of the sale as a major criterion for choosing *Loot*; "when you go to have a look at the thing, it's then that you can usually tell that it's trade dressed up as private sale, and I mean I think that's just dishonest – if I want to use a shop I'll use a shop, but this is *Loot*".

Loot's identity is based on its appeal as an unregulated free-to-advertise non-trade market place. Consequently its prices and goods are non-standardized and for some therefore overly daunting; to quote one informant, "a lot of the time the prices are so contradictory to each other . . . and the British public if they are offered something that's a bargain they automatically think there's something wrong with it". Finding a bargain among an array of unseen goods, whose product specifications are described by the partial vendor rather than through the distancing of formalized advertising and marketing terms, requires considerable skill, risk and time.

For some informants it was the appeal of preselection that made *Loot* a viable and attractive mode of consumption. The goods for sale had already been processed and evaluated by previous owners, their knowledge and selection adding a further "depth" to their profile. Each advertisement brought together a product *curriculum vitae* to decipher. Some informants consequently felt that the recently expanded newspaper had become unwieldy, its simple-to-use and localized appeal lost in its hundred-odd pages and ever increasing variety and choice. Similarly advertisers felt that this decreased their ability to make a quick sale (due to the competition and lengthening of consumers' selection process). Consequently they were encouraged to increase (and pay) for longer advertising space; "two years ago I advertised a sofa bed, there were maybe two other adverts and I sold it the same day. The other week I was looking for a sofa bed there were over twenty in there, so I gave up."

Locality and description serve as the initial enticement but information proffered is often so minimal (for example, "Sofas, 2 and 3 seaters, blue floral design") that the bulk of the selection or consumption process takes place via telephone. This transforms the advertisement into a potentially hazardous encounter where exchange and social relations merge, requiring totally different skills to those learned for formal shopping situations.

Georgie, a young single woman furnishing a newly rented home, commented that she had travelled over 50 miles tracking down sofa beds advertised in *Loot*. The first had been misrepresented as a "good condition" item and turned out to be a stained and tattered specimen. The second, more suitable item, was eventually located the other side of London. She did not regret the purchase but commented that a "real" *Loot* user would be able to distinguish truth from exaggeration during the initial telephone call. Georgie realized now that she had not "asked the right questions" and also stressed that once the seller had spent time describing the item, she felt obliged to personally view it. The experience, she felt, had undermined her social capabilities.

John, a 35-year-old systems analyst, explained how he enjoyed shopping through *Loot* as a "restricted" experience. Unlike shopping around the high street it was easier to "rank and weight your decisions" and narrow down purchase possibilities effectively. The basic telephone questions John used when purchasing a second-hand amplifier from *Loot* were brand, age, condition and size. One reason John favoured this form of purchase (other than price) was his assumption that, unlike shop assistants selling commodities, *Loot* vendors would have intimate knowledge of their possessions. However, he expressed profound surprise at the ignorance of many *Loot* advertisers who, it seemed, had spent hundreds of pounds on items they had little knowledge of. Some vendors, he pointed out, were completely unaware of the brand, quality or specifications of the items they were putting up for sale. While this led to potential misunderstandings and inefficient purchase, the mismatch in skill and knowledge of purchaser and vendor created the ambiguity of an unregulated market place, and the potential for bargains as well as disappointments.

The dangerous ambiguity of *Loot* led many informants to refer to the power of "the personal touch". Barry, for example, ascertained that his mountain bike was a real bargain through chatting to the vendor about his forthcoming trip to the Himalayas and the need to sell off much loved possessions (including the bicycle) to raise funds. This situation was validated by Barry's own personal situation; unemployed and fearful of bailiffs' intervention, he had been compelled recently to sell a professional synthesizer through *Loot* for half its original value. Barry, an avid and dedicated reader of *Loot*, firmly trusted it as a forum for real bargains: "relatives are always dying and people need a quick place to sell things off". He felt that British cynicism and suspicion made offering or appreciating a real bargain a major cultural dilemma.

The "personal touch" praised by Barry made other informants deeply nervous. Chloe felt relieved that a neighbour happened to visit when two large "Persian dealer types" arrived at her large, well-furnished house to view items of furniture she had advertised for sale in *Loot* . "It could be dangerous," she reflected, "people knowing your phone number" or "maybe giving out your address".

Similarly, Sally, a council tenant with three children, bought a piece of carpet advertised in *Loot* and felt that she had been duped by personal friendliness when making her purchase. She travelled by public transport to the home of the vendor, a young mother of a similar age, several miles away and during a friendly chat was assured that the rolled-up carpet was in "good condition". On fitting the carpet Sally found that it had a visible burn mark in the centre and felt very let down by the seller. She would not consider asking for a refund as it was too far away to travel again. More significantly she felt personally offended (and humiliated for not being more vigilant and competent).

The more confident and competent users of *Loot* did not feel embarrassed to ask personal or extensive questions about articles over the telephone to ascertain their real worth. Chloe, a middle-class informant (married, mother of two, living in a semi-detached, four-bedroom house with an au pair) frequently uses *Loot* as a kind of "home business" and hobby. When she is bored with a piece of furniture she "tries" it in *Loot* to monitor the response. Only if she receives a good enough offer will she consider a sale. Similarly she purchases items cheaply through *Loot* and resells them at a profit ("with no overheads") back through *Loot*.

In this sense, many informants acknowledged *Loot* as a potentially "subversive" arena where "things might not be what they seem". While a few informants distrusted certain types of advertisements as potentially criminal, others were unperturbed by the possibility of accidentally receiving or handling stolen goods. Chloe, for example, identified this subversive, black market potential as the linchpin of *Loot*: "After all," she asserted, "everyone appreciates a bargain, as long as it's not as traceable as a Cézanne painting".

Loot operates simultaneously as a safe, logical derivative of the community-based classified pages of local newspapers and an anarchic, potentially subversive and ambiguous means of laundering goods and services. The free-advertising policy opens up a "no loss", "free-for-all" clause encouraging impulsive sales. The fast, twenty-four-hour publication promise and lack of payment creates an instant non-formalized, fast-turnover market place where gratuitous browsing is encouraged. Previously treasured objects could, in effect, be turned into hard cash within a day. Accidental bargains from unassuming vendors co-exist alongside deliberately misleading cajolery. While the "personal contact" between buyer and seller might sanction and secure transactions, such self-regulating and non-formalized market relations for some offered too threatening a proposition.

Yet so socially pervasive is this "ungoverned", communal market place called *Loot* that one critic (an educated, middle-aged male informant) viewed it as nothing less than a front for a censorious governmental organization: "Of course . . . the police operate though *Loot* . . . what people advertise, it's constantly under surveillance . . . that's why it's free".

The following case studies reveal *Loot* as a crucial mode of alternative acquisition for specific social groups. They highlight its use in "expelling" and "laundering" material culture within the negotiation of social relations and household moral economy. Within households *Loot* is used, in particular, as a mode of acquisition and dispossession during periods of upheaval and renegotiation. Usage of *Loot* fits into a romantic aesthetic of informal provisioning where authentic objects have "histories" and negotiation of this literary, non-visual market place requires a particular urban, cultural currency and consumptive skill (for a comparative study see Soiffer & Hermann 1987).

Case study I: romancing the artefact: objects with histories

Just as *Loot* is used to "set up" new homes, with the acquisition of cheaper goods, it is also used as an effective means of "expelling" or "laundering" items made newly inappropriate to the household due to changing circumstance.

Michael and Jennifer are a couple in their late twenties. Jennifer has a 6-year-old son, Harry, from a previous marriage. Michael (her recent boyfriend) is in the process of leaving his flat and gradually moving in with Jennifer and her son. The flat is brightly painted, airy and light with informal uncluttered furniture arranged to allow optimum space. Interesting "old things" and modern ethnic artefacts decorate the apartment. The bathroom décor (featuring an original salvaged sturdy Edwardian basin) is inspired by a feature from the pages of *Elle Decoration*. Plain coloured and simple, it is decorated with real shells and starfish.

Jennifer has re-entered higher education to train as an arts administrator and Michael has a compatible career as a freelance arts journalist. Jennifer's newly formed relationship with Michael (he is several years her junior) has reintroduced her to the world of subculture and London nightclubs. There have been several emotional scenes during this process. Jennifer resents the fact that Michael retains dual status as bachelor and partner, and can always escape from the responsibilities of parenthood (which she bears the brunt of) by retreating to his own flat. Harry's natural father contributes little to the household, lives abroad, and sends only the occasional postcard and trinket to his son. As Harry places a miniature toy (given by his father) in his play house, Jennifer laments, "I may not be a very good mummy but I'm the only one he's got".

Jennifer is frustrated by the dilemma of whether or not to have a second child with Michael and attributes Harry's petulant behaviour and boredom to his status as a single child. The previous evening Jennifer, accompanied by Michael and Harry, had been babysitting for a 9 month old. Harry had enjoyed helping feed the baby its bottle. The dilemma of a second child seemed all the more poignant to Jennifer as Michael, having spent the night babysitting with Jennifer and her son, had returned to his flat the following morning to "chill out and listen to some tapes". This provoked envy, anger and resentment, ultimately directed towards Harry. Jennifer dreaded having her life "taken away" again by a second child when she seemed only just to be living it again with Michael. Her burgeoning romance with Michael conflicted with the responsibility she felt towards her son.

Recently she had regained her sexual confidence, enjoying dancing and taking drugs in nightclubs she had not visited since her teenage. She knew, however, this offered only a glimpse of an unattainable identity. Barricading the kitchen door, leaving her pleading son outside, Jennifer expressed with shame the anger she sometimes felt towards her son and a pressing desire to have "her own space". She felt totally compromised. She was neither a single, self-determining girl, a "proper" mother, nor a successful career woman.

Juxtaposed with this turmoil and emotional loneliness was the construction of a "dream home". Appreciating the idealist interiors featured in the style magazine *Elle Decoration* and browsing in antique shops in Ibis Pond, a local middle-class shopping district, fuelled her desire to move from her two-bedroom flat to begin a new life in a three-bedroom house with Michael. Car boot sales provided the ideal place for Jennifer to ponder the acquisition of interesting items for their new home. With her impatient, attention-seeking son in tow this seemed to be yet another luxury denied her. At times it seemed her son was the hindrance to the satisfactory pursuit of her dream as a whole.

Jennifer's homemaking was, she commented, "on-hold". Since the departure of her ex-husband she had refrained from redecorating their home, a two-bedroom Victorian flat conversion. Many of its ornaments and utensils were attained as wedding presents. Although her homemaking was self-avowedly suspended, she and Michael shared an expedition to Carlton antique market to find an interesting old and battered enamel bread bin.

Both Michael and Jennifer shared an attraction to "design classics", articles with known provenance and "special" aesthetic status. This was embodied in Jennifer's car, a 1969 white Mini convertible which she adores, but regrets buying from a friend. Initially she had used *Loot* to chose her vehicle. But realizing a friend desperately needed to sell her car, thought it more beneficial all round to purchase from a close friend in need of the money. The friendship ended in disaster when the engine exploded a week after the purchase. With hindsight she favours the comparative safety of *Loot* as she had subsequently lost contact with her friend. While on a rational level she believed her friend had not set out to deceive her, the car and its ensuing expenditure acted as a constant reminder of the misconceived bargain.

The attraction to special things "with history" combined with high style is manifest in Michael's Christmas gifts to Jennifer which recently included an antique perfume bottle, black and white films (*It's a Wonderful Life*, *Casablanca*) and Muji, Japanese modernist make-up accessories. Jennifer's family gifts were confined to utilitarian and electrical appliances such as a JVC stereo-system. This particular Christmas was a turning point in Jennifer and Michael's relationship as it was the first spent as a family with Harry; it included tree, trimmings and a traditional Christmas Day dinner. Jennifer stressed that only shopping for Michael had been a pleasure, the acquisition of other gifts had "been a chore". Her favourite gifts were those given by Michael, as, she said, he remembered her smallest likes and dislikes. Michael and Jennifer bought gifts for Harry individually and with little conference (choosing traditional games familiar to them as children such as Lego, Twister, Operation, Action Man, etc.). Unlike many married or established partners of their social group there was little debate around suitability and educational value of the toys (Miller 1996). Similarly the only joint gift they received, acknowledging their "coupledom", was given by Jennifer's sister. They did not shop together as they gave no joint presents, instead buying separately for respective families. Publicly and privately, then, Jennifer and Michael's relationship is in a state of major negotiation. Material culture, as home, furnishings, gifts and toys, forms an integral part of this negotiation. As this case study demonstrates, *Loot* as a mode of acquisition constitutes a vital element in the creation of this "romance".

As a single mother living on limited means, just prior to her relationship with Michael, Jennifer used *Loot* to buy a computer. Lacking expertise in this area she travelled unaccompanied to south London to view a computer; feeling obliged, she purchased this and discovered it to be wholly unsuitable and overpriced. She realized how easily the newspaper could be used to "flog off generally suspect gear". The experience seemed to reiterate her vulnerable status as a single mother, isolated for several years from practising in what she described as the "real world". Michael, on the other hand, classed himself as a "savvy" and practised *Loot* user. Indeed *Loot* had recently become the focus in the demise of his bachelor status. The previous week his guitar and leather jacket sold through *Loot* to a "nice young man" from Richmond. Nowadays Jennifer and Michael frequently read *Loot* together, at the kitchen table with a cup of tea, comparing prices, considering potential bargains and "play" arguing over fantasy purchases. Jennifer, for example, while having no intention of acquiring a pet, regularly browses the "Animal" section to fantasize about "a nice little Siamese cat".

Jennifer described her attraction to *Loot* as an appeal to her "jumble sale mentality" and its lack of association with formal marketing. She viewed regular readers of *Loot*, who understood the coded terminology of "excellent condition", "reluctant sale" and "lovely runner" like the members of football collectors' cards or train spotters' clubs understood theirs, as a subcultural group. Although it was the ideal place to get rid of "stolen and shoddy goods", Jennifer saw *Loot* as embodying a more positive ethic than commercial shopping for it encouraged a sense of "recycling" as opposed to wanton consumption.

Loot, with its variable contents and "hands on" sales method, offers the chance to practise a particular urban aesthetic and set of skills. While offering a normative medium (it is a staple means of acquiring accommodation and selling cars in London) its format allows for overt display of informal sales skills. Jennifer and Michael use *Loot* as a shared celebratory consumption activity. Whereas Jennifer's experience of *Loot*, prior to meeting Michael, was wholly negative, the skills that Michael brings to the newly developing relationship reinvent *Loot* and its material culture as an arena of mutual fantasy making. Together they can peruse their romance for "things with history" in an area of consumption deemed ethical in terms of its recycling, non-corporate dimensions. They have embraced the spontaneity of *Loot* to decisively expel the remnants of Michael's problematic "unattached" status. Michael is seen to negotiate the danger of *Loot* with the same ease and daring he uses in his association with London's club life, a world he has made newly available to Jennifer. The use of *Loot* in the contestation of these shifting social identities is premised on cultural and aesthetic, rather than economic, imperative.

Jennifer and Michael incorporate new, gendered, social skills into the household through the acquistion and dispossession of material culture. The changes and contestations of a household in flux are played out through a romancing, and expelling, of artefacts with histories.

Case study II: household hostilities and the aesthetics of consumption

Melissa and Jake have been married for four years and have a 6-month-old baby. Both are artists and Jake works as an art school lecturer. Their house (Victorian terrace, three bedrooms) was formally Jake's bachelor home which Melissa (inspired by features in *Elle Decoration* and her art school education) has transformed into a high style modern home. She is very house proud and has made painstaking attempts to capture a contemporary, almost 1950s Californian appeal. As well as contemporary furniture, Melissa has collected "interesting" ornaments and curios; the fireplace features a sculptural architectural form salvaged from the demolished local church in which the couple were married. Melissa also managed to retrieve numerous rose bushes from the church garden which now flourish and bloom around the front door.

Auctions offer an arena where Melissa can make best use of her visual skills. Before the birth of their baby the couple attended Honiton auction rooms regularly to view every month. Their most celebrated acquisition was a Charles Eames chrome chair, a "design classic" bought at a bargain price. It was now situated in the bathroom, having previously occupied the living room. Artists' easels, fire surrounds and art deco furniture proved the biggest attraction at such events. Melissa also used the same auction to get rid of Jake's unsuitable bachelor furnishings: "In fact one of my husband's horrible old Turkish carpets he sold at the auction room because I hated it, I said I like those two but that one can go". The main motive for auction going was the intrigue of "old stuff, other people's stuff, things that people don't want".

Melissa identifies her purchases as "visually led" and so while she often browses *Loot* for attractive second-hand bargains she rarely (if ever) actually initiates a purchase, "however good it might sound". When her younger brother shared the marital home, he bought *Loot* "religiously" to browse the vehicle section and discuss the merits of certain models with Jake. For them *Loot* became a common feature of household life. While Melissa had never purchased through *Loot* she was thoroughly familiar with its format, readership and sales method. This familiarity had led her to use *Loot* as the site of major contestation in the relationship. She used *Loot* in an orchestrated protest designed specifically to challenge the household status quo.

Melissa's most valued and significant possession was a Henry Dartworth painting purchased from a gallery in Ibis Pond. The item exemplified the struggles and desires of her pre-marital identity. She had saved for six months while at college, working nights in a "smelly pub" to purchase the picture, which now hangs prominently in the living room of the marital home. Recently she became disturbed by the picture; she felt that she was "not appreciating it enough", that it was being "wasted" in its present situation.

In a fit of rage, after a lengthy argument with Jake, she committed what she considered a desperate act of terrorism. She telephoned the *Loot*'s twenty-four-hour free-advertising hotline and within hours had offered her greatest fine art possession up for sale among gilt framed oil paintings of grazing sheep in "the rococo style". She joked that with hindsight *Loot* was the least appropriate place to sell contemporary fine art and that she did not receive one telephone enquiry over the sale. The gesture had not been intended as a serious sale attempt but to express the depth of Melissa's feelings. Publicly she had set out to sacrifice her most precious (pre-marital) possession through the "lowly" pages of *Loot* (with its suspect goods and used cars). The act simultaneously undermined the values and knowledge associated with Melissa and Jake's shared world; they had, after all, met at the Ibis Pond Art Club; "I was just trying to get back at Jake for something or other to make him feel bad, you know, about something horrible".

Melissa's choice of medium for the painting's sale held particular poignancy. It was a gendered consumption space shared by Jake and her brother for perusing cars. The meaning of the protest resided in the fact there would be little real risk of selling the article through such an inappropriate medium. Throwing her most prized and aesthetically superior possession, symbolically, to the wolves meant that Melissa had maligned its worth and signalled a major discontent.

Melissa and Jake share numerous other forms of informal provisioning including fishing, pick-your-own produce, handicrafts and painting. Their relationship revolves around public and private interest in art and culture and its associated values. While other forms of informal acquisition are shared, the presence of *Loot* in the household was reminiscent of Jake's carefree car-hunting days. Melissa's own pre-marital identity, built on a series of unacknowledged sacrifices, had seemed subsumed by the pending birth of their baby. Like her highly valued picture, her pre-marital worth was going to waste, taken for granted and unappreciated. *Loot*, defined by its non-visual format, provided the ideal means of "laundering" this dispute. Reducing her ultimate, inalienable possession to the stark world of commodification and low-brow, used goods, Melissa temporarily threatened the cultural values through which she shared her relationship with Jake.

Case study III: "cultural capital" and the authenticity of subversion

In the course of the ethnographic research in north London a further case, which took place outside the street, illustrated the significance of "authentication" and alternative acquisition. Phil and Spencer, both in their early thirties, share a two-bedroom flat, claim income support and have been unemployed for approximately a year. Prior to this period Phil had been employed as a temporary clerk in the professional sector and Spencer had worked in hotel restaurant kitchens. Their flat has no formal bathing facilities and is sparsely furnished with items salvaged from local skips. They pay a minimal rent and so accept this as a bearable sacrifice. The living room contains an oval marble-topped table with wrought iron legs, surrounded either side by a broken green velveteen sofa and a foam sofa bed with torn upholstery. There are no decorations or pictures on the wall. A table and four chairs stands in the window, and a bureau in the corner features the communal book and compact disc (CD) collection. Music is supplied by a Walkman CD with one speaker placed at an angle towards the ceiling. The kitchen sink has a permanent leak and a bucket has to be periodically emptied from beneath it. Spencer had just travelled to Germany and so had brought back duty-free goods including a bottle of Bombay Sapphire gin and several bulk boxes of Camel cigarettes kept on the marble coffee table for general consumption.

Despite living on limited incomes and in notably squalid surroundings, Phil and Spencer had developed an avid interest in luxury clothes and second-hand designer menswear. Their favourite shop is a gentleman's dress agency nicknamed "Fluffy Fleming's" after its camp ex-1950s couture milliner proprietor. "Fluffy Fleming" hunts out appropriate styles from his stock and often puts things aside for the boys (whom he assumes are a gay couple) until they can afford the items. An Yves Saint Laurent suit worth £700 can be picked up at "Fluffy's" for around £75 in excellent condition. Phil and Spencer usually begin their shopping trips with a strawberry milk shake in a local café and even when they have no money, they proceed to window shop at the places where their purchases normally take place. Spencer insisted that his interest in clothes had evolved through age and the ability to "carry a good suit off". Under the tutelage of Phil, who keeps a copy of *Debrett's etiquette and modern manners* and *Small talk at parties* on his bookshelf, he was continuing to learn the ropes. Phil joked that even in his native home of Urmston, Manchester, he had turned the tiny bedroom of a two-up-two-down terrace into a study equipped with pipe rack, leather chair and "other affectations". Spencer, who borrows Phil's clothes while he builds up his own collection, had, he commented, recently discovered "the merits of a distinctive cologne". Both were avid readers of P.G. Wodehouse novels.

Cheaper charity shops were used for what they described as "practice shopping" where they learned, for example, to distinguish a French cuff or a quality cotton. Mistakes proved less disastrous when made in a cheap charity shop. Both considered the "obvious" display of labels to be *gauche* and explained their attraction to designer wear as a concern for "cut" and "quality". Spencer was proud that he could now confidently visit the menswear section of any upper-end department store and "decipher" its contents without embarrassment. Phil and Spencer despised the attitudes of shop assistants in such places and defiantly shop-lifted expensive articles, using a pair of pliers to remove security tags. They once stole a small item from "Fluffy's" shop but, as they now considered him a good friend, would never conceive of doing this again and regretted the initial act. However, they occasionally stole from charity shops which they condemned as overpriced. They justified their actions by explaining the fraud and colonialism associated with many charity organizations.

While they rarely purchase from *Loot* they frequently peruse the car section and had recently planned to buy a navy blue Jaguar XJ6 with a "windfall". Ironically this "windfall" resulted from artful subversion of *Loot*'s potentially negative aspects. Phil and Spencer used *Loot* as an instrumental part of a recent, and successful, fraudulent household insurance claim. They placed a bogus advertisement in the music equipment section to sell two electric guitars. They stored Phil's massive collection of designer shirts, suits and accessories and their joint collection of CDs in a neighbour's house. They then contacted the police late that night to report a burglary.

On arrival at the scene of the "crime", the major point of contention for the police was the lack of forced entry. Spencer explained this away by testifying that two young men, seeing the advertisement in *Loot*, had visited the flat to view the guitars offered for sale. They must have gained access to the house keys when Spencer briefly left the room to make coffee for his visitors. And, the police concluded, returned later that day to steal the guitars and other property.

After Spencer had spent four hours at the police station, trying (unsuccessfully) to identify the possible culprits, the police concluded that it was an opportunist burglary that illustrated the inherent danger of unregulated publications such as *Loot*. When visited by the insurance assessor and queried on the incongruous lifestyle the couple lived (with the strange juxtaposition of designer suits, odorous furniture and generally squalid living conditions) Phil explained that his compulsive clothes buying was the result of his intolerable living conditions. The insurance claim included photographs, swatches and some receipts for the majority of the missing suits. His remaining collection of accessories and shoes substantiated the claim. A week later a joint cheque for £15,000 arrived, two-thirds of their original claim.

Phil and Spencer had already begun to spend their booty. The previous evening they spent £200 dining at a four-star hotel restaurant; Spencer boasted "we had aperitifs, Mersault, Sauternes and port" and looked "dapper in our designer suits". He was currently having a dinner jacket made-to-measure (and worked out the possible cost of each wearing in his lifetime as £150) and had that morning spent £160 on silk cravats. Still, he lamented his lack of visionary shopping skill and envied his flatmate's strategic shopping which he compared to the "skill of Karpov"; he was always at least five moves ahead in envisaging the potential of purchases. Neither has yet fully decided which Jaguar to choose from *Loot*.

Due to long-term unemployment Phil and Spencer are precluded from formulating their identities in a formal workplace. Their limited economic means logically restricts their access to forms of non-essential consumption. They are at once excluded from a world of skilled labour and by extension, a world of playful and risk-filled luxury consumption. Instead, they invert their informal economic skills of theft, fraud and alternative acquisition to its disassociated lifestyle of conservative foppery and affluence. Moneys gained are reinvested in the improvement of skills of acquisition. Unlike the "ordinary" income of the sporadic unskilled jobs otherwise available to them, their "booty" finances the material culture and aesthetics of their shared relationship with consumption.

Like Michael and Jennifer and Melissa and Jake, Phil and Spencer shared a propensity for things with history and a sense of authenticity. Although Phil and Spencer are economically impoverished, they share a romance of "authentic" masculine identity whose associated material culture has become the focal point of their lives. They are so advanced in the art of informal provisioning and alternative acquisition that they confidently invert the "dangerous" and anarchic aspects of *Loot*. They parody the potential risks of *Loot* in a display of defiant and cynical disregard, and attain the ultimate "bargain".

Argos

While *Loot* demands interaction, one-to-one negotiation of social relations and skill to mediate and comprehend a chaotic array of goods, the *Argos* catalogue seems the ultimate handbook for the inactive armchair shopper. The *Argos* catalogue is a prominent form of alternative acquisition across all social groups in the street. Unlike *Loot*, the *Argos* catalogue provides a standardized, rigid repertoire of brand-new, visually represented alienable commodities. The catalogue, of approximately 500 pages, features over 5,000 products including jewellery, three-piece suites, domestic technology, sports equipment, toys, gifts, etc. Named after the "argosy" ("a fleet of abundantly laden merchant ships") it is distinguished from other mail order catalogues in that it deals predominantly with hardware (no clothes or consumables) and acts as a portable shop window. Goods are chosen through the catalogue then ordered and purchased direct, in person, at a local showroom (larger orders, such as garden sheds, can be ordered by telephone and delivered). While the catalogue does not rely on offering a credit system, with users paying for their items in full, a £1,000 instant credit is made available through a personal account card. Some items offer six months' interest-free credit. The catalogue is published each season in full colour, spring/summer and autumn/winter. Each edition is eagerly anticipated by *Argos* users who can visit the showrooms to obtain the latest copy. The company also delivers catalogues to homes in the vicinity of the outlet.

The catalogue is designed to feature maximum products in the minimum space and locates products in a strict typology. For example, the jewellery section, beginning with diamond rings (4 pages, 132 items) progresses through "His and Her" pendants, crucifix/St Christophers (1 page, 27 items), Sovereign rings, Mizpah pendants, to gold loop earrings (4 pages, 123 items). In total there are over 1,200 jewellery items offered for sale. Inset pictures feature models of different ethnicities sporting several of the items displayed in the catalogue. The household appliance section offers everything from hostess trolleys and deep fat fryers to electric toothbrushes. It features 46 vacuum cleaners ranging from £17.95 (for a hand-held model) to £199.99 (for a *Dyson* super model) and offers a choice of 19 different ironing boards, all fully illustrated. More recently selected goods are also displayed in the *Argos* shop window, as the outlets have moved to more prominent, high street locations.

Argos seems to offer a rationalized, simple, value-for-money way to shop where the consumer is in total control. Products selected from the catalogue are entered onto an order form using a coded number. The form is taken to the service point and during the payment transaction goods are delivered to the collection counter for the customer. A 16-day money-back guarantee offers the security of a conventional shopping outlet (if not more). Although the basic product types provide the core of the *Argos* catalogue, peripheral items such as "Take That" bedspreads, "Power Ranger" collectibles, "Barbie" watches, "Baywatch" wall clocks and marble-effect telephones create a transient and fashionable dimension to the catalogue. These items circumscribe *Argos* as a contemporary, interactive catalogue as opposed to a strictly functional or blandly convenient consumptive encounter. While it provides an extensive variety of apparently mundane items, the substantial toy section denotes its significant use for child-related consumption. Luxury and gift objects, and the suggestion of gift items (certain sections show symbols and text reading "all items are gift boxed"), are prevalent throughout the catalogue.

What distinguishes *Argos* is its dual presence in homes where mail order catalogues are otherwise considered an inappropriate, even divisive, means of acquisition and those where traditional mail order catalogues are considered a staple and respectable form of consumption.

While *Argos* draws on the established working/lower-middle-class market of traditional catalogue consumers, the exclusion of clothing and 16-day money-back guarantee allows other (predominately middle-class) users to imbue its presentation and mode of purchase with the safe, respectable and educated functionalism of renowned department stores such as John Lewis (see Miller et al. 1997). The quantitative aesthetic of *Argos*, with its multiple brands and illustrations, made some informants critical of its mass "plasticy and cheap" image. Others felt that bulk of choice coupled with the omission of a biased or manipulative shop assistant made *Argos* a minimum-risk, optimum-value consumption method. While informants gave numerous examples of *Argos* products actually costing more than high street equivalents, they consciously opted for the security and self-determination offered by the pre-catalogue selection sales method. They enjoyed the *impression* of mass-produced, lowest-common-denominator goods offered at basic, understandable, stratified prices.

Argos catalogue was considered a staple of contemporary living across all social groups in the ethnography (most could locate it instantly in a convenient magazine rack or, revealingly, in their child's bedroom). However, there were vital differences in the role it played in their household provisioning. A *Financial Times* (24 August 1995) article reported a massive growth in *Argos* shares and the exceptional success of its new "Wedding List" service. While many consumers see *Argos* as an ideal source for gifts, some informants considered it as the least likely place to purchase gifts. One middle-aged woman typifying the latter view had recently used *Argos* to purchase a kettle and mattress cover, because, she pointed out emphatically, it was the only appliance store open on a Sunday: "I use it very much as convenience shopping, I would never use it to buy presents or anything because I like to see what I'm buying before ... seeing it in a picture isn't enough for me, I need to touch and feel it".

In stark opposition to this view, *Argos* was used by other informants as an essential guide for budgeting and identifying birthday, Christmas and anniversary gifts. Chris, a 19-year-old Greek/English youth working in a minimally paid government training scheme, who described himself as having a "dangerously big family", used *Argos* to ascertain appropriate Christmas gifts on a limited budget. On Christmas Eve, when buying his brother a *Pin-Pad* executive game, he remembered the "desperate scene" as people clambered to order and collect gifts.

Others viewed *Argos* as a source of consumption external (as opposed to integral) to their own provisioning, even if they made regular use of it. Some expressed an uncontainable sense of voyeurism flicking the pages of *Argos*, as if glimpsing a shopping "underworld"; "I normally find *Argos* catalogue quite entertaining because you always think 'gosh, this is cheap', so it's quite good for cheap, less important birthday presents ... I find it quite entertaining", commented one middle-class informant.

Argos, then, shares with *Loot* an appeal to self-determining acquisition. The salesperson is replaced by series of descriptive product details, the formal shopping space is reduced to a format of numbered pages. Unlike *Loot*, however, *Argos* operates as a static, secure and trustworthy form of consumption used to anchor decisions and substantiate choices. As the following case studies reveal, this medium does not automatically exclude the play and fantasy making associated with *Loot*. But they accentuate *Argos* as a vital consumptive information system which, through its normative status, opens up the sociality of consumption.

Case study I: restricted choices and familial ties

Wayne and Gillian live in a small rented council flat with their four children. They are long-term unemployed and rely on income support and welfare benefit to support their family. Wayne has just completed a six-month government retraining programme. More recently expenditure (for example, on gifts) has been confined to the immediate family due to severe financial constraints. Wayne and Gillian always shop together as a couple, and use the nearest shopping centre regularly (about three times per week). They can see no advantage in travelling to the more upmarket and supposedly better equipped mall some miles away, especially as most of their shopping involves food provisioning. They recently cancelled a milk delivery as, using four pints per day, they found it more economical to purchase in bulk from the supermarket. Similarly the local shops are out of bounds except for the occasional ice-cream for the children and the Post Office for benefit. Mr McGrudie's local hardware store, however, was praised for the wealth of information the patron offered with goods he sold. This information and service counterbalanced the slightly higher prices he was forced to charge in comparison with bulk distributorship outlets. Despite their lack of funds and inability to socialize in formal settings they are a particularly sociable couple, receiving over seventy cards at Christmas. They get on well with neighbours but friendship is generally confined to greetings and conversations. Much of their leisure activity is provided by self-provisioning: the kitchen operates as a cottage brewery and distillery for various alcoholic drinks. A substantial proportion of their weekly budget is given over exclusively to this pastime, the National Lottery and smoking.

Wayne is proud of his dual role in provisioning the family and insists that he is not embarrassed to buy anything - even sanitary towels. With a large family, shopping frequently proved stressful and on a recent shopping trip Wayne had been reprimanded by an "old dear" for hitting one of the kids in a supermarket. He felt morally justified as the child had been deliberately "winding him up all day". The children were expected to do their fair share of carrying shopping home and to learn to appreciate the cost of food. Gillian stressed, though, the nightmare of shopping with children during the summer holidays and her frustration with ill-organized shops. Places like Toys 'R' Us for example, enticed and over-excited children. In this context, *Argos* catalogue then was used as a controllable toy shop. Indeed the family relied almost exclusively on *Argos* for selection and purchase of the children's Christmas and birthday presents. As well as offering cheaper products than Toys 'R' Us, it allowed the children to indicate their choices and for their parents to respond accordingly. For them looking in *Argos* replaced the trauma of "shopping around" with a restricted income. The variety and price range offered in the catalogue was tantamount to this selection process. It was used as a price barometer and a dependable source: "If it's in *Argos* we normally get it from *Argos*". Lamenting the lack of Christmas presents requested by their eldest son, Wayne and Gillian used *Argos* to identify the most sought-after and popular toys (in this case "Power Ranger" plaster casts). Some of the children's presents are bought from bulk cut-price warehouses like Poundstretcher but Wayne and Gillian pointed out that like Kwiksave, it was a horrible but necessary shopping experience. *Argos* on the other hand encompasses the positive experiences of "shopping around" without the stress of outside intervention, but with an implicit sociality intact. The only downside to *Argos* shopping was the disappointment of out-of-stock items.

Varied and leisurely shopping is not a viable option for Wayne and Gillian. Illustrative of this position was their exclusion from "sale" shopping and their inability to risk waiting for the "right bargain". Just before Christmas, for example, the family went to buy bunk beds from *Argos*; they dare not wait until the New Year sales as they feared the money would be subsumed by Christmas expenditures. They had already saved for a year and a half and desperately needed the bunk beds as the smallest child had outgrown her cot. In a two-bedroom flat, Gillian stressed "bunk beds is the only way to get four of them in one room". They had pre-chosen the beds through the *Argos* catalogue and collected the item flat packed for self-assembly.

Wayne and Gillian have a severely limited budget and are not able to engage in varied, leisurely or experimental shopping. For them *Argos* provides a form of self-provisioning not just of goods but of shopping knowledge. *Argos* keeps them in touch with high street tastes and prices; through the normative sociality of *Argos* catalogue they prevent deeper isolation. Provisioning for a large family requires strategic action and with *Argos* they sustain a controllable, familial sociality through consumption. The children are socialized through shared food-buying trips and perusal of the *Argos* catalogue. Budgeting, Gillian pointed out, involved the use of "nightmare shops" like Poundstretcher and Kwiksave which precluded imaginative or fantasy shopping of any kind. Such shops, based around utility, could not provide the necessary social resource that *Argos* provided.

Case study II: "swings and roundabouts": sustaining sociality

Philipa and her African–Caribbean husband Roger have three children aged 7 to 14. They are both in their late thirties and live in a three-bedroom council flat that is cosily decorated with knick-knacks new and old. Old sepia photographs of the husband's family ornament the walls and the living room has a comfortable, velour three-piece suite and large television. They shop mostly at bulk outlets such as Kwiksave, Iceland frozen foods and Tesco the supermarket, but Philipa enjoys variety and happily uses markets for clothes. Recently she treated herself to £30 of Amway products, purchased direct sale from her next-door neighbour, which she justified on the pretext of "taking more care of herself at her age". "Besides which," she said, it was a question of "swings and roundabouts" - what she saved on the arduous task of food shopping she could spend on a reward for herself. And her neighbour selling Amway benefited too.

Most of the household's non-food provisioning was supplied through catalogues. Philipa subscribed to both *Kays* and *Littlewoods* mail order catalogues as she perceived them as offering slightly different, inter-changeable styles. Both mainstream catalogues, the former offered more conservative and old-fashioned clothes, and the latter, younger and more up-to-date versions. When a catalogue first arrives Philipa looks forward to browsing its pages as an enjoyable and exciting event. *Kays* catalogue provided T-shirts for the whole family in the summer and a pair of trainers for the "old man". Philipa controlled the purchase of items through catalogues but shared the browsing and decision making predominantly with the children. The Christmas provisions for the previous year, she stressed, had been almost exclusively reliant on catalogues. All the presents were purchased through catalogues which she believed forced her to keep to a fairly strict and manageable weekly credit limit. *Choice*, *Kays* and *Littlewoods* offered her a good combination of choice, and though *Littlewoods* do not offer commission, *Kays* gave a 10 per cent cash-back scheme. Accumulated "cash back" was a major purchase incentive and could either be redeemed in the form of a cheque or, for a greater amount, be redeemed against future purchases. In the past Philipa enjoyed browsing the catalogues with friends and had once collated communal orders to accrue commission. In the process she discovered that some women furnished their entire houses through the catalogue. One neighbour, for example, bought three beds, a three-piece suite, display cabinets, bedroom suite, wardrobes, "everything in one go" from *Freeman's* catalogue. The commission work however developed into a negative experience as many of her friends defaulted on their payments. Eventually she found the experience of badgering close neighbours and friends for their overdue payments too embarrassing.

Philipa's most recent large catalogue purchase was a professional sewing machine. She did not shop around for the item as she was already reliant on the catalogue's credit system. She had gained a new-found confidence, trying activities she had previously felt precluded from. She had used her sewing machine to make a costume for a jazz and tap dancing show she performed with a friend at a local dance school. There had been numerous time-consuming rehearsals and the whole family came to see the final performance. But ultimately she envisaged the sewing machine as a means to making clothes for her daughter, despite acknowledging that shop-bought clothes were cheaper in the long run. She could not yet justify the expense of the credit payments but saw the item as a major emotional and functional investment.

Her sewing machine projects had been on hold while she organized and arranged the silk flowers at her cousin's wedding. The arrangements for the wedding reception revolved around a bargain wedding dress purchased from the John Lewis department store at Brent Cross. Reduced from £500 to £250 due to being shop soiled, the dress was described as "exquisite" and "totally gorgeous", white with tiny pink sequins, glittering diamantés and a long train. This bargain, of which the bride and her relatives were extremely proud, had transformed the original decorative scheme from ivory to pink and white. This theme encompassed the bridesmaid's dresses, the bride's gown, the table settings, flowers and decorations. Philipa's mother-in-law made the dresses for the younger bridesmaids and a friend made the others. Philipa commented that her cousin's wedding had taken up a lot of energy and had been the main focus of the female relatives for the last five months. As well as creating the floral displays, Philipa had made the three tiers of the cake for her sister-in-law, a more proficient cake decorator, to ice.

Argos formed the focal point of gifting for the cousin's wedding list. With the main list placed with *Argos*, guests were asked either to choose from the catalogue or to donate *Argos* gift vouchers. Philipa had been able to afford only £20 but felt that at least her cousin could put this towards a bigger purchase. As the cousin already had an established home with two children she had preferred the notion of vouchers; but accepted that many guests would be uncomfortable giving money (despite the fact that *Argos* catalogue unequivocally indicates product prices and allows for direct comparison).

Philipa herself relied on the catalogue for the selection of gifts at birthdays and Christmas. In particular, the children used *Argos* for writing Christmas lists to Santa Claus. Their lists would include specific product selection, catalogue code number and exact price. Far from encouraging unbridled desire, Philipa used the catalogue to illustrate to the children that Christmas presents operated within a finite budget: "I told them Father Christmas couldn't afford any products over £9.99 this year". The children happily chose within the designated monetary limits.

Such comments were supported by the interviews conducted with local junior school children regarding Christmas gifting. They spoke of *Argos* catalogue as the dominant source of inspiration and identification of potential gifts. As another mother from the street noted, "they see it on TV and look it up in *Argos* book to see how much it is . . . the little one she can't write properly yet so she copies it all down including the price!" For many children, who fantasized about adulthood as the freedom to go "in any shop you wanted", the catalogue acted as their own safe, fantasy shopping space. Notably at least two-thirds of all children identified themselves as *Argos* literate. Conversations among groups of children revealed a thorough and shared knowledge of the relevant *Argos* pages. As one parent in the ethnography commented, "the children always use *Argos* . . . they all know what's on what pages and they all get their ideas what they'd like for Christmas out of it".

Philipa and the family practise varied informal and formal shopping. While they budget with limited income Philipa's social networks, partic-ularly female kin, open up numerous links through which other advantageous forms of informal provisioning are pursued. A "perk" of her work as the principal provisioner of the family is the occasional "treat". While an expensive purchase of cosmetics from the next-door neighbour seems irresponsible, such relations sustain other forms of advantageous informal provisioning. Philipa is frequently the beneficiary of stolen goods and neighbours often call on her husband Roger for paid repairs and home improvement chores which supplements an unstable family income. Like Wayne and Gillian, *Argos* is an invaluable means of controlling and mediating household consumption. It allows the children a productive and educative role in provisioning. *Argos* also forms the crux of normative consumption values within their given social group.

For Philipa her board range of provisioning supports an entire infrastructure of social and economic relations. The seemingly erratic consumption of treats and luxuries slots into a socialized web of female kin, neighbours and friends. The dual use of catalogues for acquisition and monetary provisioning, turning friendly neighbour into tiresome debt-collector proved too risky a venture as its commerciality overtly jeopardized this balanced array of vital relationships.

Within this social group *Argos* is a respectable and normative medium for self-provisioning and gifting.

Case study III: a household in rehearsal: things without meaning

Joanna is a young, middle-class married mother ostensibly responsible for the household's provisioning. At the moment her partner is retraining as a medical student and so they are living on a limited income in a maisonette. The décor mainly consists of pastel colours, stripped pine and a number of items from Ikea. There are no items in the household that Joanna would describe as having "sentimental" value or particular significance, except the ornaments and gifts given by her Canadian in-laws. The house contains predominantly new furniture and objects. Although Joanna had owned one antique, her grandmother's old chair, she had subsequently returned it to her mother as it was scruffy and too unwieldy for the small living room.

Although Joanna purchased a high ratio of brand new household products she considered *Argos* as "last resort" shopping. While the house contained numerous objects purchased through the catalogue she disassociated herself from *Argos* as a recommendable form of shopping and described its products critically. *Argos* was considered as a basic, even degrading, form of shopping used merely to supplement practical items omitted from the couple's original wedding list. The living room magazine rack held a copy of the *Argos* catalogue which Joanna emphasized would be consulted only "out of necessity, not for pleasure". While the actual reasoning behind her using *Argos* was to control the purchasing experience and avoid pressure from assistants, Joanna described the visits to the shop as too hassle-ridden and stressful. She compared the uniformity, ritual and "sheep-like behaviour" of the *Argos* users with pre-revolutionary Soviet Union bureaucracy. She did not deem *Argos* cheaper, just more instantly accessible: "You can look at home and get yourself organized at home". Her most recent purchase, a hair razor with alterable settings, was designed to save money on hair cuts for her husband and son. Three weeks after the purchase, she was still unable to operate the complicated appliance successfully.

To Joanna, *Argos* provided basic houseware at acceptably reasonable prices. In "an emergency" she once purchased a pair of gold-plated earrings, chosen from the catalogue, to match a wedding outfit. Normally dismissing *Argos* and catalogues in general, for the acquisition of personal goods, she stressed the purchase as an act of desperation. She quickly realized "the earrings were dreadful . . . horrible gold plate that tarnished quickly and were just not nice".

Her mother similarly uses *Argos* "in an emergency" where replacement, utility items are sought at a reasonable price. Neither would "dream of getting real gifts from there" but saw it as a convenience hardware store. As well as precluding *Argos* as a store for meaningful or significant gifts Joanna would not consider using *Argos* for toys for her 5 year old, Sammy. Many of his items though were purchased through more acceptable alternative modes of informal acquisition including the Ibis Pond Mother's Group jumble sales and the classifieds section of their monthly newsletter, the *Early Learning* catalogue and Usbourne and Red House educational book parties.

Joanna, living on a limited budget, consciously restricts the range of goods and methods of provisioning in the household. For Joanna the present household is merely a household in rehearsal. Its objects have no overt sentimental ties and acquisition of household goods is actively neutral. It is as if the present contents are props, mock-ups to be replaced in a more stable, affluent future. *Argos* suffices as a bridging tool while quality valued provisioning (directly associated with the desired social and cultural group) is confined to the provisioning of the child.

Although Joanna's household is limited to a tight budget it is made understood, through the acquisition of material culture, that this is a temporary state.

Argos is viewed as an involuntary option, stress-filled and aesthetically deficient. Unlike Philipa's household, here *Argos* exemplifies the tawdry aspects of modern alienated consumption – receiving no service or individual attention Joanna feels like one of many passive, mass consumers choosing from a prescribed range of goods. She uses the stock of alienable commodities to prevent attachment to a transitional life-stage.

Conclusion

Loot and *Argos* are vehicles for the restriction and elaboration of consumptive choices. As alternative, non-formal modes of acquisition, they are incorporated and manipulated into broader systems of provisioning. Both act as crucial vehicles of sociality and knowledge formation.

Loot with its demand on time, skill and risk-taking appears to call on optimum "cultural capital". Driven by the aesthetic of authenticity rather than basic thrift, *Loot* seems best "played" by those with the least at stake.

Its literary, non-visual medium requires extensive interpretative skills and, to handle the exchange, competent social interaction. *Argos*, with its standardized, price-led, easy-to-use method of acquisition, appears in contrast to be a simplified option favoured by the unskilled shopper. Here the image replaces the word as a more obvious and instantaneous response-led means of representation. Shopping through pictures, with limited social interaction, seems to challenge consumption as a culturally informed practice. Like catalogues in general, critics berate *Argos* as a "degrading" form of consumption, its users merely responding "sheep-like" to a production line of goods. Closer examination reveals, however, that users of *Argos* were as skilled and practised in their acquisition as the wily *Loot* users. Skilled *Argos* consumers effectively inverted the outlet's commodified system, using the catalogue as an effective means of self-provisioning. Far from lacking skill and competence, consumers used *Argos* to control and manage the moral economy of the household, just as users of *Loot* used the medium to practise and test theirs. These choices are value-led rather than rationally and economically driven.

Just as goods, according to Douglas and Isherwood, "are endowed with value by the agreement of fellow consumers" (1977: 75) so too are modes of consumption. While *Loot* offers an element of thrift and bargain hunting that seems ideally suited to economically restricted or working-class consumption, in effect its risk-laden and time-consuming method leaves it firmly embedded in a middle-class style of knowledge use. Although *Argos* offers a more expensive range of goods it provides a basic resource for social groups precluded from mainstream, leisure imbued formal shopping.

Loot demands high mobility and the knowledge and resources to navigate the intricacies of London's suburbs, while *Argos* is based on a fundamental notion of immobility. For poorer households and those mostly confined to the home, such as elderly people and children, it allows home-based, self-regulated and containable provisioning. These practical implications relate to conceptual ideas of space: *Loot* expands the notion of local while *Argos*, as a chain store, brings the global to the local. As this ethnographic observation illustrates, modes of acquisition and material culture are not confined to rigid social groups. Skills culled from a range of knowledges (educational, class, subcultural) are brought to bear constructively on the opportunities opened up by these new forms of acquisition.

References

Appadurai, A. 1986. *The social life of things.* Cambridge: Cambridge University Press.
Bloch, M. & J. Parry 1989. *Money and the morality of exchange.* Cambridge: Cambridge University Press.

Bourdieu, P. 1984. *Distinction: a social critique of the judgement of taste.* London: Routledge & Kegan Paul.

Caplovitz, D. 1967. *The poor pay more: consumer practices of low income families.* New York: Free Press.

Carrier, J.G. 1995. *Gifts and commodities: exchange and Western capitalism since 1700.* Routledge: London.

Cheal, D.J. 1988. *The gift economy.* London: Routledge.

Douglas, M. & B. Isherwood 1979. *The world of goods.* London: Basic Books.

Miller, D. 1986. *Material culture and mass consumption.* London: Blackwell.

Miller, D. 1995. *Acknowledging consumption.* London: Routledge.

Miller, D., P. Jackson, B. Holbrook, N. Thrift, M. Rowlands 1997. *Consumption and identity: a study of two North London shopping centres.* London: Routledge.

Miller, D. (in press) How infants grow mothers in North London. *Theory Culture and Society.*

Rutz, H.J. & B.S. Orlove (eds) 1989. *The social economy of consumption.* Lanham, MD: University Press of America.

Silverstone, R., E. Hirsch & D. Morley 1992. *Consuming technologies: media in domestic spaces.* London: Routledge.

Soiffer, S.S. & G.M. Herrmann 1987. Visions of power: ideology and practice in the American garage sale. *Sociological Review* 35(1), 48–83.

Weiner, A.B. 1992. *Inalienable possessions: the paradox of giving while keeping.* Los Angeles: University of California Press.

PART III
The public sphere

CHAPTER 5

The message in paper

Andrea Pellegram

In Western society, the debate about objects as conveyors of messages, or vehicles of expression in an iconographic language of things, has been of growing influence since it first entered academic debate in the 1960s, when structuralism drew parallels between objects and language. There is, however, another type of message that is not so evidently communicative and one that has, to some extent, been neglected in this debate. This is the latent and incidental message through which an object becomes an artefact of human interaction as a residue of a social relation. Though this is formally discussed in the field of archaeology where excavated shards of baked clay and splinters of rotten wood are used to reconstruct entire civilizations theoretically, most writers on material culture have focused on the use of objects in purposeful expression. However, in a living society, we ignore the latent and incidental message of objects at our peril, because what is not overtly intended can also be revealing.

This chapter considers the overt and latent messages borne by one class of object, paper, and how these messages are developed and manipulated. It begins with a description of the types of paper found in the office, highlighting that the physical nature of paper has much to do with the message it conveys. There follows a general discussion of how objects carry meaning that is brought down to the specific example. Stratified social positions in the office hierarchy are then shown to be expressed in roles in the execution of the production of a report. The chapter concludes with a demonstration of another form of meaning: the transformation of vital information into waste paper in office filing rituals.

The illustrative examples are drawn from a larger study of a London-based office in the local government sector. Observation was undertaken from 1990 to 1994 in an organization of approximately 22 employees. It served a committee of elected members and liaised with other departments and organizations. It was very much a closed social system since contact with these outside groups was limited to letters, telephone calls, and the formal arena of meetings. The employees are categorized into three types: managers, technical staff and administration (or admin). About half of all employees are admin, who are responsible for day-to-day office operations, providing secretarial support for the remaining staff and the committee. It is female dominated, particularly in the lower status jobs. The technical staff are all university-trained professional officers who write specialized reports for consideration by the committee. The managers oversee the entire operation, set the agenda and ensure that the final presentation to the committee and outside organizations is effective and suitable. This is a male-dominated stratum though there is one female manager.

In the office, as in any human social arena, the communications systems of verbal language are augmented by other media such as body language and object cues. Objects frame the relationships between managers, technical staff and admin, their use and manipulation giving clues about the nature of the social interaction in which they are "sound". As will be illustrated, objects can convey messages about the regard that one person shows for another: a signature on a letter shows personal esteem; juniors will show a superior person neat and tidy work in order to protect their position within the hierarchy. Status is also demonstrated with objects since only certain people may manipulate them in prescribed ways: the admin assistant does not write the letter, the manager does not file it. While the cues provided by objects are only sometimes consciously employed by social interactants, more often than not the configuration of the message is unconscious.

The office's object discourse has been developed by the workers, within their larger societal context, in response to the work they do. The local government sector by nature fosters a highly bureaucratized environment for those employed within it. The interpersonal relations are, at least at a superficial level, best described by Weber's (1978) ideal type bureaucrat (see however Beetham 1987): a technical specialist who provides a particular service to a mass public that is based upon the fair and impartial application of rational knowledge. In order for the individual working within this context to succeed in providing this service, personal identity is shoe-horned into an almost mechanical role of a task-specific service provider. The individual is controlled by the job description which is a formally composed outline of what the individual can and cannot do in the course of the work. Hierarchy within an organization is formalized and maintained through the job descriptions that exist prior to and separate from the individuals who fill the positions. The individual is therefore prevented from taking on functions and roles that exceed the parameters of the job description; frequently the only means for the individual to achieve additional power is to seek another job description in order to fill another "job".

When discussing individual motivations within a bureaucratic context it becomes necessary to extend the Weberian model to take account of the tension that arises between the job description and the personal strategies

104

adopted by the office workers themselves (see for instance Selznick 1961; Goldschmidt 1992; Cullen 1994; Wright 1994). The formal roles of the three main groups of workers discussed here – managers, technical staff and admin – are often in conflict with what they really seek to achieve: personal advancement and gratification.

The evident tension between the individual and the constraints of the job description is however often masked by an intense group loyalty. The workers, despite their interpersonal rivalries and status-specific loyalties, collude to present a unified image to the outside world (Goffman 1967, 1990). Political manoeuvring that may go on within the organization is therefore purposefully hidden from the whole outside world, and the internal cacophony is broadcast as though a single voice.

An introduction to paper

Office work is paper-based. Paper is an integral component of work process and product and is used by the workers to develop and record their ideas. It is the medium by which they create their own history and forms part of their strategies to protect themselves against unforeseen contingencies. The workers do not think much about paper, however. They are continually holding it, reading the words upon it, crinkling it up into tight balls and throwing it into plastic bins, putting it in piles and putting it away for safe keeping, but its importance is lost on them. It is so much a part of mundane existence, as necessary for their work as air for their lungs, that they pay it virtually no attention. It is simply there for them, the unnoticed comple- ment to their thoughts.

There are many forms of paper in the office, each serving a certain set of functions. The most important, most often used, is "blank" and white. It feeds the photocopying machine and the printers attached to the computers. It is delivered to the office in bulk, and every 3 months 22 more boxes arrive on the doorstep. Each box contains 5 reams of paper which are composed of 500 individual sheets. Thus, these 22 people consume over 4,000 sheets of such paper each week. White paper is everyday and common. It is nothing special and is used for nothing special. White paper and its sister, lined paper, which differs in that script is applied to the surface manually and not mechanically, is generally reserved for purposes internal to the office. Most of this paper never leaves the office except in the form of photocopies. More often than not, either it is used to progress an idea and becomes "scrap" paper after a short time, or it is stored for later reference.

A different calibre of paper is used to visit the outside world. Like children dressed by their parents in their "Sunday best" for when they will be seen by other parents, so the office's letters are dressed in fine inks and textures designed to reflect well on their authors. As the name implies,

105

letterhead stationery is used for correspondence sent officially from the office as an entity to other offices or individuals within them. Personal communications do not find their way onto these sheets because what is official is also public. Letterhead forms part of the office's wardrobe. Just as individuals have their own unique and often identifiable taste in dress, so every office has its own style of letter and printed report, a "house style", made up of grain, paper quality, logo, text and colour. Each firm or organization, and sometimes departments within them, have their own letterhead designed to leave a unique mark on memory.

Letterhead fosters recognition in regular recipients of written communications. Most of what is received in the post by an office is first distributed to individuals then somehow acted upon, and finally in most instances, put into storage. If the origin of a letter is easily discernible it is easier to locate. When the workers try to find a piece of paper in a file or pile, they try to match what they imagine its sensory qualities to be. People remember what a letter "looks like" not because of the words written on it, which are so small, numerous and regular as to require slow concentration to make distinctions between them, but by impression. What a letter looks like is determined by its colour, the way light bounces off its surface, the shapes of things printed upon it, the amount of printed area and the way it feels to the touch.

Most of the surface of letterhead stationery has nothing printed upon it. The office workers thus consider this category of paper to be another form of "blank" paper. Letterhead paper is high quality bond that is slightly closer to the colour of cream than white: it is thicker than the paper used for the photocopier and has tiny bumps and ridges along the surface. Everything about it says "special purpose": it does not flop around as much as other papers and the little ridges make it feel rough between the fingertips that hold it.

The form that the letterhead takes has been adapted to fit the prevailing office technology. The first page of the letterhead is printed with the office logo and in small lettering, the name, professional qualifications and job title of the most senior manager, and the address, telephone and fax numbers. The upper right corner was the chosen position for this information since it was assumed that letters are fastened into files by holes punched in the left side: the upper right corner would thus be most likely to catch the eye of somebody searching a file. Words are applied to the surface of the paper via a word processing software package. "Date:", "Our reference:", "Your reference:" and "Contact name:" are printed onto the letterhead and the complementary information is aligned by the word processing software.

The computer system was set up with a standard template that allows the author to supply this information with key strokes, which then perfectly align with their green printed mates. Likewise, the keyed address aligns with a tiny green triangle printed on the letterhead that is 14 cursor movements down. This little marker in its turn aligns with a "window" in the envelope, saving the extra step of typing or writing the address for the second time on the outside of the envelope. Finally, along the left edge of the sheet are printed two tiny green marks, each the width of a hair and 2mm in length that divide the sheet into thirds. These marks remain unnoticed most of the time. However, their purpose becomes obvious when a letter is put into the envelope. Folding a letter into thirds so that the address fits squarely into the window in the envelope requires practice. By using the little marks as a guide, the letter can be folded correctly the first time.

Once all the words have been printed on the page in all the right places, using continuation sheets as necessary, the single outstanding element is the signature. Signatures make the standard office letter personal. People often reserve specific pens for writing them, particularly those who sign many letters and feel that they have an image to maintain. These pens are "special", perhaps distinguishable from others by being heavier, or because they are encased in metal or enamel. Their tips may be higher quality "roller balls" or "gold plated medium width nib fountain pens" rather than "ordinary" felt tips or ball points. They leave their trails of ink in a different manner: more expensive pens do not create indentations in the paper's surface and there may be some variation in line width.

The signature is proof that the letter is one of a kind, or at least is being sent to a particular individual or for a specific purpose. If a signature is put onto a letter in any other way, this individuality is lost, and the letter becomes impersonal. A photocopied signature is stale in comparison with a fresh one from a pen and the letter is accorded less attention by the recipient. A letter with an artificial signature, for instance one that is printed onto the page with a rubber stamp, is even easier to disregard. Signing a letter by hand is an act of courtesy which indicates that the sender has some personal regard for the recipient.

From a purely physical standpoint, a letter is "finished" and ready to be sent into the world as an emissary of inter-office politics when the words are all printed in the right places on the special letterhead paper, the margins neat, the paragraphs clearly defined, the salutations properly executed, the bottom signed, the folding at the marks on the edge, the address in the envelope's window, the stamp or franking mark on the envelope. It becomes a tight little package, full of detail and information, easy to recognize, easy to use, tucked discreetly in its anonymous envelope, its message hidden from eyes not meant to see it. The sealed envelope with the address in the window speaks of "office" and "authorized" and "professional" and is clearly something to be taken seriously.

Blank white paper and letterhead are the most important types of office paper but not the only ones. As an example, the "typing form" is specially printed on blue paper and held together with a gummed hinge to form a pad.

These forms are required when something is to be processed for typing by admin. It is stapled or clipped to the top of a pile of writing or revised typing to be put into the office manager's in-tray. There are numerous blank sections where information must be inserted such as the author's name, when the work needs to be finished, the date it was submitted, if it is required urgently, and where it is filed in the computer system. Most people do not bother to fill in all the sections but supply only as much information as they believe is necessary. The most important messages to be conveyed by the form to those for whom it is prepared are that it is blue and says who wrote it. The colour allows it to be identified as something that must be processed by the typists; the name allows the office manager to prioritize which request gets done first.

The most important colour in the office is blue. Every official letter that leaves the office is copied onto this paper and kept in a filing system separate from that for the white paper. Blue copies of letters are referred to whenever there is some question about when a letter was sent or if it was sent at all. Light green paper is used to summarize the main points of the committee meetings and is sent out to individuals who need to have a quick overview of what the office's main output has been. Yellow paper is used for a form that is a check-list of steps towards completion of public relations procedures. Some members of staff use salmon paper for certain memos and reminders in the hope that their colleagues will notice these messages and not lose them. The problem with coloured paper is that everyone who uses it wants to make their message stand out, and if too many people are using it at once, the uniqueness is lost and it might as well be white.

Post-it® Notes are the most loved form of paper. A sheet can be peeled off the pad and stuck anywhere: on telephones, in diaries, on papers, in books to mark pages, on a colleague's back. They are small so using them does not seem wasteful. They are sticky so they do not need to be stapled onto things in order to get them to stay, but they are not sticky enough to damage what they are stuck to. Because they are yellow (or other bright colours), they are easy to see. They are used to make notes to oneself or to give short messages to others. Most of the short messages that are sent around the office are on this form of paper. They have an air of informality and friendliness; they are for jotting, not writing. Their relationship to letterhead paper is the same as that between a casual comment between friends to a formal speech in front of a large group of people.

Carrying the message

In one of his best-known works, *Mythologies*, Barthes (1989) explored the way in which mundane objects such as soap powders and cars can bear messages as "signs". Following Saussure (1974), Barthes developed

108

semiology to explore the modern myths of society as conveyed by the object environment. Everything in his view serves as a sign when used socially. The sign is a symbolic representation of a referent: it is the conceptualization of an idea that is based on its two component elements, the signifier or the object, and the signified expression. Barthes' myths devolved from the Marxist notion of ideology, and are the dominant ideological underpinning of the hegemonic elements of society that are virtually taken for granted by its participants (Olsen 1990: 167).

Jean Baudrillard (1988) also attributed sign-like qualities to objects. Objects by their nature have a greater internal coherence, he argued, than human needs and desires that are more difficult to define cognitively (1988: 15). Products of serial production create a "lexicon of forms and colours" that can approximate speech, but speech that lacks a true syntax. Baudrillard's thesis continued that in contemporary society, particularly in the USA, the sign (the commodity) has taken on greater importance than the signified (the original social relation) and that the important element of the commodity is not its object self but the image or meaning it portrays (see Harvey 1989: 287–8; Featherstone 1991: 68).

Both authors relied heavily upon a linguistic metaphor, attributing objects with units of meaning. Barthes took this to its logical extreme in *The Fashion System* (1990) when he considered the implicit meanings of elements of clothing as presented in the pages of women's magazines, so that for instance "raw silk = summer" and "a thick wool sweater = an autumn weekend in the country". This approach, though now considered dated by some, provides a useful model for evaluating the intimate meanings of objects and as Barthes noted, and I shall elaborate below, the message attributed to an object may appear in various subforms yet within an overarching and coherent total message. Using this approach with a class of object such as paper can only be taken so far however, and it fails when objects are considered within their total socio-cultural milieu.

Barthes and Baudrillard overemphasized the importance of the end product, the sign, and paid insufficient attention to how the sign was developed, or how meanings become attached to objects. The Post-it® Note is not selected by the office worker because it conveys a sense of informality: it is selected because it is convenient to the purpose of writing a short note, and it is that purpose, generally informal in character, that has become associated with the object through habitual reiterations of the act.

This approach is therefore most useful in critiquing objects that are purposefully selected by those who manipulate them, objects that could be termed commodities, whose defining feature is their socially relevant exchange value (Appadurai 1988; Keane 1994). But not all things that bear meaning are exchanged. Some are merely used, either by a single individual, or within social transactions, and not as the transaction's focus but only as an element of it. It is difficult to use this model of commodity value in regard to a class of objects that is not selected but is available in what is virtually an endless supply and at no cost for those who use it, such as paper in the office.

It is therefore necessary to temper the sign/signified/signifier relationship with arguments concerned with the social production of meaning. In order to do this, it will prove useful to examine the critique of Berger and Luckmann (1991) by Miller (1987). Berger and Luckmann posited that there are three moments in the generation of cultural phenomena: externalization, objectivation and internalization (1991; 149). Their argument is that the collective and the socially defined world interact upon one another in a kind of self-affirming loop. The subject externalizes a given relation into some objective reality and this in its turn acts back upon the subject and is internalized (1991: 78–9). Miller argued that Berger and Luckmann took the existence of society as prior to the conceptualization, so that the social relation exists and this is then somehow cognitively linked with an object (Miller 1987: 65). Miller argues that there is "no subject prior to the process of objectification",[1] implying that any meaning derives spontaneously at the time of attribution to the symbolic carrier, the object. Miller wrote:

> Objectification describes the inevitable process by which all expression, conscious or unconscious, social or individual, takes specific form. It is only through the giving of form that something can be conceived of. (Miller 1987: 81).

Unfortunately, the use of paper in the office would support either thesis. On the one hand, using the Berger and Luckmann model, if society preceded objectivation, then we could expect to see examples in practice of a social relation being codified symbolically in an object. This was indeed the case with letterhead paper which was specifically designed by the office workers in order to present their unique group identity to the outside world. Objectivation can also be identified in the preparation of a report, which is described below, which is meant to give an impression of professionalism to the outside world. In both these examples, the concept of the relation existed first, and was expressed within a material medium. But the model put forward by Miller works equally well, albeit with a different set of examples. For Miller, the message would be created by its attribution. Going back to the Post-it® Notes, they were not specifically designed to mean "this is informal", but because they are used informally, they have become associated with that sort of social liaison. It is the social context in which the message was developed in conjunction with the use of the object that led to the understanding among these specific people that Post-its® are for informal communication.

What we are beginning to see here is that there are a number of ways in which the message-bearing qualities of an object can be viewed (see Csikszentmihalyi and Rochberg-Halton 1981) and I would argue that it is futile to devise a single model by which to analyse the significance of objects.

In her article on the use of white cloth by the Banu Yoruba, Renne (1991) demonstrated how the physical quality of an object lends itself to certain symbolic uses. Among these people white cloth is used to denote various relationships and states of being. She wrote:

> In Banu society, the particular qualities of white cloth – for example, its colour, its absorbency and its susceptibility to decay – make it an evocative symbolic vehicle for mediating relations. ... However, white cloth's opacity and impermanence also suggest less benign associations, such as hiding and desertion. (Renne 1991: 710–11)

This would indicate that the unique physical qualities of white cloth are interpreted in the Banu culture to meet the needs of certain forms of social expression. Direct correlations of this example can be identified with the use of paper in the office. Thick, creamy coloured, textured and expensive paper is used to lend an air of professionalism to business letters. Coloured paper indicates that what is on its surface is an extraordinary type of communication.

Battaglia concluded that human reality is a material reality, and sensual stimulation should be the starting point for any analysis of material culture. "The real is distinguished from the thought and imagined ... in no uncertain terms ... physicality has priority and its value is positive and absolute" (1994: 639). She suggested that anthropologists should "get real" by considering the role of objects in social relations and thus gain access to indigenous processes of valuation and knowledge (639–40). I adopt this approach here. Paper as a message system can be understood only in terms of the thing that is paper: the type of message that it can or cannot convey is limited by its physical attributes. Before continuing with my discussion of the physical aspect of paper's message, however, I wish to clarify my earlier assertion that there are two sorts of messages that can be identified.

The message that the workers create and disseminate with purposive intent, and for which they employ paper as a tool, is what I term the overt message. Beyond the actual words that have been applied to the surface of sheets of paper, examples of the overt message can be extended to include letterhead which contains pattern, text and the office logo to foster recognition in recipients; and the house style, which is consciously created and defended in order to make the office's work easier to digest. The overt message is complemented by the latent message, and it is the latter that is determined by physical and sensory qualities. The content of the overt message can be easily discussed and analysed by the office workers, it can be changed, modified and refined. Since the overt message is composed of words and rules, the units of meaning are discrete and identifiable. They provide something distinct and bounded for the mind to latch onto, and can be easily conveyed.

In contrast, the content of the latent message could probably not be easily described by the office workers. They would sense that these meanings existed, yet be unable to define them. While the overt message is purposive, the latent message is incidental. It is an emotional and primitive response to something that provides a sensory stimulus and is characterized by unformed perceptions and assumptions: it is what "seems right" or "feels wrong" in the social and material context of a situation. Miller's work would also support this notion of objects as carriers of unspoken meaning. He argued that objects have "a particularly close relation to emotions, feelings and basic orientations to the world" (1987: 107). An example can be drawn from the signature on the letter: the recipient can discern the ink laid down from a cheap or expensive pen and it is sensed that a signature in blue ink with a line that varies in thickness as it traces the curves of the name is somehow better quality than one that is black, of even line width, and follows scratches in the surface of the paper caused by a minute metal ball. It is unlikely that the recipient of the letter will actually comment on the pen used for the signature but the feeling of "wrongness" will remain.

Latent qualities could otherwise be regarded as akin to the concept of "keys", defined by Goffman as "the set of conventions by which a given activity ... is transformed into something patterned on this activity but seen by the participants to be something quite else" (1986: 43–4). The physical qualities of paper are used to indicate the framework for the discourse at hand. Keys such as colour and size are used to set off contrasts and to indicate internal relationships (see Bateson 1980: 67–8): they indicate the character and flavour of a communication, usually interweaving in and complementing the overt message.

Perhaps a useful way of summarizing this idea of the latent message is to draw a set of contrasts in how paper is perceived by the office workers. I shall make the distinction between formal and informal. Broadly, it can be argued that there are two main types of "primary frameworks" (Goffman 1986) for all office activities: the formal, characterized by bureaucratic relations and aimed at "outside" consumption, and the informal, characterized by personal relationships, the actual practice of daily working and generally geared towards "inside" interactions. Taking these two frameworks, a typology of paper types and characteristics can be drawn as shown in Table 5.1.

This can be extended to the relationships, emotional responses and assumptions made regarding these physical qualities as shown in Table 5.2.

Latent messages can thus act as keys for the genre of expression linked to the physical thing that is a piece of paper. Specific situations dictate that

Table 5.1   Paper types and characteristics

Formal (outside)	Informal (inside)
letterhead paper	blank white paper
A4 size	other than A4 size
signed	unsigned
typed/mechanically printed	handwritten

Table 5.2   Assumption regarding paper types

bland and standardized	idiosyncratic and personal
group/corporate	individual
professional	unprofessional

papers with particular characteristics are employed in order to increase the order of the whole communication system and to allow the participant to categorize, and thus mentally sort into neat and manageable piles, the wealth of information that is received daily.

Producing the overt message

This office's mission is to develop and disseminate information that furthers a particular political and ideological stance. To do this as effectively as possible the workers believe that they must develop a reputation for the group that will make their audience respect and follow their recommendations. Any overt message that the office produces, for instance a report or a press release commenting on government programmes, also conveys other abstruse messages to do with reputation. This is another example of what Goffman (1990) referred to as "impression management" and the production of information for outside consumption extends beyond words on paper into the realm of public presentation.

The paper-based release of the overt message into the outside world is generally restricted to two main categories: the business letter and the committee report. Others include the newsletter, survey forms, published reports and press releases as well as those that are not made tangible such as words spoken in meetings or over the telephone. The committee report provides the best illustration of how the overt message is carefully dressed to visit the external world and how its latent qualities are manipulated and new levels of meaning are added in order to present the best possible impact on outsiders. The content of these reports is highly standardized and, to be simplistic, consists of an introduction, background to an argument, the development of the argument, and a recommended course of action. The reports are in the public domain once they have been considered and serve as the basis for the office's ongoing work. They are thus the very heart of office activity.

The final committee report, itself only a few sheets of paper, covered in dense printed black text and fastened at the upper left corner with a staple, is the culmination in a production process of many steps. Each report that is held in a committee member's hands can represent hundreds of sheets of paper.

Committee reports are initially conceived in management meetings, most typically in response to some interest expressed by the members. When the topic has been identified, it is assigned to an appropriate member of the technical staff. Instructions are usually delivered orally and because of the spoken word's ephemeral nature, there is no means of going back and verifying what was actually said should a misunderstanding between manager and subordinate later emerge. It is because of this potential problem that one party or the other might decide that there is a need to record the decision in a memo. When this occurs, it is almost always the result of mistrust: either that the instructions will not be heeded, or that what was expressed will be transformed from today's instruction into tomorrow's gaffe. Memos are passed in photocopied triplets across the in-trays and desktops of the office. They go in multiples of three or more so that the originator has a copy, the recipient has a copy, and the witness has a copy. A wise office worker will always have a witness.

The "expert" then begins the process of writing the report. Reference to other paper-bound information is critical in the preparatory stage of research which requires that previously released reports have been checked thoroughly for background context, and other relevant data are gathered. Authors have been given lengthy instructions on the precise format of each report, complete with the font style, line spacing, paragraphing conventions, heading style, and order of presentation, together composing further elements of the house style. If each report is structured in like manner, the habitual reader (the committee member) will know which predefined sections might be of interest. It is hoped therefore that this repetitiveness of structure will lead to at least certain parts being read. The author of the first draft tries to follow these conventions even at the earliest stage because these are the bones upon which the flesh will rest; it is easier to follow the conventions in the first stage than to change it later, and most importantly, if anyone else sees the draft and it is not in the required format, it will seem incomplete, amateurish, and runs the risk of not being taken seriously. If the author is in any way unclear as to what the exact formatting requirements are, there is a paper copy of the set of instructions that was circulated to all members of staff for reference.

Once complete in concept if not presentational form, the first draft is an emerging "professional" document. If written by hand, it must be "sent down to typing" to be neatened up and have any outstanding elements of the format put into place. Nobody ever shows a superior a copy of a draft report that is not typed, though such a report may be passed to more junior staff. There is a real anxiety that if the boss sees anything that does not look final, the author's credibility will suffer. Even if the author is certain that the superior will change the contents dramatically, the draft is clothed as the final, almost as a dare to spot the mistakes or differences of view.

Sending a draft down to typing is thus very important for a person who is not able to command a word processor through either physical access or technical skill. The draft is taken by the author, photocopied at least once (in case anything happens to the draft), a blue typing form stapled onto the front, and is dropped into the special in-tray reserved for typing processing. This is a crucial link in the paper chain since the drafting process cannot continue until this step has been successfully completed. It is at this stage more than any other that the author is vulnerable. All reports go to the same meeting and all reports to the same meeting must be despatched together. It is not uncommon for 18 reports to have the same deadline. Admin gives ample warning of what these deadlines are, particularly when draft reports should be put into the word processing in-tray if there will be sufficient time to type them all. However, it always seems the case that authors regard it as a deadline only for their own report, and they may want to push that deadline to its very limits. About a week before every despatch of papers, admin, and particularly those involved in typing, are subjected to severe strain as papers come pouring into the in-tray in frightening bulk. It is here that the blue typing forms become important. The office manager must decide what gets typed first, and the more senior staff take priority, though all papers must be typed in time for the despatch. The juniors' work will also be typed, albeit the last of the lot, but their work, suffering under the exigencies of hierarchy, will be met with knitted eyebrows and tut-tutting since it is late.

Once the typists have converted the draft into something more tidy and presentable, they print a copy onto paper and give it back to the author with the now redundant blue form and original draft attached. The author then re-reads it, makes changes or corrections by scribbling in the margins, and returns it again to typing for a final brush-up where the cycle repeats itself. When the author is satisfied that it is ready, the report is photocopied again, one copy for the boss and other copies for witnesses or referees, as necessary. The boss checks it, making sure that it is what the members will want to read, then returns it (scribbled upon) to the author. The author makes the changes, sends it down to typing again, and then, at last, the report is finished. After this stage has been reached, the report is assigned a unique number that refers to the date of the meeting and the report's agenda item, a reward for having successfully cleared the many hurdles during its production.

Paper generation has not ended yet. Once the report is final, it is bundled with all the other reports for that particular meeting and photocopied many times. There must be a copy for the file, a copy for the records of the meeting, copies for each of the politicians, copies for all of the managers, for relevant people in other offices, for the author, and there must be spare copies for just in case.

The women of admin reserve a half-day for each despatch. A table is set up in the middle of their work area next to the photocopier and each report is placed in copied stacks around the table's edge in the same order as they appear on the committee agenda. The women walk a continual loop around the table, again and again, picking up each report and adding it to those they already hold in their hands, finally bundling them with a rubber band, putting the bundle in the pre-addressed brown envelope, and putting that in the post-bag. Often after a large despatch the admin manager will buy cakes to show her appreciation for a job well done. The women from admin are pleased that no members of the technical staff are invited to share in their treat. Relieved that their task is completed, they may forget that their technical colleagues also worked hard.

Paper and status

The committee report is a collaborative construction and the overt message is presented to the world in a way that shows off the office as a group of people with a joint reputation. The accuracy, style and competence of the delivery of the message builds their professional identity and is confirmation of their unique place in the world. They, like their rival offices, are elbowing for a place at the front where they can influence those with the power to bring about change. The spoken word is too informal, too ephemeral and fleeting, to bear lasting testament to their corporate character. Inchoate thought must be developed into something that conveys the public message and this they do together. But their joint face is only for the benefit of those not employed in the office. What is co-operation in the final result is achieved only through fractured component roles and each contributor's position is regulated by their social status.

The overt message has a more prominent place in the minds of the office workers and is a "high order" or high status element of the final total message. Also, the overt message, subject to precise definition and scrutiny, is assigned commensurate higher status and is reserved for those with personal status to match. It comes as no surprise then that the overt message can be identified most strongly with those highest in the office hierarchy. The job of the managers is to initiate and finalize the process by which a committee report is produced. Only they are in the position to identify a topic and assign a technical person to begin the drafting stage. Their opinions are always sought on the emerging report and their concerns take precedence over those of their juniors. Theirs is the realm of the overt message – they need not be too involved with the details of the latent. They are responsible for the complete impact of the message on the audience but their focus is on the words on the paper and the ideas that these convey. The managers can afford to be somewhat cavalier with the latent message because they trust that their juniors will apply it in the end.

The latent message gains in importance as an individual's status decreases within the organization. This was illustrated with the example of the technical person who passed on a draft to a superior for consideration only after it had been typed, i.e. once the latent element had been put into place, whereas it was of no great concern to a superior whether a junior saw something in handwritten form. This would indicate that while the primary status that can be derived from a paper-borne message is based upon its overt content, additions of the latent can increase credibility, by for instance taking a good argument and adding a layer of seeming professionalism in order to strengthen it. Taking this one step farther, typing transforms the technical person's handwritten prose into a higher order product. But such is the manager's status that his or her handwritten comments scribbled illegibly in the margins of a draft take precedence over words that are typed.

The production of the latent message requires the least amount of concerted thought or skill since this is applied by following automated processes and predefined conventions and routines. This, added to its undefinable qualities, makes it very low order, low status. The final placement of the latent message onto the overt is reserved for the least powerful people in the office: the admin staff. Within the production process, they are restricted to the lowest status elements such as transcribing the handwriting of their superiors into typed letters, photocopying the reports for the despatch, packaging the reports into bundles with staples and rubber bands, and putting copies in the filing system.

Only the audience, the recipients of the report, is able to fully and objectively judge the final efficacy of the office group's efforts. Only they can appreciate the coherent, total, message. They make their judgements on the basis of how well the overt and latent messages dovetail together. Despite the fractured and in some cases opposing roles inherent in the production, the final message as received by the audience reflects more upon the office group than any individual. If any part of the production were ineptly executed, for instance if factual errors were identified in the overt message, or if the latent message were marred by too many typos, the whole group is branded as "unprofessional" or "amateurish" by the audience. The outsider does not care who the typist was, and only considers the annoyance caused by misspelt words. Equally, the telephonist will be treated with marginally less respect when taking the irate call of somebody expressing a complaint about an inaccurate statement, even though the telephonist did not write it.

But with all this effort, the final product is standardized and bureaucratic. Like their speech, attire and posture, they clothe their written message in blandness, their group reputation based on the impersonalism of the formatting functions on a word processing package. True professionalism is devoid of human frailty. The blandness sets off the precision of the words.

Epilogue: filing paper

Only rarely is all the paper that has been generated thrown away as waste: more often it is stored. Great importance is placed by the workers on saving things for the future. All this paper – too much to read, too much to remember – is put away safely for later reference. It is kept just in case it needs to be reread, in case it will prove useful evidence in an intellectual or professional debate, in case a false accusation should be raised or in case there will finally be time to give it the attention that it deserves now.

Saving paper is something that is done in degrees of privacy. Desk drawers are the most private repositories. Less distant and personal are the bookshelves that accompany each desk. These are classified as "my bookshelf" and "your bookshelf". The only collective bookshelves are in the technical library where nobody hunts or in the reception area where nobody reads. Personal bookshelves are stores of knowledge built up over years by their owners and contain much of the technical references needed to write a report that will impress and influence. Much of what is on these shelves has been requisitioned from the main technical library on the grounds that the owner "really" needs the materials and that keeping them saves time since they must be referred to so often. If something is required from somebody else's bookshelf, permission must first be granted and the owner will usually personally retrieve the necessary item, extracting promises that it will be promptly returned. Much effort is put into filling a book shelf: plunder it and the same will happen to the owner's ability to do the job.

The main filing system in the office is a paper one and is fully public. Even documents from the computer are stored here as copies in their hard form. Paper is the filing method of preference because of its practical qualities. Five hundred sheets can take up a space as small as nine inches by eleven by three. So many words stored in so little space: and it can all be seen, smelled, touched and leafed through, photocopied and saved for later, just in case. The paper filing system is the biggest thing in the office in any physical sense. There are seven metal double-doored filing cabinets six feet high devoted exclusively to paper storage. Within them are virtually thousands of sheets of paper, each organized according to general topic, subtopic, and temporality. Seven file cabinets all in a row, providing the comfort of orderly structure for the history of the office.

Each office worker, particularly the technical staff and the senior admin, are responsible for marking important documents with the correct filing code and putting them into the specially marked "filing tray" in the admin area. There are 641 separate files, arranged in 18 main branches or topic areas. Each employee has a 29-page photocopied list of all the file codes. It is the job of the most junior admin staff to match the codes with the correct files. Everyone forced to do this menial job hates it but it is done regularly nonetheless because of the importance accorded it.

At the time my observations were made, the office had been saving paper for almost six years. During that time the workers and their predecessors managed to save innumerable sheets – more than the filing cabinets and the hanging sleeves within them could safely hold. Indeed, some files were near to bursting and it was generally felt that no matter how many "just in cases" there might be, enough was enough. Admin decreed that the system needed a clear out. And so the first "Filing Day" was announced. With the full approval of the managers, memos announcing the event were circulated. Three weeks in advance everyone was instructed to keep Friday 3 April free in their diaries. No subsequently booked leave or meetings would be allowed. The memo made it clear that all unnecessary paper would be cleared from the files and that it would be fun (a pizza lunch was planned to break up the day). Casual attire was acceptable.

The day arrived. Even those with pressing work to do were not allowed to do it. Files were to be thinned and there would be no argument. As penance for saving too much paper for too many unrealized contingencies, each person was assigned a two-foot-thick pile of papers with the instructions to start sorting. Everything that was not reasonably needed would have to be thrown out. Some people became very enthusiastic cullers, pulling out sheet after sheet, challenging their colleagues to see who could accumulate the largest pile of scrap. Others were more cautious and threw out only duplicates. Everyone threw away something. By the end of the day, when they still had not managed to go through all the files, the newly defined waste that had been vital documentation only a day before, climbed in precarious stacks in a mountain before the door. It was a glorious sight and everyone, most notably those who had spent years putting all those words on all those sheets in the first place, felt a great surge of pride. Look how much they had thrown away! All that paper would leave the office forever.

The managers declared Filing Day to be a "resounding success". This point was minuted in a memo after a management meeting that was held a few days later. A copy was circulated to all the staff. It would become an annual event. With pizza.

Note

1. Note that this term differs from that used by Berger and Luckmann (1991).

References

Appadurai, A, 1988 [1986]. Introduction: commodities and the politics of value. In *The social life of things*, A. Appadurai (ed.). Cambridge: Cambridge University Press.
Barthes, R. 1989 [1957]. *Mythologies*. London: Paladin.
Barthes, R. 1990 [1967]. *The fashion system*. Berkeley: University of California Press.
Bateson, G. 1980 [1979]. *Mind and nature*. New York: Bantam.
Battaglia, D. 1994. Retaining reality: some practical problems with objects as property. *Man* 29 631–44.
Baudrillard, J. 1988. *Jean Baudrillard: selected writings*, M. Poster (ed.). Cambridge: Polity.
Beetham, D. 1987. *Bureaucracy*. Milton Keynes: Open University Press.
Berger, P. & T. Luckmann 1991 [1966]. *The social construction of reality*. Harmondsworth: Penguin.
Csikszentmihalyi, M. & E. Rochberg-Halton 1981. *The meaning of things: domestic symbols and the self*. Cambridge: Cambridge University Press.
Cullen, S. 1994. Culture, gender and organizational change in British welfare benefits services. In *Anthropology of organizations*, S. Wright (ed.). London: Routledge.
Featherstone, M. 1991. *Consumer culture and postmodernism*. London: Sage.
Goffman, I. 1967. *Interaction ritual: essays on face-to-face behavior*. New York: Pantheon.
Goffman, I. 1986 [1974]. *Frame analysis*, Harmondsworth: Peregrine.
Goffman, I. 1990 [1959]. *The presentation of self in everyday life*. Harmondsworth: Penguin.
Goldschmidt, W. 1992 [1990]. *The human career: the self in the symbolic world*. Cambridge, MA: Blackwell.
Harvey, D. 1989. *The condition of postmodernity*. Oxford: Blackwell.
Keane, W. 1994. The value of words and the meaning of things in eastern Indonesian exchange. *Man* **29**, 605–29.
Miller, D. 1987. *Material culture and mass consumption*. Oxford: Basil Blackwell.
Olsen, B. 1990 [1991]. Roland Barthes: from sign to text. In *Reading Material Culture*, C. Tilley (ed.). Oxford: Blackwell.
Renne, E. 1991. Water, spirits, and plain white cloth: the ambiguity of things in Banu social life. *Man* **26**, 709–22.
Saussure, F. de 1974 [1916]. *Course in general linguistics*, C. Bally & A. Sechehaye (eds). London: Fontana.
Selznick, P. 1961. Foundations of a theory of organization. In *Complex organizations*, A. Etzioni (ed.). New York: Holt, Rinehart & Winston.
Weber, M. 1978. *Economy and society*. Berkeley: University of California Press.
Wright, S. 1994. "Culture" in anthropology and organizational studies. In *Anthropology of organizations*, S. Wright (ed.). London: Routledge.

CHAPTER 6

Material of culture, fabric of identity

Neil Jarman

Ceremonial, commemorative and recreational parading through city, town and village streets is one of the principal means of expressing and consolidating a sense of communal identity in Northern Ireland. There are over 2,700 parades held every year, about 90 per cent of which are organized within the Protestant-Unionist community. These parades are not simply about mobilizing numbers or affirming territorial rights, they are the principal opportunity and medium for displaying and elaborating the nuances of collective identity. At each of the major parades held during the summer months a range of banners, bannerettes and flags are a central part of the colour and display. At the Orange Order's Twelfth of July parade in Belfast, over 100 large banners are carried by the various lodges, most of the bands accompanying them are led by a colour party carrying a bannerette. Both lodges and bands also carry an array of flags. These banners, bannerettes and flags bear a range of images that elaborate on the ideological and political nature of the Ulster Protestant identity.[1]

In this chapter I want to explore the importance of fabric, and in particular its use in decorative banners, for the Ulster Protestants, by discussing the history of banners as social objects and by analysing the individual history of banners from manufacture through to collective display. In so doing I aim to show how the banners have become the visible and material repository of the Orange tradition. Tradition is a concept that is widely evoked by Protestants. Tradition is used to signify the historical and unchanging basis for their status and customs, traditional practices are assumed to have greater validity than non-traditional practices, and tradition is assumed to bestow rights and obligations. In this instance I do not wish to undermine the idea of tradition, by exposing its social invention, but rather I wish to explore the emergence and ongoing development of one tradition. Tradition itself becomes the underlying focus.

In the first part I shall trace aspects of the social history of the custom of using banners, and other forms of visual display, as part of the wider social and economic development of the north of Ireland. This will reveal how material culture has been central to the creation, expression and distribution of the developing Ulster Protestant sense of collective identity and their allegiance to Great Britain. In particular I focus on the role of the textile industry as the object through which economic development and prosperity were achieved and also how fabric was adopted as a medium for the symbolic expression of their changing status. Somewhat similar analyses have been undertaken by Bayly (1986), Bean (1989) and Schneider (1989) on the significance of textiles in the economic and symbolic transformations in India and early modern Europe. Initially there was a close relation between the economic importance of linen and its significance as a symbolic medium. Over a period of 150 years linen lost its central economic status in the Northern Irish economy, but the symbolic displays of Britishness were still expressed through the medium of cloth; now transformed into silk, it became the embodiment of tradition. The silken banner is now both a traditional artefact and bearer of traditional meanings.

In the second section of the chapter I turn to the ethnographic present to explore what Kopytoff (1986) refers to as the cultural biography of the artefact. He considers the transformations that are involved as an object moves through the process of production and consumption and into the public arena. In this instance the transition from manufactured artefact to paraded banner follows a pathway from commoditization to singularization, in which the act of purchase and transfer of possession transforms the artefact from commodity into an inalienable object. In particular I shall consider how the entry of the banner into the public domain of the Orange parade has become surrounded by ritual, and how this sacralization of the object emerged at a particular historical moment as the banners were transformed from the product of local craft skills to a specialist and standardized item. Finally I consider how the intense local focus of these rituals, and often the images on the banners, feed back into the wider discourse of Ulster Protestant identity when they are taken to the large parades, the ongoing arena in which identity is reconstituted. Again the role of ritual, with its (unspoken) emphasis on continuity and the unchanging links with the past, serves to silently enforce the status and significance of the traditional artefact.

The third section of this chapter runs simultaneously with the first two; it is a photographic exploration of the importance of fabric through its use in the banners, in uniforms and in regalia displayed at loyalist parades. The photographs are not presented as apt illustrations to the text: there is no image of the specific banner or ritual that is discussed in the second section. Instead, the aim of the photographs is to illustrate the use and significance of material artefacts in Orange culture in a less direct way than words permit. It has been said many times that images are more resistant at definition, more ambiguous in meaning, more open to diverging interpretations. I am trying to work with these understandings to offer a parallel, visual interpretation of my subject. These photographs also deal with a wider range of artefacts than there was

room to address directly in the ethnographic section of the text, they are being used to link the ethnography with the wider themes addressed in the historical section. The images are not presented in any particular order, there is no development or narrative running through them in a systematic way – in this they also parallel the displays of Orange banners and regalia: as randomly ordered yet symbolically connected images. I will only add that they are part of a much larger body of images gathered in the course of ongoing fieldwork. These particular photographs were taken at a range of loyalist parades in Ireland between July 1990 and August 1994.

The fabric of Irish history

The victory of King William III, at the Battle of the Boyne in 1690, confirmed the ascendancy of the Protestant faith in both Britain and Ireland. For the next century Ireland was largely peaceful. The majority Catholic population were excluded from political and economic influence by the Penal Laws, enacted in 1710, and Ulster, with its large population of Protestant colonists from England and Scotland, grew relatively prosperous. This prosperity was based on the growth of the linen industry in the south of the region, between Dungannon, Armagh and Newry. As linen manufacturing became industrialized and capitalized, its networks of trade expanded and this encouraged the growth of roads, navigations and urban centres. Belfast in particular grew rapidly from an insignificant settlement to a population of 18,000 in 1791. This expansion was based largely on trade, and in particular the export of linen. The newly built White Linen Hall, opened in 1784, emphasized the importance of this trade to the town. Besides linen, cotton mills were also an important element in the town's early growth. By the end of the century Belfast was the premier port in Ulster and the third largest port in Ireland. But this industrial development was not without problems. Ireland was effectively ruled from London, its parliament was subservient to Westminster, and its trade was heavily regulated (Foster 1988; Bardon 1992). This unequal relationship with Britain generated resentment throughout the century. It was publicized initially by Jonathan Swift in the 1720s, but open political opposition became most insistently expressed only during the 1770s. This was done through the supporters of the Patriot party in the parliament in Dublin, and the public displays of the Volunteer movement on the streets. Volunteer companies were initially raised among the Protestant middle classes in 1778, in order to counter a feared French invasion during the American War of Independence. They then joined with the politicians and, as an extra-parliamentary force, campaigned for political and economic reform in Ireland. The combination of the force of rhetoric and the threat of force of arms secured a victory for their political demands for both constitutional and trading reforms in 1782.

The Volunteer companies were, from the first, concerned to present themselves as a legitimate military organization and each company underwent formal military training and carried out manoeuvres. Volunteering was immensely popular wherever there was a large Protestant population. In Ulster, where Protestants accounted for some 50 per cent of the population, more than 300 companies were formed by 1783 (Smyth 1974). Each company adopted military-styled uniforms and insignia to identify themselves when taking to the streets on their many parades. These were held throughout the year, to mark numerous anniversaries, for visits to church and as part of routine manoeuvres. Although parading had long been a feature of Irish social and political life, the Volunteer period marks the beginnings of the modern practice of holding parades to commemorate secular anniversaries in Ulster. These parades announced the entry of the northern bourgeoisie into the public sphere, and they marked out the Protestant middle classes as a distinct group with a distinct agenda.

But besides the practical aims, Volunteering was also the fashionable activity for young Protestant gentlemen in the late 1770s. Parading in brightly coloured uniforms to the beat of a drum was the thing to be seen to do. The numerous parades were popular public events and attracted large crowds of spectators who came to admire their menfolk. The *Belfast News Letter* (*BNL*) often described the uniforms when reporting Volunteer parades and this practice of presenting oneself for public display seemed to have become the *raison d'être* of Volunteering for some. The press carried advertisements for

fabrics and all types of badges, buttons, frills and accessories that were necessary for the well-dressed company. In the summer of 1778 ladies in Dublin and Bridgetown, Co. Wexford, were reported as favouring scarlet and green, the commonest Volunteer colours, for the season's fashions (*BNL 4/7 August 1778*). In perhaps the most extreme example the *News Letter* reported the proposed formation of a new Dublin Company of light cavalry:

> the horses are, it is said, to be large sized bay hunters, and the uniform a light green faced with white with silver buttons holes and epaulets. (*BNL* 23/27 July 1779)

Here it seems that the uniform was seen as the primary attraction for possible members. The anonymous author of a letter to the *Londonderry Journal* in June 1779 acknowledged the importance of this element of frivolity and display to the movement, when describing the Volunteers as:

> Our Cloud-cap't Grenediers and our gorgeous infantry ... [who] after the amusements of a year ... rest satisfied with a fine coat and firelock. (Smyth 1979)

When the Belfast Company paraded through the town in June 1778 the *News Letter* noted the smartness of the uniform: "scarlet turned up with black velvet, white waistcoat and breeches", but, more significantly:

125

The clothing of the majority of the Company was of IRISH MANUFACTURE; and the whole made a brilliant and pleasing appearance. (Bardon 1992: 211)

One might even speculate that it was the economic crisis and surplus of production in the preceding years that made local fabric affordable on such a scale. Nevertheless the cost of Volunteering was high even for wealthy people. For those of lesser means, but great expectations, participation in the movement might mean having to choose between a uniform or ammunition. In such a case it was often the uniform that took priority (Smyth 1974: 74–7).

When the brightly uniformed men marched out in their companies, they were preceded by an (often elaborately) embroidered flag. This was used to identify the particular group and also to depict something of their political aspirations. There are isolated references to visual displays at early eighteenth-century public processions in Dublin, but these were largely restricted to decorating one's everyday clothing, or sometimes houses, with orange lilies, shamrocks, orange or blue cockades or coloured ribbons (Jarman 1995). It was only with the appearance of the Volunteers that a more elaborate and formalized display was established. Their flags were based on military styles but they bore a range of symbolic devices and figures. These included Hibernia (the female personification of Ireland) wearing a Liberty cap and holding a pike, King William III on horseback, the Irish harp and shamrock and the masonic sunburst (Hayes-McCoy

1979). All of these emblems can be found at contemporary parades, but the Volunteer period represents the last time that symbols which have subsequently come to signify the divergent aspirations of nationalism and unionism would appear together. Although the Volunteers drew on an existing custom of parading to publicize their position, they transformed it, both by utilizing it for overt political ends and by turning the event into a visual feast, a spectacle of wealth and status. The Volunteers spoke for and demanded an audience for the "Protestant Interest" but it was very much an interest that was rooted in Ireland. Their parades established a tradition but they were not to direct its future course.

Textile manufacture and trade had underpinned the rise of the Protestant bourgeoisie in the north and it was their fabric that enabled the Volunteers to make such impressive displays. Where eighteenth-century agrarian rebellious groups such as the Oakboys, the Strawboys and the Whiteboys drew on facets of the natural world for their symbolic repertoire, the Volunteers could emphasize their status and difference through their most readily accessible commodity – cloth. It was cloth that had helped to create the raised interests and expectations in the north and provided the economic base of the Protestant community, cloth that formed the basis for the Irish industrial revolution and helped mark Ulster in a positive light in relation to the rest of the country, cloth that drew the northern ports into closer economic relationship with Britain and made more stark the discrepancy between the two constitutional positions, and it was cloth that was the medium to express these resentments. Dean Swift had already cloaked himself in the metaphor of fabric when he protested earlier in the century against the unequal relationship between Britain and Ireland through the anonymity of the Drapiers Letters. Drawing on their own resources to form a defence force, it was perhaps unexceptional that the Volunteers should therefore utilize the most accessible of local resources to present themselves in public in their turn.

The Volunteers peaked as a popular political movement with the establishment of Gratton's parliament in 1782. With their political and economic power confirmed, their more radical demands for Catholic emancipation were rapidly abandoned and the Volunteer movement fragmented. Although the radical rump continued to campaign for political reform until its demise in 1792, the middle-class Protestants, who had formed the majority of the Volunteer companies, largely abandoned public displays and commemorative parades to the lower classes. However, the custom was continued by the Orange Order, which was formed in County Armagh in 1795. The Order was the most prominent of the brotherhoods established in Ulster in the late eighteenth and early nineteenth centuries. It aimed to protect the economic and social interests of the rural, Protestant, farmer–weaver community at a time when new industrial technology and a growing Catholic population was leading to both rapid change and increased sectarian tension (Gibbon 1975). By the early nineteenth century the Orange Order was widely established throughout rural Ulster and the Orangemen consolidated and extended the custom of parading *en masse* and with elaborate visual displays. The individual expense of a uniform clothing was reduced to the minimum of an orange sash,[2] but on the anniversary of the Battle of the Boyne, 12 July, their banners and flags were often numerous, with a hundred or more reported at the larger parades.

> The banners were of the most costly fabric and the most elegant design and as they floated in the morning breeze they presented a spectacle of great beauty and splendour. (*BNL* 13 July 1848)

The images were largely restricted to representations of King William, and other symbols of loyalty to the Crown and to the Bible while Hibernia was abandoned as a symbol by the Protestant community. The quality and the style of their displays varied considerably:

> There was ... a number of orange banners and colours, more remarkable for loyalty than taste or variety, for King William on horseback, as grim as a saracen on a signpost, was painted or wrought on all of them. (Gamble 1812, quoted in McClelland 1980)

Several of the flags were really of a most artistic and beautiful character

... Ballynakelly LOL No 157 with the word "No Surrender" at the bottom, wrought in gold, on a scarlet ground, encircled the painting of King William III on a white charger. ... Newmills LOL No 138, the figure of King William on horseback was encircled with a wreath of lilies wrought in gold and orange on a purple ground, the insignia of the Star and Garter was emblazoned on each corner. (*BNL* 13 July 1860)

The banners came in all shapes and sizes, in a variety of materials and colours and drew on a range of design techniques. They were produced locally, utilizing the skills and materials that came to hand, and can be seen as examples of the art of "bricolage" (Lévi-Strauss 1966). In some cases this meant using the skills of the local haberdasher who would run up numerous items in the days preceding the parade. In other cases, local women embroidered elaborate and extensive designs on a flag that then had pride of place within the lodge. The banners would be displayed only once a year but would be expected to last for some time, accompanying the lodge on parade year after year.

Tailoring Ulster Unionists

From the late 1880s these rural traditions were transformed by two developments: the emergence of the Home Rule movement, and the professionalization of banner painting. The demand for Home Rule had

widespread support among Catholics, but was virulently opposed by the Protestant middle classes whose economic activities had become more closely entwined with Britain and its global empire. The industrialization of the textile industry, which had begun to distinguish the Ulster economic base in the eighteenth century, continued apace. This further distanced the economy of the north from the rest of Ireland, which remained largely agricultural. Although the cotton industry collapsed under competition from England, the linen industry rollercoastered through cycles of boom and bust. With shipbuilding and engineering, linen provided the foundations of local prosperity. Linen dominated the local economy. The industry employed nearly 70,000 people by the end of the century and as late as 1924 over 51 per cent of the labour force was employed making linen (Bardon 1992). Many of the major mills were in Belfast, but the industry was spread throughout the north, replacing the economy of independent farmer–weavers with a network of rural factory towns (see Cohen 1993 for a case study of one such development).

Extensions to the franchise in 1884 increased the importance of the working classes in the political process. The Orange Order was recognized by the political leadership of the Unionists as an important instrument for increasing and strengthening vertical solidarity within the Protestant community. The public celebrations through the summer months were an annual opportunity to mobilize opposition to the proposed constitutional changes. The Twelfth of July parades became important platforms for political speeches and exhortations in the Unionist cause. But this was not merely a one-way process; the membership of the Order began, in turn, to use their displays to elaborate, refine and extend the meaning of the newly emerging identity of Protestant Ulster Unionists as British rather than as Irish. While nationalist Ireland rediscovered its Gaelic traditions and emphasized its Catholic base, the Unionists turned to the Protestant past and their contemporary links with Britain to form the basis of their re-imagined selves.

In England banner production had become professionalized, com-mercialized and standardized as a result of the demand from the growing trade union movement. This was largely the work of one man, George Tutill, who by the 1860s had devised a method of using oil painting on silk which retained both plasticity in the banner and brightness in the colours. Having patented his technique, Tutill's company established the standards for the medium and dominated the market (Gorman 1986). Irish groups ordered banners from Tutill's workshop but before the end of the century professional banner painters established themselves in Ireland. The Orange banners became homogenized in form as they were brought within the industrial ethos. A standardized style, form and size of banner replaced the heterogenous mixture of local customs. The new banners were now made of 100 per cent silk, with a different design on each side, surrounded by scrolled mottoes and identifying names, and trimmed with a silk border of a contrasting colour. For Tutill, the choice of silk was based on its strength and lightness. But in east London it was also a readily available material as he exploited the skills of the local silk-weaving community. Although many Ulster banners were still made of local fabric, there was a steady move to imported silk, an extension of the already extensive trade between Britain and Ireland.

The most prominent of the Irish banner makers was William Bridgett of Belfast. Bridgett was himself an Orangeman and around the turn of the century he almost single-handedly transformed the corpus of Orange banners from the two or three designs that had persisted through the century to an extensive array of political, historical and religious figures, biblical stories, local churches and buildings and a range of symbols specific to Ulster. These designs still form the basis for the majority of Orange banners. As the Home Rule crisis continued between 1886 and 1914 the designs were extended to include a wider range of scenes from the Williamite campaigns in Ireland, and in particular those that emphasized William's personal connection with Ulster, depicting his arrival and journey through the region on his way to the Boyne. The images also stressed the resilience of their Protestant faith with numerous representations of Martin Luther and the martyred Bishops Latimer and Ridley. This will to active resistance was further highlighted by the increased prominence of the Siege of Derry on banners and street decorations. The motto of "No Surrender" served to connect the successful resistance of 1688–9 with the campaign

being waged against Home Rule. Finally while portraits of the monarch and leading English politicians were numerous, there was a rapid increase in the number of local figures who were held up as exemplars to action. These included a diverse range of firebrand Presbyterian preachers like the Reverends Kane and Hanna, politicians like William Johnston, Edward Saunderson and Edward Carson and industrialists like Edward Harland.

Collectively these images, which were paraded in increasing numbers and seen by huge crowds of people, presented a complex version of the history, identity and ideology of the Ulster Protestants. Their identity became less commensurate with Ireland and more specifically located in an Ulster that was historically, religiously and economically a part of Britain. These displays presented a view of recurrent persecution of the Protestant faith by Roman Catholics, which was balanced only by an equal determination to resistance. As biblical stories came to ever greater prominence on the banners of both the Orange Order and its sister organization, the Royal Black Institution, the self-identification of the Ulster Protestants as God's Chosen People, an undercurrent in Protestant thinking since the seventeenth century, became explicit (Buckley 1985–6; Bartlett 1992; Buckley and Kenney 1995).

The banners were the most overt medium of expressing the Unionist ideology but this period also saw the consolidation of a formal, if unofficial, code of dress for public occasions. Throughout the nineteenth century the Orangeman was identified by his orange sash. This was worn at all parades and has been immortalized as a traditional artefact in the parading anthem

recognize by political views by colour

"The Sash (my father wore)". Apart from the sash, dress was expected to be smart – "Sunday best" – but there was no standardization. The intensification of the campaign against Home Rule saw the formation of the paramilitary Ulster Volunteer Force (UVF) in 1912 which was consciously based on the practices of the eighteenth-century Volunteer movement (Foster 1988: 468). Some units of the UVF adopted military uniforms for parades and training (although khaki lacked the glamour of the scarlet, favoured during the Volunteer period), but for most large-scale events a uniform civilian dress was adopted (Kee 1982; Lucy 1989). In particular, the bowler hat became the ubiquitous symbol of Orangeism. In style it was somewhere between the top hat favoured by the leadership of the Unionists and the cloth cap of the working-class membership. As well as providing a uniformity of dress, it served as a symbolic reference to the formal, "civilized" dress styles of the English middle classes, while emphasized the social solidarity of the Orangemen. The bowler hat was another symbol that connoted the Protestant sense of Britishness. Although the bowler is by no means worn by all Orangemen at contemporary parades it remains a clearly recognized symbol of the Order. In 1995, when protests were made against Orange parades along Belfast's lower Ormeau Road, local residents erected signs depicting a silhouetted figure wearing a bowler hat and an Orange sash with a bar across it signifying no Orange parades (*Sunday Life* 19 February 1995).

The start of the First World War (in 1914) brought a pause to Home Rule proceedings. The UVF, which had been held up as a threat to Westminster, was now offered in the cause of Britain. When Kitchener agreed to keep the Ulstermen together in the 36th (Ulster) Division, the Unionist leader Craig immediately went to Moss Bros and ordered 10,000 uniforms. As the sons of Protestant Ulster strode off to war clad in British uniforms, the Ulster linen industry enjoyed its final boom as it struggled to meet the military demands for its products (Bardon 1992). In July 1916 the Battle of the Somme provided an immediate, contemporary example of willingness to sacrifice oneself for king and country that had been missing from the historiography and iconography of Unionism. At the first Twelfth of July parade after the war, in 1919, the first (of many) banners appeared with the "Heroic charge of the Ulster Division at the Somme" backed by the traditional "Battle of the Boyne". The Ulster Protestant identity was now fused and condensed in those two events and the history, faith and determination that linked them and which irrevocably linked Ulster to Britain. The British government was forced to acknowledge the patriotic sacrifice at the Somme but given the equally unstoppable demands for independence, partition of Ireland, which had been resisted before the war, went ahead.

In tracing the social history of banners and uniforms I have tried to show how style, form and substance not only were linked to the economic structure of the community, but also served as a flexible and adaptable vehicle for a symbolic expression of faith and unity. The initially close allegiance between the Volunteers and the fabric of their political expression has become increasingly tenuous. Since the 1920s the linen industry has steadily contracted and is now but a fragment of its former importance. In contrast the visual displays, initially based on that fabric, remain a vital part of popular political culture. They are an essential and traditional part of the Orange parades, if now long removed from being a direct expression of economic vitality. Over a period of 150 years textiles moved from being a direct expression of Protestant interest to little more than the ghost of an illusion to the past. The silken fabric that once signified British industrial skill and power is now imported from elsewhere in Europe. While the direct connections are no longer considered important, the banners, as objects, have instead become the bearers of what are regarded as traditional values. Traditional practice itself has become the medium of continuity, the bearer of tradition. While social history suggests something of the complexity and variability underpinning the widely prevalent notion of tradition, it is a somewhat broad brush to explore the centrality and meaning of these displays to the actors involved. In the second section of this chapter I want to turn to the ethnographic present and explore the importance of the Orange banners for the contemporary Ulster Protestant community.

The fabric of tradition

The contemporary banners of the Orange Order are based on the styles and designs established in the early years of the twentieth century. The banners are rectangular in shape, some 7 foot long by 6 foot wide. A central square of silk is finished with a contrasting border on three sides. Orange, blue, red and purple account for over 80 per cent of the colours used for Orange Order banners. Above the central painting the banner carries the name and warrant number of the lodge and below it there is often a motto or religious quotation. The image is further framed with heraldic-style foliage or scroll designs. The painting is done in oil and sometimes gold leaf or silver foil is added to make the banner shine in the sunlight. On parade the banner is hung between two poles which are topped with religious or Orange symbols. The banner alone costs between £1,200 and £2,000.

The main focus of interest are the central images. The choice of subject matter is left to lodge members. The most widespread representations relate to the Williamite wars, but a wide range of historical, religious and political figures and events as well as many more parochial subjects can be found on banners (Jarman 1992). A catalogue produced by Bridgett Bros in 1930 shows that the majority of the present-day images had been established by this time. The overall conservatism reflects the centrality of history and the sense of tradition within the aims and ideals of the Institution itself, but this tradition is also sustained through the banner-making process. Banners last upwards of 25 years if they are well looked after and an old or damaged banner often then serves as a template for its replacement. Some lodges have had the same images on their three previous banners, that is for the best part of the century. Because of their longevity banners rarely carry references to contemporary political events. Nevertheless the contemporary painter (there are less than a dozen working professional banner painters) still has influence on the appearance of the banner. A local building or a recently deceased lodge member may be chosen as the subject for a new banner and so the corpus gradually expands. Some customers request a general theme but leave it to the painter to interpret their wishes. In this way the style or composition of the images will change even when the subject remains the same. When new subjects do appear they are rarely original images: personal photographs, postcards and illustrations from a children's Bible are all commonly used. These images serve as the starting point from which the banner painter interprets the customer's desires: repositioning or removing characters, working with the shadows, shading and colour to effect the best translation from one medium to the other. The new banner should not surprise. It draws on tradition and extends it. They are the material repository of the Orange tradition.

Unveiling the future

Before a new banner is publicly paraded for the first time, it is customary to unfurl it at a dedication ceremony. These are small-scale local affairs but prominent public figures are often invited and they use the occasion to make political speeches. The format of the event varies from place to place; some take place in the open air, others are held in a church or an Orange Hall. All involve a parade as part of the occasion. In the weeks preceding the Twelfth of July parades there are numerous banner unfurlings that help to focus local attention on the build-up to the big parade.

One such ceremony was held on Saturday 4 July 1992 when a new Orange banner was dedicated and unfurled at Bessbrook, Co. Armagh, a village two miles north of Newry. Bessbrook was laid out in the 1840s as a model village for the employees of John Grubb Richardson's linen mill, which remained the dominant employer until production ceased in 1986. During the Troubles, Bessbrook was clearly identified as a Protestant stronghold in what is popularly known as "bandit country". The village became headquarters for the British Army in South Armagh and the border zone. Consequently, it was heavily fortified, which served to accentuate the feeling of being a besieged community. Prior to the paramilitary ceasefires of 1994, the general area was considered so unsafe for the security forces that all troop and supply movements were made by helicopter. The base was reputed to be the busiest heliport in Europe. On the day of the unfurling, helicopters seemed to arrive and depart almost continuously, often drowning the ceremonies taking place.

136

The Orangemen gathered outside the Orange Hall, just beyond the security cordon. All vehicles entering the village were checked by soldiers, army footpatrols checked the hedgerows and watched the open spaces while police officers patrolled within the village. At 3pm the Orangemen, accompanied by a local flute band, carried the still furled banner the few hundred metres into Bessbrook, watched by the soldiers and a few locals. A crowd of perhaps 150 people gathered in front of an open-sided articulated lorry trailer, which served as a platform for the officials, in the village square. On the platform were the officers of the local lodge, Orange officials from Belfast, the local vicar and the widows of the two Orangemen who were commemorated on the banner. The main speaker was the Revd Martin Smyth, MP for South Belfast and Grand Master of the Orange Lodge of Ireland.

The proceedings began with a short introductory speech by the Master of the local lodge, who told people that it had been 30 years since the previous banner had been unfurled, and that they had chosen to commemorate their dead colleagues this year because Bessbrook was to host the Twelfth of July parade for the first time since 1981. The ceremony continued with the hymn "O God, our help in ages past" (something of an anthem for the Ulster Protestants since it was sung at the occasion of the signing of the Ulster Covenant to oppose Home Rule in Belfast in September 1912: Kee 1989: 180), a prayer and a scripture reading. The banner was then unfurled. This particular banner commemorated two local members of the Orange Order who were among ten men killed by the IRA at nearby Kingsmill in January 1976. The two men, Joseph Lemmon and James McWhirter, were portrayed wearing their Orange regalia, while between them was a memorial stone bearing the names of all ten men who died at Kingsmill. The painting was underlined with the words "We Will Remember Them". The unfurling, held immediately in front of the stone memorial depicted on the banner, was carried out by the widows of the two men. The banner was then dedicated by Martin Smyth. There was a pause in the proceedings as spectators photographed the new banner. A second hymn was sung and a final prayer said before a round of speeches was made from the platform. The introduction and the dedication speech had focused on the memory of the two men, and their relationship with the Order and their Protestant religion, but the final speech was used by Martin Smyth to reiterate the Ulster Unionist Party position on the current political situation. The ceremony ended with a singing of the National Anthem and the public events concluded with the new banner being paraded up and down the main streets of the town by the Orangemen accompanied by two bands. Most people who had not already seen the banner were at this stage lining the streets to watch the procession. The proceedings had taken up the entire Saturday afternoon.

Cocooned in ritual

Contemporary unfurling ceremonies are seemingly inseparably interwoven
with religious sentiments and practices, presided over by churchmen and
often held in church premises. This linkage between Christianity, banners
and militaristic parades is enhanced by the words of two of the hymns often
used on these occasions:

> Stand up! stand up for Jesus,
> Ye soldiers of the Cross!
> Lift high his royal banner,
> It must not suffer loss.

and:

> Onward Christian soldiers,
> Marching on to war,
> With the Cross of Jesus
> Going on before.
> Christ the Royal Master,
> Leads against the foe,
> Forward into battle,
> See his banners go.

From these sentiments, the carrying of banners on parades can be literally interpreted, justified and demanded as an extension of religious belief. And if the religious images depicted on many banners make an analogy between the Ulster Protestants and God's Chosen People then this is extended and enhanced by the practice of actually carrying "his royal banner" across the Province. However, this connection is still a somewhat recent development. Formal ceremonies to mark the unfurling of Orange banners are recorded from the early years of the twentieth century. At the same time as the iconography was being expanded and production professionalized, the banners were also becoming enveloped in ceremony and ritual. At the earliest reports the banner was unfurled by lodge members and some speeches were made but there was no formal religious ritual. But at a more formal ceremony in 1901 the banner of Cleland Royal Standard was unfurled with the words "In the name of God the Father, God the Son and God the Holy Ghost I dedicate this banner" (*Belfast Weekly News* 4 July 1901) and from this time on formal unveiling was rapidly adopted for all Orange banners. So too were other facets of material culture such as Orange arches and the first murals. Although religious dedications were introduced early into the ritual, churchmen were not involved; instead a local woman unfurled the banner and she would invariably receive a pair of silver scissors as thanks. Sometimes in acknowledgement of political patronage, local dignitaries were invited to unfurl banners that bore their own portraits. But although politicians were involved and made speeches these do not seem to have been openly political occasions. Instead unfurling provided a public focus to view and admire the images and to commemorate the day in a local setting before setting off for the big parade, when the new banner would become just one of any number on display.

After the First World War banner unfurlings were further ritualized by holding the event on, or near to, the anniversary of the Somme, on 1 July, rather than immediately prior to the Twelfth of July parade. An unfurling became an event in its own right and linked the commemoration of the devastation and sacrifice of the war with the celebration of the continued vitality of the loyal orders. Although an occasional unfurling did include some form of religious dedication, they apparently remained largely secular events until after the Second World War. If the religious trappings of banner presentations were somewhat slow on being taken up in the inter-war years, the events were significant in extending the localization of rituals. The images also emphasized individuals, places and historical events of local importance, and the regular and numerous unfurling ceremonies stressed the connection between the local branch and its home domain rather than the branch as small part of the large parade.

In a discussion of a similar ceremony in the Spanish enclave of Melilla in North Africa, Driessen describes the presentation ceremony of a new national flag to the military garrison. As part of the ceremony the flag was dedicated to God, whose support and protection was requested; it was consecrated with holy water and then carried in a military parade through the town. Besides the obvious similarities with Ulster banner dedications described above, Melilla is in a geographically similar position (from the Loyalist perspective), being physically separated from the Spanish mainland and surrounded by those of a different faith. The ceremony in Melilla took place at a time of heightened inter-ethnic tensions and Driessen argues that, by evoking national honour and local pride, the ceremony helped to restore a unified sense of community to the Catholic Spanish population in Melilla and by invoking divine patronage, it legitimized Catholic political domination (Driessen 1992: ch. 6).

Driessen sees the event as similar to a baptism or marriage ceremony, in which the flag is a metaphor of rebirth, of the renewal and confirmation of the bond between Melilla and the motherland. At the same time as it confirms the essential family-like unity of the Catholic population, it also makes clear that the Muslim population were, and would remain, excluded both from this united family and from the power and authority it maintains over the city. The elements that Driessen emphasizes, of birth or rebirth and communal unity, can be seen as features of Ulster banner ceremonies but one can also take the analysis in another direction by focusing on the relationship between the banner and the local lodge. The unfurling ceremony for a first banner announces the public existence of the group of men as a collective entity. Although lodges can, and do, parade without any form of distinguishing regalia, they are effectively invisible if they do. Without a banner to display at public events the men are a nameless group of individuals, lacking a collective identity and lacking a history: it is the banner that announces the name of the body, its geographical base, its political and religious orientation and, from its warrant number and images, its history. Orange banners have been likened to regimental flags, being both the focal point and a rallying point. It is only with a banner that the group of individuals are incorporated as a single body with their own identity that enables them to represent themselves on parade to a wider public; without the banner they would be anonymous and the parades would have no more form than the anonymous mass of a crowd. It is therefore the banners that give order, structure and meaning to the parade.

The dedication of a banner or a replacement is an opportunity to announce and celebrate this existence within the community that has brought it forth. While all fraternal organizations have an initiation ceremony for their members, these are private affairs and the exact details often remain secret. It is only with the appearance of a banner that such bodies cease to be secret organizations and announce their formal existence. The unfurling is the time when this hitherto secret and private gathering of individuals declare their existence collectively in public. When the collective body of brethren display their unity and parade their existence among their friends and neighbours and through their neighbourhoods, it makes the distinction and marks their transformation from a secret organization to an "organisation with secrets" (Buckley 1985–6).

While the banners are an objectification of the men, the ceremony is also important stage in the biography of the banner itself. The time of its first public display marks the culmination of many months of hard work to raise the money for the banner through raffles, dances, socials and collections. The unfurling ceremony offers the members, and supporters who have helped pay for the banner, the first opportunity to scrutinize what will be the public face of the lodge for perhaps the next 25 years. The event is therefore a time of transition, for the banner as much as for the lodge. The dedication ceremony also marks the transformation of the banner from a secular commodity to a sacred object, of a commercial product into an inalienable possession of the lodge.[3] It was not mere chance that the introduction of formal unfurling ceremonies and religious dedications occurred at the same time as regalia manufacture was being removed from the local community and undertaken by professionals. The dedication removes the taint of commercialism by offering the banner to God and asking for His blessing to the object and its community. Driessen (1992) compares this process of dedication to the ritual of Christian baptism, whereby the original sin is washed away and the individual is adopted into a new moral community. The religious dedication transforms the nature of the object but also transforms the body of men who will be represented by the object, and who are thus similarly confirmed and sanctified in their new status. Both Driessen (1992) and Bloch and Guggenheim (1981) have emphasized the importance of the role of "godparents" in these events. They act as mediators, as guarantors and as overseers in the ritual. The painters and the new owners of the banner have little role to play at this dedication stage; instead it is godparent who performs the actual rites of transformation. In this case Martin Smyth, who is a politician, a religious figure and a representative of the larger community of allegiance, acted as a surrogate, or as an intermediatory between the painter and the purchasers.

Dedication ceremonies therefore also draw attention to the larger body to which the men belong, while allowing it to focus on its local presence. Unfurling a new banner should be a positive occasion. It declares a success: this may be for the appearance of a new lodge as a symbol of a general resurgence, a local triumph over tragedy and adversity (as at Bessbrook), or it may signify the continued strength and success of a local group – when a new banner is unfurled to replace one worn out through age. Whatever the reason the appearance of a new banner is a mark of a success and needs to be celebrated. Much of this celebration and congratulation is done at the ceremony itself, in the most private part of a public event, when the meaning, importance and symbolic value of the banner is discussed and conveyed to onlookers. Apart from the celebration of the local lodge, these

events also offer an attentive local audience for members of the various institutions to make political rallying speeches.

Conclusion: the threads of tradition

After the unfurling ceremony, a banner will be seen no more than twice each year. At the major parades a new banner is one among many; the image is divorced from its local relevance and resituated within the broader tradition of Orangeism. A parade is always a chaotic jumble of colour and paintings, in which the core images of the Orange Order are over-duplicated and dominate the display. However, the unusual events and those individuals of erstwhile local significance will in turn be brought to the attention of a wider audience and established within the canon of Orange history. The Bessbrook banner depicted two Orangemen killed by the IRA in 1976, an event commemorated permanently by a stone memorial but its transposal onto a banner means that those attending Orange parades over the next 25 or more years will now be reminded of the event. However, while the Protestant victims of IRA violence are now remembered, the wider context of that violence, as a revenge attack after killings of a Catholic showband by the loyalist paramilitaries of the Ulster Volunteer Force, will be forgotten (Bruce 1992). Within the complex, sectarian politics of Northern Ireland, the commemoration and remembrance of these dead civilians and their elevation to the status of Protestant martyrs can be structured only on loss of local relevance and the communal forgetting of the Catholic dead who preceded them.

What is presented by the totality of the display of banners is a sense of history embodied as tradition. A commemoration and celebration of past heroes, of glories and sacrifices is displayed as both a morality and exemplar to the living. Each Protestant is encompassed within a singular tradition, which remains fixed as tradition but pliable as practice. Every display of banners is but one of a number of variations of a celebratory remembrance of times past. The range of images varies at each parade and from year to year, and, with the range of banners constantly being added to, every parade involves an annual public re-presentation of history. Always different, always the same. As part of a continuously developing tradition each Orange parade displays its own reading of history. But Orangeism is itself part of a wider political process that has generated a number of alternative, and sometimes contrasting, versions of the same events. The banners, and the images they bear, create their meaning within the wider context of the commemorative celebrations, and through which the meaningful histories of Ulster are re-created and remembered.

Few of the myriad events of Irish history are publicly commemorated in any way. Many minor events and personalities of Irish and Ulster history remain in the public eye solely on the banners. It is only at the major parades that the wide range of historical events and personalities are gathered together for the general public to be shown the full sweep of history. In this manner the lack of any coherent narrative among the jumble of banners is an important factor in equalizing events of apparently vastly different significance, a means of condensing several hundred years of history by denying and refusing any temporal order. The juxtaposition of events of major significance, the Battle of the Boyne and the Battle of the Somme, creates an equality of value between events of the recent past, still recalled by the living and remembered in oral histories and those of the distant, almost mythological past. History and time are condensed into a single concept of the past, an entity constructed of categories of events: sacrifice, martyrdom, betrayal, faith. This past has not ended; it continues to structure the feelings, expectations and fears of those acting in the present, who experience it as tradition. This tradition is extended with the commemoration of each new local hero whose modest faith and sacrifice are publicly recalled each year as they are displayed through the streets of Ulster.

Notes

1. The Orange Order, the Royal Black Institution and the Apprentice Boys of Derry are the main organizations that organize parades to celebrate the status of

Protestant in Ireland. The Twelfth of July commemorates the Battle of the Boyne in 1690, which ensured that the British monarchy would be Protestant. The three orders are all male organizations or brotherhoods and much of their structure and regalia derives from Freemasonry. Local branches of the Orange Order are called lodges; these are organized hierarchically within the Grand Lodge of Ireland, but each lodge retains a considerable degree of local autonomy. For more details on the organization structure and the extent of the parading culture see Jarman (1995) and Jarman & Bryan (1996).

2. The traditional sash was worn across the chest. In the seventeenth century it was used by horsemen to carry their sword. The sash is the symbol of membership for all loyal orders; most are now worn around the neck as a collarette. The styles and colours vary, but all are used to display badges of office and symbols of the institution.

3. Most banners are used until they are damaged beyond repair or until enough money is raised to buy a new one. Old banners usually end up, neglected, in the local Orange Hall. Occasionally a banner is donated to a newly formed lodge, some have been sent to Canada or Togo for this purpose. In such cases the banner will be partially repainted with a new name and then rededicated. As a gift, it will still bear the trace of its original lodge.

References

Bardon, J. 1992. *A history of Ulster*. Belfast: Blackstaff.

Bartlett, T. 1992. *The fall and rise of the Protestant nation: the Catholic question 1690–1830*. Dublin: Gill & Macmillan.

Bayly, C.A. 1986. The origins of swadeshi (home industry): cloth and Indian society, 1700–1930. In *The social life of things: commodities in cultural perspective*, A. Appadurai (ed.) Cambridge: Cambridge University Press.

Bean, S. 1989. Ghandi and Khadi: the fabric of Indian independence. In *Cloth and the human experience*, A. Weiner & J. Schneider (eds). Washington, DC: Smithsonian Institute Press.

Bloch, M. & S. Guggenheim 1981. Campadrazgo, baptism and the symbolism of a second birth. *Man* **16**.

Bruce, S. 1992. *The red hand: Protestant paramilitaries in Northern Ireland*. Oxford: Oxford University Press.

Buckley, A. 1985–6. The Chosen Few: biblical texts in the regalia of an Ulster secret society. *Folklife* **24**.

Buckley, A. & M. Kenney 1995. *Negotiating identity: rhetoric, metaphor and social drama in Northern Ireland*. Washington, DC: Smithsonian Institute Press.

Cohen, M. 1993. Urbanisation and the milieux of factory life: Gilford/Dunbarton, 1825–1914. In *Irish Urban Cultures*, C. Curtin, H. Donnan & T. Wilson (eds). Belfast: Institute of Irish Studies.

Driessen, H. 1992. *On the Spanish Moroccan frontier: a study in ritual, power and ethnicity*. Oxford: Berg.

Foster, R. 1988. *Modern Ireland 1600–1972*. Harmondsworth: Penguin.

Gibbon, P. 1975. *The origins of Ulster Unionism*. Manchester: Manchester

University Press.

Gorman, J. 1986. *Banner bright: an illustrated history of trade union banners*. Buckhurst Hill: Scorpion.

Hayes-McCoy, G.A. 1979. *A history of Irish flags from earliest times*. Dublin: Academy Press.

Jarman, N. 1992. Troubled images: the iconography of loyalism. *Critique of Anthropology* **12** (2).

Jarman, N. 1995. *Parading culture: parades and visual displays in Northern Ireland*. PhD thesis, University College London.

Jarman, N. & D. Bryan 1996. *Parade and protest: a discussion of parading disputes in Northern Ireland*. Coleraine: Centre for the Study of Conflict, University of Ulster.

Kee, R. 1982. *Ireland: a history*. London: Abacus.

Kee, R. 1989. *The bold Fenian men: the green flag*, vol. II. Harmondsworth: Penguin.

Kopytoff, I. 1986. The cultural biography of things: commoditization as process. In *The social life of things: commodities in cultural perspective*, A. Appadurai (ed.). Cambridge: Cambridge University Press.

Lévi-Strauss, C. 1966. *The savage mind*. London: Weidenfeld & Nicolson.

Lucy, G. 1989. *The Ulster Covenant: a pictorial history of the 1912 Home Rule crisis*. Lurgan: New Ulster.

McClelland, A. 1980. *Orange arches of the past: in the Twelfth 1980*. Belfast: Grand Orange Lodge of Belfast.

Schneider, J. 1989. Rumpelstiltskin's bargain: folklore and the merchant capitalist intensification of linen manufacture in early modern Europe. In *Cloth and the human experience*, A. Weiner & J. Schneider (eds). Washington, DC: Smithsonian Institute Press.

Smyth, D.H. 1974. *The Volunteer movement in Ulster: background and development 1745–85*. PhD thesis, Queen's University, Belfast.

Smyth, P.D.H. 1979. The Volunteers and Parliament, 1779–84. In *Penal era and Golden Age: essays in Irish history 1690–1800*, T. Bartlett & D.W. Hayton (eds). Belfast: Ulster Historical Foundation.

CHAPTER 7

Calypso's consequences
Justin Finden-Crofts

This chapter will attempt to show, using Trinidadian calypso music as its primary source of example, the part that popular music can and does play in a society and how it can actually form the context for social processes against which everyday life is played out. It will take a different approach, attempting to go beyond the common forms of ethnomusicological analysis that concentrate on the composition and performance of music, to look at the more far-reaching effects of its consumption. The concern is not with how music is created but with what may happen to it after it has been conceived, performed, packaged and released for the general public to buy or hear; that is, how a calypso can embed itself in the public consciousness, and as such exert an influence over social processes.

Calypso and politics

In the 1940s, Albert Gomes, a major politician of the time who was later unsuccessfully to contest Eric Williams for the position of prime minister, described calypso as "the most effective political weapon in Trinidad. . . . The fact that the tents are so sedulously supervised by the police reveals the extent to which the calypso singers influence political thought" (see Warner 1982: 61). At that time police were sent to listen to calypsonians performing in the tents with a pen and paper to record the content of their calypsos as a check for subversive lyrics. Politicians then clearly feared the potential power of the calypsonian to speak to the masses, as they still do today. As one elderly informant put it: "Ministers have to be very careful with their sexual relations around Carnival. Yuh cah escape the calypsonians yuh know". Of course today it is just as difficult to escape the journalists.

The project is ultimately concerned with contemporary calypso and will return to use more recent examples of how it can work in society, but so as to put these in perspective a few notable examples from its post-war past, as well as from another Caribbean island, will be cited first.

In 1958 Sparrow won the Road March with a calypso about tax entitled

"Pay As You Earn". This itself is unusual in that a calypso that is essentially a political commentary should win the Road March (which is usually the best calypso for dancing), but he also sang another tune that year entitled "You Can't Get Away From The Tax". Both calypsos were a reaction to new tax laws introduced by Eric Williams. However, far from criticizing the government, these calypsos backed them up by making the point that they still compare favourably with foreign tax rates. Sparrow had achieved his first major success as a calypsonian in 1956, which was also the year that Eric Williams first came into power. He consistently supported the People's National Movement (PNM, which was led by Williams) and for the 1961 elections he advised the people to vote PNM with his calypso "Wear Your Balisier On Election Day", the balisier being a plant taken by the PNM as its emblem. The belief that the public had in Sparrow is perhaps best shown by a common saying of the time that can still be heard today: "if Sparrow say so, is so". It may show the playful boasting of the calypsonian and his routine, but it also suggests the authority and influence that the calypsonian can have.

The people also sensed, in the words of Gordon Rohlehr, "an implicit [and explicit] link between Sparrow and the PNM" (Rohlehr 1990: 527). The PNM had won the elections and were not to lose power until 1985. In 1965 Sparrow sang a calypso "Get To Hell Out'a Here" which was taken as a direct quote from Williams. The minister for external affairs, Dr Solomon, had been accused by a corporal in the police force of personally setting his stepson free from jail and as a result had resigned his post. Williams wanted him reinstated, however, and these words were reputedly his reply to anyone who disagreed. As a result, the Eric Williams character in Sparrow's calypso is made to say these words as a refrain. The effect is that although Williams may come across as a strong leader, Sparrow reduces him to the level of a "badjohn" by putting such harsh, hooligan-like words in his mouth. It is interesting that after this song Sparrow's commentaries became rather more social than political.

In 1979 came one of the most controversial calypsos to date, which this time was to be quoted by Eric Williams. The calypso "Caribbean Man" was sung by Black Stalin and was a call for Caribbean unity following the failure and confusion caused by the attempts at unification through one federation, Caricom and then Carifta. To unite successfully, Stalin advises the politicians to "rap to you people and tell them like me" before singing the chorus:

Dem is one race – De Caribbean man
From de same place – De Caribbean man
That make the same trip – De Caribbean man
On the same ship – De Caribbean man
So we must push one common intention.

148

The calypso came in for heavy criticism for allegedly being racist and sexist and outraged certain members of the Indian community further when Stalin won the Calypso Monarch singing "Caribbean Unity" as one of his calypsos in that year's final (see Warner 1982). The Indian social psychologist Ramesh Deosoran, who wrote for the *Trinidad Express*, one of the two national newspapers of Trinidad, was one of the most outspoken critics, claiming that the calypso implied that only Africans could take part in Caribbean unity and thus neglected people from other boats and places. The Caribbean woman was also represented as having to wait before she could follow. The *Express*, however, found it necessary to publish their own opinion, which found Stalin to be "not guilty", preferring to take the view that although in Trinidad and Tobago those of African origin may represent only some 41 per cent of the population, looking at the Caribbean as a whole those of African origin were in a large majority. This obviously does not mean that all those of other origins should be disregarded but the *Express* were praising Stalin for attempting to break down the petty island rivalries, especially what may be termed the "big island–small island complex", the tendency for larger islands to look down on those from smaller islands than themselves, which the paper described as "one of the biggest barriers to Caricom becoming a vibrant entity" (*Trinidad Express* 6 March 1979).

After the end of that season the calypso found its way into an address given by Eric Williams to his PNM party. Williams, himself a reputed historian, had decided to present them with an historical account of how each ethnic group had come to be in Trinidad while punctuating each account with the words "Dem too is one race . . . from de same place . . . dat make de same trip . . . on de same ship"(see Warner 1982: 85). Williams too had given his own interpretation to the calypso as well as having appropriated it into his speech to make it more effective. This is an example of the weight that may be attached to a calypso and the depth of feeling that there is in Trinidad for calypso. It also indicates how meaning may be added to a calypso after it has been taken on by the public.

Gordon Rohlehr (1992) goes as far as to suggest that given the role of the calypsonians in the years of the National Alliance for Reconstruction (NAR), the party did not have a chance, no matter what positive contribution it made or could have made. The power of the calypsonian may extend from portraying public opinion, to the actual legitimization or delegitimization of political leaders. The NAR party had little support from the calypsonians and were unable to remain in power for more than just the one term. It was primarily internal party disputes that led to the NAR being only an alliance in name and consequently being ousted from office by the PNM. However, there were exceptions; if any calypso in recent times has had its effect on political processes it is probably "The Sinking Ship" in 1986, by Gypsy (Winston Peters). Some Trinidadians will even claim that "if Gypsy not singing dat song, de NAR not getting in yuh know". The brief coming to power of the NAR was a significant event in Trinidad's post-independence history as it was the only party ever to have beaten the PNM in a general election. People were disillusioned with 30 years of the PNM. It was this feeling that the calypsonians clarified. By using the metaphor of a sinking ship, Gypsy created a powerful image of the failings of the PNM:

> This is an SOS from the Trinidad,
> Location 7 miles off the coast of Venezuela
> SOS May Day May Day. Help. Help.
> The Trinidad is a luxury liner
> Sailing in the Caribbean Sea
> With an old captain named Eric Williams
> For years sailed smooth and free
> But suddenly Eric Williams passed away
> The ship hit rock bottom
> That day someone turned the bridge over
> To a captain named Chambers.

> *Chorus*
> Captain the ship is sinking
> Captain the seas are rough
> We gas tank almost empty
> No electricity, we oil pressure reading low.
> Shall we abandon ship or shall we stay on it
> Or perish slow, we don't know, we don't know.
> Captain you tell me what to do.

The NAR party had promised open government and ran their campaign using the slogan "one love" in reference to the ethnic boundaries that the party felt it had overcome. The analogy of a sinking ship provided a dissatisfied nation with an image they could identify with. Gypsy himself later claimed in his 1988 calypso "Respect for the Calypsonian" that "I could write a song to make government strong. I could write a song to bring government down". Black Stalin, one of the foremost social commentators, describes his perception of the calypsonian's role as "the people's watchdog/ Elected for life" and concludes "So I must be on yuh back" (L. Caliste, "No Ease Up", 1990). That is he feels that it is the calypsonian's duty to be "on the backs" of the politicians. More recently the calypsonian Bally (Errol Ballyantine) emphasized the need for impartiality in calypsos for more practical purposes:

Politicians in this country
Me ent telling them who is my party
Cause if they doh get my vote
They might want to cut my throat
Like poor Sugar Aloes who feel hurt.

Sugar Aloes is another prominent social commentator in the calypso arena who is one of the most outspoken calypsonians and a self-confessed supporter of the PNM. In the last verse Bally, six years on, refers back to Gypsy's calypso and the effects it had for him:

When Gypsy tell the world the ship sinking
Robinson [the NAR leader] hug he up like he darling
Put a medal round he neck
Send him to Skinner Park fete
Poor Gypsy ent ketch he self yet.

Bally finds that this calypso has also had far-reaching effects for Gypsy who, having been openly serenaded by the NAR, must now suffer the consequences of being associated with an effectively redundant political party.
His conclusion comes in the chorus:

Tell all ah dem ah bad
Tell them keep dey party card
I voting Tobago and Trinidad.
(E. Ballantyne, "Who I Voting For", 1992)

Despite this it is quite apparent that while most calypsonians inclined towards social commentary may criticize the PNM from time to time, they have done so with the belief that the power base of that party is unshakeable and many would undoubtedly be uncomfortable with the thought of any other government taking over, especially one made up primarily of IndoTrinidadians. In fact it has been more and more noticeable in recent years that many of the more prominent social commentators seem to have neglected their right or even their "duty" to attack the government. This was recently pointed out in *Bomb* (a weekly newspaper) in the well-known and rather cheekily named column "Snake in the Balisier" which significantly derived its name from the calypso by The Mighty Shadow and itself stands as an example of the far-reaching effects of a calypso. The column, addressing itself to the prime minister, Patrick Manning, asked "Patrick, what magic spell you have on them? . . . Kaiso [another word for calypso] men 'fraid you in 95" (*Bomb* 3 March 1995). The column highlighted the fact that while the NAR were in power many calypsonians were constantly hitting out at the senior members of the party but with the reinstated PNM there was instead "a plethora of acidic tunes swiping at people who have little or no say in the affairs of State". This may be because most calypsonians, if pressed, would give their vote to the PNM, but this does not mean that they cannot criticize them; the column probably gets nearer to the heart of the matter when it hints at Patrick Manning having "friends who are influential in the NCC" who appoint the calypso judges. This would account for the low positioning in 1995 of those calypsonians like Luta, the defending champion, who dared to sing against the government. Rigging, corruption and political interference in calypso competitions are commonly complained about by calypsonians and listeners alike, sometimes with justification and sometimes merely as an excuse to explain a lower than expected placing by the judges. In any case the fear of political interference in the judging of calypso competitions may be enough to deter some calypsonians but there are many that are known to be above this and will not be silenced but others may be guilty of restraining themselves through fear of damaging the party that ultimately has their support.

Despite Gypsy's "Sinking Ship" it is hard to talk of anything as extreme as calypsonians bringing down governments or changing the course of elections in Trinidad. However, examples from other Caribbean islands where calypso is also an important form of musical expression illustrate how this may happen. Calypsonians are liminal or liminoid figures, as defined by Turner (1982: 52), and as such are anti-structural in nature in that they have at their disposal the ability to represent any of the latent potential alternatives to the ones employed by a society in the present moment. In this sense, as Turner also points out, anything that can employ elements from anti-structure may also be proto-structural as it becomes the source for any emerging cultural forms.

The development of the Trinidad-type carnival in several eastern Caribbean countries has stimulated and provided a context for the emergence of local calypso forms. Frank Manning (1986) takes a smaller island community, where the causes and effects of events are highlighted and more easily traceable, and presents an excellent example of the effect calypso can have. He finds that in St Vincent, calypso played a major part in shaping the outcome of a startling electoral upset in 1984 (Manning 1986: 169). The calypsonian Becket sang a calypso for that year entitled "Horn for Them" which was adopted by the minority New Democratic Party (NDP) as their slogan for the elections. To "Horn" someone refers to having sexual relations with someone who is not your usual sexual partner. The strength of the calypso, as is so often the case, lay in its use of *double entendre*. The leader of the NDP was James Mitchell, but John Horn was a NDP candidate contesting a seat against the ruling Labour Party deputy leader, Hudson Tannis. Lyrics from the calypso went:

"Horn for them; Horn for the Sheriff and the Deputy". Horn won his seat beating a man who as deputy was expected to win comfortably by his party. The NDP also won the election convincingly, taking nine out of a possible thirteen seats. Previously the Labour party had held ten out of the thirteen seats. This alone cannot be regarded as so unusual but what was significant was the record 89 per cent turnout from the electorate. Those who would not usually vote were inspired to do so at this election. What is also particularly interesting here is that while there are many calypsos written that are intended as serious social commentary, this calypso relied far more on humour for its popularity. This may account for its effect, especially as the same calypsonian also had two other calypsos around this time entitled "Oppression" and "Love is the Answer". These were far more serious in nature but also far less effective. The effectiveness arose from the simple *double entendre* which was easily recognized by the NDP who fully utilized "Horn for Them" in their election campaign.

In Barbados the celebrated calypsonian The Mighty Gabby has been engaged in lively controversy with its prime minister, Tom Adams, since 1987, and has emerged as the *de facto* leader of the popular opposition to the incumbent government. Calypso has yet to sway the outcome of an election in Barbados but its overall role in partisan politics is greater than in St Vincent (Manning 1986: 177). Gabby has his tent at the ruling Democratic Labour Party headquarters but he has so far refused to stand as a political candidate (unlike the Trinidadian calypsonian "Atilla the Hun" Raymond Quevedo, who became an MP in the 1950s) since he believes that he has more power as a calypsonian.

Manning concludes from his study of these islands that "If Caribbean politics are theatrical, it is in part because Caribbean performance is political. Genres like calypso shape politics to their form and style, inject themselves in myriad ways into the political arena, and at times decisively affect the direction and outcome of political processes" (1986: 177). The effect of calypso on political processes is here apparent and its influence in other areas may also be traced. I shall now demonstrate how its influence often extends to a more general commercial and social afterlife.

Calypso and advertising

One of the most obvious medium through which calypso is utilized, and in turn has been utilized by calypsonians, is in advertising. In the past many calypsonians have written calypso-like jingles for the express purpose of selling them to certain companies or small businesses. With the commercialization of the tents in the 1920s and 1930s calypsonians competed with each other in front of audiences that were paying for the privilege of listening. Tents, like the steelbands, were often sponsored with the sponsors donating the prize money. Often companies would hold their own competitions, supplying prize money for the calypsonian who could sing the best jingle about their product. One of the most famous and successful calypsos in Trinidad, "Jean and Dinah", the one responsible for breaking the most successful calypsonian of all time, the Mighty Sparrow, onto the calypso scene, was itself originally composed as a commercial jingle. Sparrow had written the calypso in the hope of selling it to Salvatori's but as they were not interested he set new lyrics to the melody (see Rohlehr 1990: 448). In more recent times Sparrow actually sang a calypso "Stag, The Recession Fighter" which was written as a promotion for Stag beer and David Rudder's "Rally Round The West Indies" is presently employed to promote television coverage of the West Indies cricket team in action.

Generally today, this process has been reversed. That is, the calypso is written as a song in its own right first and then may be taken up by a business in order to help sell their product. The lyrics may be slightly altered or even totally changed so that they bear some relevance to the product. In Western markets it is of course commonplace for big businesses to use excerpts from popular songs in a similar way to help advertise their products, often even using lyrical catchphrases from the songs. The singers themselves are also used, for example, Michael Jackson by Pepsi Cola. For the 1993 calypso season in Trinidad one particular calypso achieved a great deal of air play both on the radio and the television, not so much because it was popular with listeners or disc jockeys (in fact it had relatively little chart success) but because it was used as the music for a telephone commercial. The calypso was entitled "Call Me" and was performed by the past Road March winning calypsonian Scrunter. For the television commercial Scrunter himself appeared singing the song. Lyrically the calypso had been tampered with but its original theme was what had appealed to the telephone company. The calypso had as part of its music a superimposed sound of a ringing telephone and was about a man's plea to a woman to call him at any time. The idea behind the advertisements was essentially to get everybody to pay their telephone bills on time. To do this TSTT (Telecommunications Services of Trinidad and Tobago) tried to point out, through the reworded calypso, the benefits of having a phone, with a sharp reminder from the calypsonian at the end to "pay your telephone bill". The newspaper advertisement (Fig. 7.1) features the calypsonian Scrunter and was used in the daily and weekly newspapers.

The caption "pay before you play" refers to playing *mas* at carnival. Playing *mas* is often very expensive especially if it is with one of the larger bands. The advertisement then implies that it is therefore a good idea to pay the phone bill before you spend all your money on a costume or whatever other "calls" there may be on your finances. This will lead to your keeping your phone connected and a more enjoyable carnival free from the worry of unpaid bills. It will also lead to a more prosperous telephone company.

Calypso was also used by T&TEC (Fig. 7.2), the suppliers of the nation's electricity, to encourage the nation to pay their bills that year too. T&TEC, like TSTT, is a state-controlled industry. While there was no calypso that lent itself as readily to T&TEC's purposes as "Call Me" did to TSTT's, theirs was still an easy decision. Although the Road March winner for 1993 was Superblue's (Austin Lyons) "Bacchanal Time", the craze for that year was a dance called "The Donkey". This phenomenon will be examined a little later in this section, but suffice to say there were several calypsos written that year about this dance which consistently excited the crowds. One of these calypsos by Ronnie McIntosh and his band Massive Chandelier was called "Whoa Donkey" and the other by the United Sisters

Figure 7.1

Figure 7.2

was called simply "Donkey". The lyrics of the former used the constant refrain "Whoa Donkey" and this became, for the carnival season, a kind of catchphrase, used by the media and the public alike. Usually it was used in a friendly manner as a way of telling someone to calm down, or "steady on", or to not get too out of control especially if they are partying. As can be seen from the copy of the advertisement (Fig. 7.2), the phrase was quickly picked up by T&TEC who otherwise ran a very similar campaign to TSTT. They also use the carnival as a deadline for payment.

> The onset of the carnival is a reason for prompt payment lest you "get carried away in the frenzy of Carnival" and either forget to pay or, worse still, find that you spend too much and then find that you cannot pay.

The advertisement (Fig. 7.2) or reminder could be found in all the national newspapers, usually occupying a full page. However, the music from the calypso itself was not used, the campaign relying completely on the phrase inspired by the song and a rather literal pictoral interpretation that makes no allusions to the dance that the song is about. The use of the phrase though could hardly have failed to signify to any Trinidadian both the song and the dance from which it came, but it also embodies the new meanings for which the phrase has come to be used.

Before considering the 1993 calypsos it is worth looking at an important calypso from 1992 by the calypsonian Crazy, who has been consistently both controversial and popular in recent years. In 1992 the most talked-about calypso was Crazy's "Penelope", which had as a refrain the words "if you can't take a woman, take a man", meaning if you cannot bring a woman to the party bring a man instead. However, the *double entendre* was considered by many as too controversial and, as usual, Crazy found that he had a calypso that was banned from most radio stations. Despite its popularity it also held little appeal for advertisers. In 1993 Crazy again provided the most talked-about calypso which was, despite being banned by most radio stations, used in many different advertisements. The calypso was entitled "Paul, Yuh Mudder Come", which was also the refrain of the calypso. The calypso is about the arrival of "Paul's" mother in Trinidad from the USA but it also worked on a phonetic *double entendre*; substitute "Paul, yuh mudder come" for "haul, yuh mudder cunt". Despite the controversy, or in spite of it, this calypso was one of the most commonly used calypsos by advertisers (see Fig. 7.3).

Other popular calypsos to be found in advertisements in 1993 were Superblue's "Bacchanal Time" (also that year's Road March winner), Shadow's (Winston Bailey) "Swing de Ting", Sparrow's "The More the Merrier", Wayne T's "Doye Doye", Ajala's "Jump Up and Get on Bad".

Figure 7.3

Figures 7.3 and 7.6 are advertisements for public parties or fêtes where an entry fee is required. Calypso is generally used to promote fêtes at carnival time as it is calypso music that will be played at them. Advertisements for fêtes will commonly be heard on the radio and many people will listen in order to find out what is on. Figure 7.5 uses the title of Sparrow's calypso "The More the Merrier", not to promote a fête this time, but a shopping mall or plaza. The plaza is itself using carnival entertainment which will include live calypso music, in order to attract more people. The play on Sparrow's calypso ("The More The Merrier") is returned to at the bottom of the advertisement: "More Variety! More Bargains!" and so on.

Figures 7.6 and 7.7 use the straightforward method of employing words from well-known contemporary calypsos for the promotion of company products. Figure 7.4 is an advertisement for MacFoods who use Superblue's "Bacchanal Time". Although this tune eventually turned out to be the Road March winner, at the time of these advertisements nobody could know for sure what calypso would win. The Road March winner is announced at the end of the carnival season. Probably the most comprehensive example of calypso use in a printed advertisement found by the researcher is in the one quoted in full on page 160:

Figure 7.4

Figure 7.5

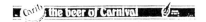

Figure 7.6

Figure 7.7

RIDE YUH DONKEY
to Carnival City 93
Ishmael M Khan
Where there are big bargains on the latest Carnival clothes, shoes and accessories to JUMP UP AND GET ON BAD in.
And just so that you can SWING DE TING you get a free quality printed T-shirt.
Visit Ishmael M Khan's and join DE BACCHANAL LIME.

Here Ishmael M Khan has made humorous use of four of the most popular calypsos from 1993, though the last one has been slightly altered from "Bacchanal Time" to "Bacchanal Lime", a lime being a Trinidadian word used to describe a group of friends or people spending leisure time together.

The advertisement for Queensway (Fig 7.7) plays on Shadow's "Swing de Ting", adjusting it to "Swing de prices down".

Carnival is often used as a time for sales. Some other advertisements that illustrate the extent to which some companies may go in their use of carnival as a sales promotion are: "Every man wants the perfect partner for Carnival – Gator Shoes", or "o.b. Tampons are so secure I don't have to worry about accidents when I play mas – Johnson & Johnson"; or "Don't be a Donkey this Carnival. Shop at Detour . . . Dress like a man not a Donkey". These advertisements all appeared in the national newspapers over the 1993 carnival season.

Finally calypso is often used in advertisements as an incentive for people to buy certain products. For example the company Sharp used the offer of two free calypso LPs (long-playing vinyl discs) as an incentive to buy one of their products. Singer used a similar offer of two free tickets for one of the largest calypso tents, Calypso Revue, run by Lord Kitchener, for the purchase of any bed or mattress.

Calypso and society

So far this section has been concerned with the recognition of the persuasive power of calypso by commercial enterprises and the way it has then been utilized to fit these purposes. The rest of this section will now look at some contemporary examples of how certain calypsos have alone been able to alter social processes or are in fact at the centre of a new social phenomenon. The first example is taken from 1992 and arose from a comment made by a calypsonian in 1989 usually associated with serious social commentary and the second, from 1993, arose from a party calypso orientated toward the Road March.

On Wednesday 8 January 1992 the weather-vane that sat on the peak of the Red House in Port of Spain, Trinidad's government headquarters, was removed and replaced by a white dove. The old weather-vane was commonly believed to be in the shape of a dragon but was actually a sea serpent. This appeared to be the culmination of a comment made in 1989 by one of the more controversial but popular calypsonians, Sugar Aloes (Michael Osouna). At this time the NAR government were in power and this calypsonian was, and still is, a self-confessed supporter of the PNM. Sugar Aloes had cause to refer to this "dragon" as an evil omen that was harming the country. The fact that it had been on top of the Red House since 1907 and therefore survived through many PNM governments seems to have escaped him. However, an article printed in one of Trinidad's foremost national newspapers explains how this oversight came about and is worth quoting at length:

> Then, after years of neglect and exposure to the elements, and of being tarnished by polluting agents, the high-placed weather vane became more conspicuous as a result of the Red House renovations. The acquired patina was carefully removed and the whole body repainted in gleaming white.
>
> Now in a more noticeable new colour, the dragon, which incidentally was not a dragon, got a new image. In 1989 a calypsonian, bereft of other ideas called attention to the dragon, labelling it an evil omen. Although false, that stigma struck a responsive chord in the superstitious breasts of many in the country.
>
> The calypsonian, seemingly ignorant of the fact that the repainted weather vane had been in place since 1907, treated it as a newly installed device and associated it with several tragic events in the country.
>
> The innocent dragon, which had never done anything to anyone, now gained a whole army of enemies. Many who before did not even deign to glance heavenwards at its elevated roost, now threw hateful stares in its direction. (*Sunday Guardian* 12 January 1992)

This article was written in 1992 just after the dragon had been removed and some two years after the calypsonian's original comment when the NAR were in power. At the time of the elections in 1991 Sugar Aloes had cause to make a reference to the dragon again, this time in a calypso entitled "My Decision", which delivers a damning indictment on the NAR period of government:

> ... It really look like the dragon breathing fire on this nation.
> But tell him [A. Robinson, leader of NAR] from me,
> If he don't want this nation to hit rock bottom,

Take down the dragon and try to put back the clock.
That might work.

The PNM went on to win this election and the question then remained as to whether they would yield to those members of the public that had been stirred up by the calypsonian, and remove the offending dragon. In the event it was indeed removed under cover of the night and made front-page headlines. Three days later it was replaced by a dove with an olive branch in its beak. This headline appeared the following Monday:

Dove replaces DRAGON (*Trinidad Guardian* 13 January 1992)

The minister for public works, Colin Imbert, was reported as saying that the reason for the removal of the dragon had nothing to do with "hocus pocus" or superstition. His reasoning was that the serpent was not properly designed to function as a wind-vane and therefore had been replaced by a "more aero-dynamically suited object. The old wind vane did not have a [steel] bearing so it couldn't function properly" (*Trinidad Guardian* 13 January 1992). The point here though would seem to be that, in reality, the PNM had essentially yielded to the advice of a calypsonian and some would say pandered to the superstitious whims of the population and needlessly defaced one of the national monuments of Trinidad and Tobago. The removal of something as minor as a weather-vane was an event that had been transformed into headline news and the disputes over it continued. The removal of the dragon provoked a continual influx of letters to both national daily newspapers. The letters page of the 12 January edition of the *Sunday Guardian* was completely given over to complaints about the dragon affair. An extract from one letter reads: "we allowed ourselves to be misguided by a calypsonian who was looking for anything with which to incite displeasure with a government he obviously hated. . . . We showed our immaturity by believing his misinformation and building on it to the point of blaming all of our misfortune on a simple OBJECT".
    Gerry Besson, a Trinidadian historian, described its removal as the sign of an insecure government (ibid.). He also pointed out that it had an irreplaceable aesthetic value as part of a deliberate overall plan by the architect to match it with the mermaids and mermen that adorn the fountain in Woodford Square opposite the Red House. Therefore, for some, to remove it was akin almost to vandalism. It naturally begs the question: why did the PNM have the serpent replaced if not to appease superstitions aroused by a calypsonian? Either way, what would otherwise have been an event of minor importance that would probably not even have been noticed by public and media alike, became an issue for almost two years that eventually finished as headline news.

The dragon that was not a dragon even ended up in use as an adjective that came back to haunt the PNM when scarcely a week after its removal the government announced its budget. Here is a copy of the headline that appeared in the paper (see also Fig. 7.8).

DRAGON BUDGET (*Trinidad Guardian* 18 January 1993)

The dragon finally completed its entrance into mainstream popular culture when, like the many examples above, it had become well enough known to be used for advertising purposes.

Out of most carnival seasons there will arise something that makes that particular carnival in some way different and there will be a certain amount of expectation and speculation throughout Trinidad as to what this will be. The 1993 season was no exception and was in fact host to a quite unusual trend known as "Donkeymania". This trend has already been mentioned in reference to the T&TEC advertisements for which it was used in an effort to persuade the public to pay their electricity bills. It chiefly revolved around two calypsos, "Whoa Donkey" by Ronnie McIntosh, from which arose the donkey dance, and "Donkey" by the United Sisters, a group of four usually solo female calypsonians.

The fact that there were two calypsos based around the same topic certainly added to the carnival by providing some additional competition. Competition is very much part of carnival and apart from the official competitions the media will play up any personal differences that may exist between calypsonians to try to create some sort of picong (picong being the name given to a rivalry or argument between calypsonians). Calypsonians

Figure 7.8

often refer to each other in their calypsos and even criticize each other in their songs which will usually be exaggerated by the media to add an extra interest for the listening public. The two "donkey" calypsos were often billed together as the "donkey derby" and it was for the crowd to determine which was the better calypso or "ride". At the time there was was some dispute as to whose was the original "donkey", not between the United Sisters and Ronnie McIntosh, the latter's clearly being first, but between McIntosh and a calypsonian from the US Virgin Islands known as Mighty Pat, who had sang a calypso the previous year about a runaway donkey belonging to someone named Jenny. From this calypso McIntosh derived his chant "Whoa Donkey" which he was already using for the 1992 carnival before developing it into a full calypso for 1993. To capitalize on this the Mighty Pat was flown over by the largest of the calypso fête venues, the Spectrum (previously known as Soca Village), to compete in a three-way clash. The fact that calypsos have been written about donkeys since the 1930s did not seem to affect the dispute.

The popularity of the donkey, or "donkeymania" as the press liked to call it, led to a now notorious fête at the Cruise Ship Complex billed as the "donkey derby". The United Sisters and Ronnie McIntosh were billed together for the first time that year, and at a venue that had a capacity of 5,000, more than 12,000 showed up. The *Express* reported:

> As McIntosh started his version of the song, the crowd started to move in the direction of the band and threw down some of Chandelier's [his band] speaker boxes. People who were attempting to get inside the venue outside the Wrightson Road compound broke down a gate and a fence. Hundreds of bottles were thrown by people in the compound. Several people were hurt and had to be treated for cuts at the Port of Spain General Hospital. (*Express* 18 January 1993)

As an eye-witness to the event, it may be added to this that the crowd began to get out of control only when Ronnie McIntosh had told them to "take any new donkey"; in other words, that everyone should find themselves a different partner. The people on the outside then also became more desperate to get in, thinking they were missing out on something.

Wherever the donkey calypsos originated from, Ronnie McIntosh was certainly responsible for bringing "donkeymania" to Trinidad in 1993. However, the popularity of these calypsos was seen by many as an example of the decline of calypso and, as usual, there were plenty of complaints about there being too many "wine and jam" calypsos with poor lyrics. To many who feel that they appreciate good calypso the donkey calypsos were nothing but "chupidness" and they could not understand the mass appeal. Raymond Ramcharitar, one of the most respected columnists for the *Sunday Guardian*, asked, "what is the fascination with the damned donkey? Ronnie McIntosh's version does not stop anywhere short of a slapstick neanderthal warcry. He yells 'Whoa Donkey' and everybody starts screaming and working themselves into a frenzy" (*Sunday Guardian Magazine* 24 January 1993). This is an attitude common to many who have little interest in those tunes that are generally in competition for the Road March. The complaints are often aimed at either the general poor quality or banality of the lyrics, or at their smuttyness. What is not often appreciated is that the Road March or party calypsos serve a different function to the social commentary calypsos which are judged primarily on their lyrics. But lyrics are both necessary and important for party calypsos too. The appeal of Ronnie McIntosh's calypso can be found in the very lyrics that were derided for their lack of meaning. If listened to, it will be realized that the words of Ronnie McIntosh's "Whoa Donkey" are nothing other than a set of instructions for a new dance – the Donkey Dance. Many successful carnival calypsos issue sets of physical instructions for the people, one of the most simple coming from the 1993 Road March winner "Bacchanal Time" by Superblue, which gave the command "jump up, jump up, jump up, jump up", etc., to which so many willingly obliged. Others included "Wine on a Bumsee" or "Jump Up and Get on Bad". McIntosh takes the party reveller through a precise set of instructions for a new dance, an alternative to the now traditional wining that dominates carnival: "Put toes together and knees apart. Put two fists together out in front . . . and yuh calling whoa donkey". This is the first part of a dance that is in three stages. The second part involves a man placing a woman on his shoulders and the third is described by McIntosh as the "back-to-front donkey", which is when the man turns around so that his face is between the legs of the woman writhing on his shoulders, making the dance end up as a kind of mimicked act of airborne oral sex. Sex is nearly always the primary appeal of Road March or fête calypsos, where people go to dance. The sexual appeal of the dance combined with its novelty value were at the centre of its mass appeal. The song, like so many carnival tunes, has much less effect outside of the live performance and therefore lives and dies with carnival. Its popularity was its novelty especially as an alternative dance, although whether it has the appeal to be taken up in future carnivals is another matter.

Like the dragon of the previous years, the donkey found its way into the local vocabulary. The phrase "whoa donkey" could have been used in a number of varying situations, but usually it inferred that someone should "calm down", "steady on", or "don't get too excited". A headline for an article in the *Trinidad Guardian* (3 February 1993) reporting a parliamentary motion brought by the opposition to debate corruption and the government's inability to handle it, appeared as "Nobody can resist the donkey", referring to the bad behaviour of the politicians present and the farce that the debate turned into. What had originally began as a chant at a fête had developed into a set of popular calypsos, a dance, an addition to local Trinidadian dialect, a method of persuading people to pay their bills, and finally a term used to describe the behaviour of politicians.

To conclude, various impacts made by calypsos are quite different in nature from one another. The "Donkey" and the "Sinking Ship", for example, underline the duality that exists within calypso between, in simple terms, the serious social commentary exemplified in the Calypso Monarch competition, and the fun party calypsos exemplified in the Road March and Soca Monarch competitions. It has been shown that political and social commentary in calypso can influence social processes while the more popular "catchy" calypsos can find another life in advertising. However, these latter calypsos can also have a political impact, most notably shown by the calypsonian Becket from St. Vincent. Despite the obvious polar categories that may be assigned to calypso and its various social impacts it would be a mistake to focus on either one in isolation. Carnival includes them all and gives the music its own power while at the same time the music helps to shape and define each carnival. Cohen refers to carnival as a "contested event" that is "precariously poised between the affirmation and validation of the established order and its rejection" (Cohen 1982: 34). This provides some understanding as to the essence of carnival and therefore calypso. Carnival works by remaining ambiguous so that although there are given categories such as social commentary and wine and jam, or Calypso Monarch and Road March, there is always the opportunity to exploit the areas between these by such devices as the use of *double entendre* which are capable of drawing politics down to the people and also making entertainment an activity with political and social consequence.

References

Cohen, A. 1982. A polyethnic London carnival as a contested cultural performance. *Ethnic and Racial Studies* **5**, 23–42

Manning, F. 1986. Challenging authority: calypso and politics in the Caribbean. *Political Anthropology* **5**, 167–79.

Rohlehr, G. 1990. *Calypso and society in pre independence Trinidad*. St Augustine: G. Rohlehr.

Rohlehr, G. 1992. Calypso 92. In *Calypso and politics*, M. Narine (ed.). Port of Spain: Caribbean Imprint.

Turner, V. 1982. *From ritual to theatre: the human seriousness of play*. New York: PAJ.

Warner, K. 1982. *Kaiso: the Trinidad calypso*. Washington, DC: Three Continents Press.

PART IV

The global sphere
(or the World Wide West)

CHAPTER 8

Coca-Cola: a black sweet drink from Trinidad[1]

Daniel Miller

The context for much of the current interest in material culture is a fear. It is a fear of objects supplanting people. That this is currently happening is the explicit contention of much of the debate over postmodernism which is one of the most fashionable approaches within contemporary social science. It provides the continuity between recent discussions and earlier critical debates within Marxism over issues of fetishism and reification, where objects were held to stand as congealed and unrecognized human labour. As most of the chapters in this book demonstrate, this is often an exaggerated and unsubstantiated fear, based upon the reification not of objects but of persons. It often implies and assumes a humanity that arises in some kind of pure pre-cultural state in opposition to the material world, although there is no evidence to support such a construction from either studies of the past or from comparative ethnography, where societies are usually understood as even more enmeshed within cultural media than ourselves. Rather our stance is one that takes society to be always a cultural project in which we come to be ourselves in our humanity through the medium of things.

This fear, at least in its earlier Marxist form, was not, however, a fear of material objects *per se* but of the commodity as vehicle for capitalist dominance, and this raises a key issue as to whether and when societies might be able to resist this particular form of object domination. Although this is a general issue, there are certain objects which have come to stand with particular clarity for this fear, and to in some sense encapsulate it. A few key commodities have come to signify the whole problematic status of commodities. Recently a new theory has been developed to consider this kind of "meta-"status in the form of a book on the history of the swastika by Malcolm Quinn (1994). Quinn provides what he calls a theory of the meta-symbol. The swastika is unusual in that instead of standing as the icon for a specific reference it has tended to stand more generally for a meta-symbolic level that evokes the idea that there exists a higher, more mystical level of symbolization. At first after discoveries at Troy and elsewhere this was the power of symbolism in the ancient past or mystic East, but later this kind of empty but latent status allowed the Nazis to

169

appropriate it as a generalized sign that their higher level and cultic beliefs stemmed from some deep historicity of the swastika itself. Quinn argues that the reason the swastika could achieve such importance is that whatever its particular evocation at a given time, it had come to stand above all for the the general sense that there exists a symbolic quality of things above and beyond the ordinary world. This allowed people to attach a variety of mystical beliefs with particular ease to the swastika.

There may well be a parallel here to a few commodities that also occupy the position of meta-symbol. Coca-Cola is one of three or four commodities that have obtained this status. In much political, academic and conversational rhetoric the term Coca-Cola comes to stand, not just for a particular soft drink, but also for the problematic nature of commodities in general. It is a meta-commodity. On analogy with the swastika this may make it a rather dangerous symbol. It allows it to be filled with almost anything those who wish to either embody or critique a form of symbolic domination might ascribe to it. It may stand for commodities or capitalism, but equally Imperialism or Americanization. Such meta-symbols are among the most difficult objects of analytical enquiry since they operate through a powerful expressive and emotive foundation such that it becomes very difficult to contradict their claimed status. So Coca-Cola is not merely material culture, it is a symbol that stands for a debate about the materiality of culture.

The title of this chapter has therefore a specific intention. It is a joke, designed to plunge us down from a level where Coke is a dangerous icon that encourages rhetoric of the type West versus Islam, or Art versus Commodity, and encourages insead the slower building up of a stance towards capitalism which is informed and complex, so that any new critique has firm foundations resting on the comparative ethnogaphy of practice within commodity worlds.

The literature on Coke that is most readily available is that which best supports the expectations raised by the meta-symbolic status of this drink. These are the many books and articles about the Coca-Cola company and its attempts to market the product. Almost all are concerned with seeing the drink as essentially the embodiment of the corporate plans of the Coca-Cola company. A good example of this is an interview published in *Public Culture* (O'Barr 1989). This is held with the head of the advertising team of the transnational agency McCann Erickson, the firm used by Coke. It focuses upon the specific question of local–global articulation. The interview traces the gradual centralization of advertising as a means to control the manner in which its image became localized regionally. In fact the advertiser notes, "it wasn't until the late '70s that the need for advertising specifically designed for the international markets was identified". In a sense this meant more centralization since "the benchmark comes from the centre and anybody that needs to produce locally, for a cultural reason, a legal reason, a religious reason, or a marketing reason, has to beat it". Many examples are given in the interview as to re-takes around a core advertisement, e.g. re-shot with more clothed models for Muslim countries. The interview also included discussions about the phrase "I feel Coke" which represents a kind of Japanesed English for that market and about what attitude worked for Black Africa. Although the advertiser claims, "I don't think Coca-Cola projects. I think that Coca-Cola reflects", the interview satisfies our desire to know what this product is by having exposed the underlying corporate strategies for global localization.

Most of the literature on the company, irrespective of whether it is enthusiastically in favour or constructed as a diatribe against the drink, acts to affirm the assumption that the significance of the drink is best approached through knowledge of company strategy. The literature is extensive and probably few companies and their advertising campaigns are as well documented today as Coca-Cola.

There are, however, many reasons for questioning this focus and questioning the theory of commodity power that is involved in assuming that the company controls its own effects. Indeed Coca-Cola could be argued to be a remarkably unsuitable candidate for this role as the key globalized corporation. Two reasons for this emerge through the recent comprehensive history of the company, Pendergrast's book *For God, Country and Coca-Cola* (1993). The first piece of evidence was that which Pendergrast (1993: 354–71; see also Oliver 1986) calls the greatest marketing blunder of the century. His account (and there are many others) shows clearly that the company had absolutely no idea of what the response might be to their decision to change the composition of the drink in the 1980s in response to the increasing popularity of Pepsi. The enforced restitution of Classic Coke was surely one of the most explicit examples of consumer resistance to the will of a giant corporation we have on record. After all, the company had behaved impeccably with respect to the goal of profitability. The new taste scored well in blind tests, it responded to a change in the market shown in the increasing market share of Pepsi and seemed to be a sensitive response that acknowledged the authority of the consumer. Despite this, when Coke tried to change the formula, in marketing terms all hell broke loose, and the company was publicly humiliated.

The second reason why Coca-Cola is not typical of globalization is that from its inception it was based upon a system of franchising. The company developed through the strategy of agreeing with local bottling plants that they would have exclusivity for a particular region and then simply selling the concentrate to that bottler. It is only in the last few years that Coke and Pepsi have begun centralizing the bottling system and then only within the USA. There are of course obligations by the bottlers to the company. The most important are the quality control which is common to most franchising operations and the second is control over the use of the company logo.

Indeed this was one of the major early sources of contention resolved in a US Supreme Court decision. In other respects the franchise system allows for a considerable degree of local flexibility, as will be shown in this chapter. Felstead (1993) documents the relationship between the specific case of Coke and more general trends in business franchising.

Coca-Cola in Trinidad

In some ways Coca-Cola is perhaps less directly associated with the States within the USA, where its presence is taken for granted, than in an island such as Trinidad, where its arrival coincided with that of an actual US presence. Coke came to Trinidad in 1939. In 1941 the British government agreed to lease certain bases in Trinidad for 99 years. As a result US troops arrived in some force. This had a profound effect upon Trinidad, no less traumatic because of core contradictions in the way in which Trinidadians perceived these events. Trinidad was already relatively affluent compared to other West Indian islands, thanks to its oil industry, but the wage levels available on the US bases were of quite a different order, leading to a mini-boom. Furthermore the US soldiers were seen as highly egalitarian and informal compared with the aloof and hierarchical British colonial authorities. In addition there was the presence of Black American soldiers and particularly a few well-remembered Black soldiers who took a sympathetic and active role in assisting the development of local Trinidadian institutions such as education.

The Americans reflected back upon themselves this benign side of the relationship in extracting the Trinidadian calypso "Rum and Coca-Cola", which was a tremendous hit within the USA. There was, however, another side to "Rum and Coca-Cola" that was evident within the lyrics of the calypso itself, as in the lines "mother and daughter working for the Yankee dollar", but are found in more detail in the resentment echoed in the book with the same title written by the Trinidadian novelist Ralph de Boissiere (1984). There were many US soldiers who looked upon Trinidadians merely as a resource and were remembered as brutal and exploitative. At the time many Trinidadians felt that it was the commoditization of local sexuality and labour that was objectified through the mix of rum and Coke.

In general, however, given the ideological needs of the independence movement from Britain that followed, it was the benign side of the American presence that is remembered today. Another legacy is the drink rum and Coke which has remained ever after as the primary drink for most Trinidadians. This not only secures the market for Coke but also makes it, in this combination, an intensely local nationalist drink, whose only rival might be the beer Carib. Before reflecting on the meaning of the drink in consumption, however, we need to examine the commercial localization of Coke.

172

The Trinidadian soft drink industry

Since Coke always works by franchise, its localization as a business comes through the selection of a local bottling plant. In Trinidad Coke is bottled by the firm of Cannings. This is one of the oldest grocery firms in the island. Established in 1912, it was described in 1922 as follows:

> His establishment became the leading place in Port of Spain for groceries, provisions, wines and spirits. It gives employment to about one hundred and ten persons. ... It would be difficult to find anywhere a stock more representative of the world's preserved food products. ... An example of the firm's progressive policy in all they undertake is also found in the electrical machinery equipment of their contiguous aerated water factory, where all kinds of delicious non-alcoholic beverages are made from carefully purified waters. (Macmillan 1922: 188)

The franchise for Coca-Cola was obtained in 1939 and was later expanded with the bottling of Diet Coke and Sprite. Coke by no means dominated Cannings, which continued to expand in its own right and developed with Hi-Lo what remains the largest chain of grocery stores on the island. An interesting vicarious insight into this relationship is provided by the Trinidadian novelist V.S. Naipaul (1967). The protagonist of his book *The mimic men* is a member of the family that own the Bella Bella bottling works which holds the Coca-Cola franchise for the semi-fictional island of Isabella. In the book a child of the owner is shown taking immense pride and personal prestige from the relationship, viewing the presence of Pepsi as a discourtesy to his family, and showing school groups around the Coke bottling works. The novel thereby provides a glimpse into the earlier localization of Coca-Cola manufacture into local circuits of status (1967: 83–6).

In 1975, Cannings was taken over, as were many of the older colonial firms, by one of the two local corporations that were becoming dominant in Trinidadian business. Unlike many developing countries which are clearly controlled by foreign transnationals, the firm of Neil & Massey along with ANSA McAl together represent the result of decades of mergers of Trinidadian firms (for details see Miller 1997: ch. 3). Both are locally owned and managed and are more than a match for the power of foreign transnationals. Indeed Neil & Massey, which took over Cannings, is clearly itself a transnational although retaining its Trinidadian base. Begun in 1958 and becoming a public company in 1975, it is now the largest firm in the Caribbean. The 1992 annual report noted assets of over TT$1.5 billion, 7,000 employees and subsidiary companies in 16 countries including the USA.[2]

Although ownership lies with Neil & Massey, the bottling section is still, in the public mind, largely identified with Cannings. This relationship is long standing and it cannot be assumed that the local company is dominated by Coke. Cannings represents reliability and quality of a kind that Coke needs from its bottlers. So while Coke would like to push Fanta as its product, and thus increase its own profits, Cannings, which makes good money on its own orange flavour, has simply refused to allow the product into Trinidad. At times it has also bottled for other companies with complementary products such as Schweppes and Canada Dry.

In effect the services offered by Coke Atlanta are largely paid for in the cost of the concentrate which is the most tax-efficient way of representing their financial relationship. In marketing, pricing, etc. the bottler has considerable autonomy to pursue its own strategies. But Cannings has little incentive to do other than follow Atlanta which will often put up 50 per cent of the costs for any particular marketing venture, and can provide materials of much higher quality than the local company could produce. As it happens McCann Erikson, which is Coca-Cola's global advertiser, is present as the sole transnational advertising agency at present operating in Trinidad.

Cannings and in turn Neil & Massey do not, however, represent localization in any simple sense, since both derive from old colonial firms. While they may therefore be seen as representing national interests as against foreign interests they may also be seen as representing white elite interests as against those of the dominant populations in the country which is split between a 40 per cent ex-African, originally mainly though by no means entirely ex-slave, and a 40 per cent ex-South Asian, almost entirely originally ex-indentured labourers (for further details on Trinidad see Miller 1994).

The importance of this identification is clarified when its competitors are brought into the picture. There are six main bottlers of soft drinks in Trinidad. Each has a specific reputation which bears on the drinks they produce. Solo is owned by an Indian family, which started in the 1930s with the wife boiling up the syrup and the husband bottling by hand. It then become one of the earlier larger firms to be outside of the control of whites and it has been either the market leader or at least a key player in the soft drink market ever since. Its main product is a flavour range called Solo and it has one franchise called RC Cola. In a sense while Solo is seen as a local "as opposed to white", the firm of S.M. Jaleel is generally regarded as more specifically "Indian". This is because it has the only factory in the South which is the area most dominated by the Indian population, and historically it grew from roots in a red drink that was sold mainly to Indians. Today its own flavour range is called Cole Cold but it has tried out various franchises such as for Schweppes, Seven Up and Dixi Cola.

The firm of L.J. Williams is regarded locally as the "Chinese" bottlers. As traders and importers they are not associated with their own label but with the brand of White Rock, together with franchises for drinks including Peardrax and Ribena from Britain. The final major company is called Bottlers, though it was recently taken over by a larger firm called Amar. Bottlers have the contract for Pepsi Cola, which at times has had a significant presence in Trinidad but has been languishing with a smaller market share mainly through its inability to find ties with a reliable distributor. Its presence is mainly felt through its links with Kentucky Fried Chicken and the large amount of advertising that has continued despite its lack of market share. It also has a flavour range called USA Pop.

Marketing materials suggest that brand share would be around 35 per cent Coke, 20 per cent Solo, 10 per cent each for Cannings and Cole Cold, with the rest divided between both the other brands mentioned and various minor brands. The industry was probably worth around TT$200 million with a bottle costing 1 dollar to the consumer. The industry sees itself as an earner of foreign currency for Trinidad. This is because the only major imported element is the concentrate. Trinidad is a sugar producer; it also has a highly efficient local producer of glass bottles which manufactures for companies around the Caribbean and sometimes even for Florida. The gas is also produced as a by-product of a local factory. Soft drinks are in turn exported to a number of Caribbean islands, for example nearby Grenada is largely dominated by Trinidadian products and there is some exporting to ex-patriate populations in, for example, Toronto, New York and London. All the main companies involved are Trinidadian. Indeed even the local Coca-Cola representative is a Trinidadian who is responsible for the company's operations not only in Trinidad but also in five other countries including Guyana in South America. There is also a representative from Atlanta based in Puerto Rico.

When sitting in the offices of the companies concerned, the overwhelming impression is of an obsession with the competition between these firms. Indeed I argue elsewhere (Miller 1997) that it is the actions of rival companies rather than the actions of the consumers that is the key to understanding what companies choose to do. Money spent on advertising, for example, is justified in terms of one's rival's advertising budget rather than the needs of the product in the market. The competition is intense, so that the price in Trinidad is significantly lower than in Barbados where there are only three soft drink companies.

In studying the industry in detail a number of generalizations emerge that seem to command the logic of operations almost irrespective of the desires of particular companies. The first is the cola-flavours structure. Virtually all the companies involved consist of a range of flavours usually made by the companies and a franchised Coke such as Coca-Cola, Dixi Cola, RC Cola or Pepsi. The cola product has become essential to the self-respect of the company as a serious operator, but being a franchise the profits to be made are somewhat less than the flavour ranges where the concentrate is much cheaper.

The second feature seems to be the law of range expansion. Since the 1970s each year has tended to see the entry of a new flavour such as grape, pear, banana, etc., but also a more gradual increase in choice of containers, from bottles to cans to plastic, from 10 oz to 1 litre and 2 litre to 16 oz. In general the company that starts the innovation makes either a significant profit as Solo did with canning or Jaleel did with the litre bottle, or the innovation flops and a loss is incurred. Where there is success all the other companies follow behind so that the final range for the major companies is now very similar. Taking all combinations together they may produce around 60 different products.

This logic is actually counterproductive in relation to the third law, which seems to be that the key bottleneck in company success is distribution. Some of the major advances made by companies have been in finding better ways to distribute their products to the countless small retailers, known as parlours, which are often located as part of someone's house in rural areas. Jaleel, which was a pioneer here through using smaller 3 ton trucks, developed the slogan "zero in on a Cole Cold" precisely to draw attention to its greater availability. This need to streamline delivery is, however, undermined by the increasing diversity of product, since the latter means that a greater number of crates are required to restock the needs of any particular location. This is only one example of the way in which the imperatives within the industry may act in contradiction to each other rather than as a streamlined set of strategic possibilities.

What is Trinidadian about these business operations? Well, if, as in some anthropology, local particularity is always something that derives from some prior original diversity that somehow resists the effects of recent homogenized tendencies, then the answer is "very little". If, however, one regards the new differentiation of global institutions such as bureaucracy and education as they are manifested in regions, as just as an authentic and important form of what might be called a posteriori diversity, then the case is not without interest. Although the various details of how business operates may not be tremendously surprising, it is actually quite distinct from any generalized models that business management with its reliance of universalized models from economics and psychology would like to promote.

In almost any area of business, such as for example, the conditions that control entry of new companies to the market, the situation in the Trinidadian soft drink industry would be quite different from the situation described in the business literature in, for example, the USA (e.g. Tollison et al. 1986). Partly for that reason I found that executives with business training abroad often pontificated in a manner that clearly showed little understanding of their own local conditions.

Some of the particularities, for example the degree to which the public retains knowledge about the ownership of companies or as another example the fluctuating between competition and price fixing, may have to do with the relatively small size of the market and indeed the country. Others, such as the constant link between franchised colas and local flavour groups, have to do with more fortuitous aspects of the way this industry has been developing locally. Overall this industry, as so much of Trinidadian capitalism, no more follows from general models of business and capitalism than would the particular operation of kinship in the region follow from knowing general models and theories of kinship. Profitability, like biology in kinship, may be a factor but only as manifested through politics, personal prestige, affiliation, particular historical trajectories and so forth.

To give one last example, ethnicity alone might seem an important consideration, but Solo, although Indian, is not seen as ethnic in the same way as Jaleel, which is Indian and operates in the South. Yet in terms of politics the positions are reversed. The family that owns Solo has been associated with opposition to a government that has largely been dominated by African elements and severe difficulties have been put in its way from time to time as a result, as for example preventing it from introducing diet drinks; while Jaleel, being Muslim and thus a minority within a minority, has historically been associated politically with the government against the dominant Hindu group of the dominated Indian party.

To conclude – to understand the details of marketing Coke in Trinidad demands knowledge of these local, contingent and often contradictory concerns that make up the way capitalism operates locally, together with the way these affect the relationship between local imperatives and the demands emanating from the global strategists based in Atlanta. Often the net result was that Coke representatives in Trinidad were often extremely uncertain as to the best marketing strategies to pursue even when it came to choosing between entirely opposing possibilities such as emphasized its American or its Trinidadian identity.

The consumption of sweet drinks

The companies produce soft drinks. The public consume sweet drinks. This semantic distinction is symptomatic of the surprising gulf between the two localized contexts. The meaning of these drinks in consumption can easily be overgeneralized and the following points may not apply well to local elites whose categories are closer to those of the manufacturers. But to understand how the mass middle-class and working-class population perceive these drinks, one needs a different starting point. For example, sweet drinks are never viewed as imported luxuries that the country or people cannot afford. On the contrary they are viewed as Trinidadian, as basic necessities and as the common person's drink.

Apart from this being evident ethnographically, it is also consistent with the policy of the state. For many years the industry was under price control. This meant that prices could be raised only by government agreement and, since this severely restricted profitability, price control was thoroughly opposed by the industry. The grounds given were that this was a basic necessity for the common person and as such needed to be controlled. The reality was that to the extent that this was true (and still today consumption is around 170 bottles per person per annum), the government saw this as a politically astute and popular move. Furthermore until the IMF (International Monetary Fund) recently ended all protectionism, Coke was protected as a locally made drink through a ban on importing all foreign-made soft drinks.

As a non-alcoholic beverage, sweet drinks compete largely with fruit juices and milk drinks such as peanut punch. All are available as commodities but also have home equivalents as in diluted squeezed fruit, home-made milk drinks, and sweet drinks made from water and packet crystals. Water competes inside the home, but no-one but the most destitute would request water *per se* while ordering a meal or snack. Unlike their rivals sweet drinks are also important as mixers for alcohol.

The importance of understanding the local context of consumption as opposed to production is also evident when we turn to more specific qualities of the drinks. From the point of view of consumers, the key conceptual categories are not the flavours and colas constantly referred to by the producers. In ordinary discourse much more important are the "black" sweet drink and the "red" sweet drink.

The "red" sweet drink is a traditional category and in most Trinidadian historical accounts or novels that make mention of sweet drinks it is the red drink that is referred to. The attraction of this drink to novelists is probably not only the sense of nostalgia generally but the feeling that the red drink stands in some sense for a transformation of the East Indian. While the African has become the non-marked population, the Indian has been seen as an ethnic group with its own material culture. The red sweet drink was a relatively early example of the community being objectified in relation to a commodity as opposed to a self-produced object. The red drink is the quintessential sweet drink inasmuch as it is considered by consumers to be in fact the drink highest in sugar content. The Indian population is also generally supposed to be particularly fond of sugar and sweet products and this in turn is supposed to relate to their entry into Trinidad largely as indentured labourers in the sugar cane fields. They are also supposed to have a high rate of diabetes which folk wisdom claims to be a result of their overindulgence of these preferences.

The present connotation of the red drink contains this element of nostalgia. Partly there is the reference to older red drinks such as the Jaleel's original "red spot". There is also the presence of the common flavour "Kola Champagne" which is itself merely a red sweet drink.[3] Adverts that provide consumption shots will most often refer to a "red and a roti" as the proper combination; the implication being that non-Indians also would most appropriately take a red drink with their roti when eating out, since the roti[4] has become a general "fast food" item that appeals to all communities within Trinidad.

The centrality of the black sweet drink to Trinidadian drinking is above all summed up in the notion of a "rum and Coke" as the core alcoholic drink for most people of the island. This is important as rum is never drunk neat or simply on the rocks but always with some mixer. Coke does not stand on this relationship alone, however. The concept of the "black" sweet drink as something to be drunk in itself is nearly as common as the "red" sweet drink. Coke is probably the most common drink to be conceptualized as the embodiment of the "black" sweet drink, but any black drink will do. This is most evident at the cheapest end of the market. In a squatting community where I worked, a local product from a nearby industrial estate called "bubble up" was the main drink. This company simply produced two drinks: a black (which it did not even bother calling a cola) and a red. People would go to the parlour and say "gimme a black" or "gimme a red". At this level Coke becomes merely a high status example of the black sweet drink of my title.

This distinction between drinks relates in part to the general discourse of ethnicity that pervades Trinidadian conversation and social interaction (see Yelvington 1993). Thus an Indian talked of seeing Coke as a more white and "white oriented people" drink. The term "white oriented" is here a synonym for Black African Trinidadians. Many Indians assume that Africans have a much greater aptitude for simply emulating white taste and customs to become what is locally termed "Afro-Saxons". Africans in turn would refute this and claim that while they lay claim to white culture Indians are much more deferential to white persons.

Similarly an African informant suggested that "[a certain] Cola is poor quality stuff. It would only sell in the South, but would not sell in the North". The implication here is that sophisticated Africans would not drink this substitute for "the real thing", while Indians generally accept lower quality goods. In many respects there is a sense that Black culture has replaced colonial culture as mainstream while it is Indians that represent cultural difference. Thus a white executive noted that in terms of advertising spots on the radio "we want an Indian programme, since marketing soft drinks has become very ethnic".

The semiotic may or may not become explicit. One of the most successful local advertising campaigns in the sweet drink industry to occur during the period of fieldwork was for Canada Dry, which was marketed not as a ginger ale but as the "tough soft drink". The advert was produced in

179

two versions. One had a black cowboy shooting at several bottles, as on a range, and finding that Canada Dry deflected his bullets. The other had an American Indian having his tomahawk blunted by this brand, having smashed the others. As the company told me, the idea was to cover the diversity of communities and the (as it were) "red" Indian was adopted only after marketing tests had shown that there would be empathy and not offence from the South Asian Indian community of Trinidad.

I do not want to give the impression that there is some simple semiotic relationship between ethnicity and drinks. What has been described here is merely the dominant association of these drinks, red with Indian, black with African. This does not, however, reflect consumption. Indeed marketing research shows that if anything a higher proportion of Indians drink Colas, while Kola champagne as a red drink is more commonly drunk by Africans. Many Indians explicitly identify with Coke and its modern image. This must be taken into account when comprehending the associated advertising. In many respects the "Indian" connoted by the red drink today is in some ways the African's more nostalgic image of how Indians either used to be or perhaps still should be. It may well be therefore that the appeal of the phrase "a red and a roti" is actually more to African Trinidadians, who are today avid consumers of roti. Meanwhile segments of the Indian population have used foreign education and local commercial success to sometimes overtrump the African population in their search for images of modernity and thus readily claim an affinity with Coke.

In examining the connotations of such drinks we are not therefore exploring some coded version of actual populations. Rather, as I argued in more detail elsewhere (Miller 1994: 257–90), both ethnic groups and commodities are better regarded as objectifications that are used to create and explore projects of value for the population. These often relate more to aspects or potential images of the person than actual persons. What must be rejected is the argument of those debating about "postmodernism" that somehow there is an authentic discourse of persons and this is reduced through the inauthentic field of commodities. Indeed such academics tend to pick on Coca-Cola as their favourite image of the superficial globality that has replaced these local arguments.

Nothing could be further from the Trinidadian case. Here Coca-Cola both as brand and in its generic form as "black" sweet drink becomes an image that develops as much through the local contradictions of popular culture as part of an implicit debate about how people should be. If one grants that the red sweet drink stands for an image of Indianness then its mythic potential (as in Lévi-Strauss 1966) emerges. This is an image of Indianness with which some Indians will identify, some will not, and more commonly some will identify with only on certain occasions. But equally for Africans and others the identity of being Trinidadian includes this presence of Indian as a kind of "otherness" which at one level they define themselves against, but at a superordinate level they incorporate as an essential part of their Trinidadianness. The importance of the ethnicity ascribed to drinks is that individual non-Indians cannot literally apply a piece of Indianness to themselves to resolve this contradiction of alterity. Instead they can consume mythic forms which in their ingestion in a sense provide for an identification with an otherness which therefore "completes" this aspect of the drinker's identity. To summarize the attraction of such adverts is that Africans drinking a red sweet drink consume what for them is a highly acceptable image of Indianness that is an essential part of their sense of being Trinidadian.

Ethnicity is only one such dimension, where Coca-Cola as myth resolves a contradiction in value. Drinks also carry temporal connotations. Coke retains a notion of modernness fostered by its advertising. But it has actually been a presence in Trinidad for several generations. It has therefore become an almost nostalgic, traditional image of being modern. For the Indians or indeed for any group where the desire not to lose a sense of tradition is complemented by a desire to feel modern, this is then an objectification of the modern that is literally very easily ingested. Solo retains its high market share precisely because it provides the opposite polarity. Although as a mass product it is less old than Coke, it is perceived as nostalgic. The Solo returnable is the old squat variety of glass bottle, and I cannot count the number of times I was regaled with the anecdote about how this was the bottle used a generation before to give babies their milk in. The desire for particular commodities are often like myth (following Lévi-Strauss 1966, rather than Roland Barthes 1973) an attempt to resolve contradictions in society and identity. This is nothing new; it is exactly the conclusion Marchand (1985) comes to with regard to his excellent study of advertising in the USA in the 1930s.

Consumption v. production

These are just examples from the complex context of consumption which often frustrate the producers who are looking for a consistency in the population that they can commoditize. The problem was evident in a conversation with a Coke executive. He started by noting with pleasure a survey suggesting that the highly sophisticated advertising campaign currently being run by Coke was actually the most popular campaign at that time. But he then noted that what came second was a very amateur-looking ad for Det insecticide which had a particularly ugly calypsonian frightening the insects to death. His problem was in drawing conclusions from this survey that he could use for marketing.

In discussing this issue of production's articulation with consumption, it is hard to escape the constant question of "active" or "passive" consumers, i.e. how far consumers themselves determined the success of particular commodities. For example, I do not believe that the idea that sweet drinks are considered a basic necessity to be the result of a successful company promotion that results in people "wasting" their money on what "ought" to be a superfluous luxury. Nor was it an invention by government that became accepted. This assertion as to the past autonomy of the consumer derives partly from historical evidence in this case but also on the basis of what can be observed of the response to current campaigns.

Perhaps the primary target of soft drink advertising in 1988–9 was the return of the returnable bottle. Here what was at issue was precisely the industry attempting to second-guess the consumer's concern, in this case for thrift and price. The industry reasoned that its own profitability would be best served by trying to save the consumer money. But it was the executives who felt that the public "ought" to respond to the depths of recession by favouring the returnable bottle. The problem was that despite heavy advertising by more than one company, the consumers seemed unwilling to respond to what all the agencies were loudly announcing to be the inevitable movement in the market. The campaigns were generally a failure, especially given that they were intended to collude with a trend rather than "distort" public demand.

Companies can, of course, often respond well to complexity. They also compensate for those attributes that have become taken for granted. Thus Jaleel as a highly localized company used the most global style high-quality advertising, while Coke often tried to compensate for its given globality by emphasizing its links to Trinidad through sponsorship of a multitude of small regional events or organizations.

That, however, a gulf can exist between producer and consumer context is most evident when each rests upon different conceptualizations of the drinks. A prime example is the distinction between the sweet drink and the soft drink. Localisms such as sweet drink are not necessarily fostered by company executives who come from a different social milieu, and whose social prejudices often outweigh some abstract notion of profitability. The producers are part of an international cosmopolitanism within which high sugar content is increasingly looked upon as unhealthy. In connection with this, sweetness increasingly stands for vulgarity and in some sense older outdated traditions. The executives would wish to see themselves, by contrast, as trying to be in the vanguard of current trends.

There were, therefore, several cases of companies trying to reduce the sugar content of their drinks, and finding this resulted in complaints and loss of market share. As a result the sugar content remains in some cases extremely high. A good proportion of the cases of failure in the market that were recorded during fieldwork seemed to be of drinks with relatively high juice content and low sugar content. As one executive noted, "we can do 10 per cent fruit as in Caribbean Cool. We are following the international trend here to higher juice, but this is not a particularly popular move within Trinidad. Maybe because it not sweet enough".

Indeed while the executives consider the drinks in relation to the international beverages market, this may not be entirely correct for Trinidad. The term "sweet" as opposed to "soft" drink may have further connotations. The food category of "sweets" and its associated category of chocolates is here a much smaller domain in the market than is found in many other areas such as Europe or the USA. Although sweets are sold in supermarkets and parlours they do not seem to be quite as ubiquitous as in many other countries and there are virtually no sweet shops *per se*. Given that the most important milk drink is actually chocolate milk, there is good reason to see drinks as constituting as much the local equivalent of the sweets and chocolates domain of other countries as of their soft drinks. But once again this emerges only out of the consumption context and one would have a hard time trying to convince local Trinidadian executives that they might actually be selling in liquid form that which other countries sell as solids.

It is this that justifies the point made earlier that to endeavour to investigate a commodity in its local context, there are actually two such contexts, one of production and distribution and the other of consumption. These are not the same and they may actually contradict each other to a surprising extent. There is an important general point here in that Fine and Leopold (1993) have argued with considerable force that consumption studies have suffered by failing to appreciate the importance of the link to production which may be specific to each of what they call "systems of provision", i.e. domains such as clothing, food and utilities. What this case study shows is that while production and consumption should be linked, they may be wrong to assume that this is because each domain evolves its own local consistency as an economic process. Quite often they do not.

The reason that this is possible is that, although the formal goal of company practice is profitability, there are simply too many factors that can easily be blamed for the failures of campaigns. At best companies have marketing information such as blind tests on particular brands, and point-of-sale statistics. But even this information is little used except as *post-hoc* justification for decisions that are most often based on the personal opinions and generalized "gut" feelings of the key executives. Given peer pressure based on often irrelevant knowledge of the international beverage market, producers often manage to fail to capitalize on developments in popular culture that are available for commoditization.

Similarly consumers do not regard companies as merely functional providers. In a small island such as Trinidad consumers often have decided views, prejudices, and experiences with regard to each particular company as well as their products. As such the reaction of consumers to a particular new flavour may be determined in large measure by those factors that make the consumer feel that it is or is not the "appropriate" firm with which to associate this flavour. So there are cases of several firms trying out a new flavour until one succeeds. What the ethnography suggests is that there are often underlying reasons that one particular company's flavour tasted right.

Conclusion

This case study has attempted to localize production and consumption separately and in relation to each other. The effect has been one of relativism, using ethnography to insist upon the local contextualization of a global form. It follows that Coke consumption might be very different elsewhere. Gillespie (1995: 191–7) has analyzed the response to Coke among a group of West London youths from families with South Asian origins. The attraction to Coke is if anything greater in London than in Trinidad, but the grounds are quite different. In London, where immigration from South Asia is a much more recent experience, the focus was on the portrayal of the relative freedom enjoyed by youth in the USA as a state to be envied and emulated. There is no local contextualization to the consumption of the drink comparable to Trinidad. Furthermore the primary emphasis in London was on the advertisements rather than the drink itself.

The point of engaging in these demonstrations of relativism was declared at the beginning of this chapter to be an attempt to confront the dangers of Coke as meta-symbol. I confess I wanted to localize Coke partly because I was disenchanted with tedious anecdotes, often from academics, about Coke and global homogenization and sensed that the kind of glib academia that employed such anecdotes was possibly serving a rather more sinister end.

Anthropology seemed a useful tool in asserting the importance of a posteriori diversity in the specificity of particular capitalisms. A critical appraisal of capitalism requires something beyond the lazy term that ascribes it a purity of instrumentality in relation to profitability as goal seeking which does not usually bear closer inspection, any more than kinship can be reduced to biology. I therefore felt that prior to embarking upon a reformulated critique of capitalism it was important first to encounter capitalism as a comparative practice, not just a formal economistic logic (see Miller 1997).

But such a point could be made with many commodities. Coke is special because of its particular ability to objectify globality. This chapter has not questioned this ability, it has argued only that globality is itself a localized image, held within a larger frame of spatialized identity. As has been shown within media studies (Morley 1992: 270–89), an image of the global is not thereby a universal image. The particular place of globality and its associated modernity must be determined by local setting. Indeed Caribbean peoples with their extraordinarily transnational families and connections juxtaposed with often passionate local attachments well exemplify such contradictions in the terms "local" and "global". Trinidadians do not and will not choose between being American and being Trinidadian. Most reject parochial nationalism or neo-Africanized roots that threaten to diminish their sense of rights of access to global goods, such as computers or blue jeans. But they will fiercely maintain those localisms they wish to retain, not because they are hypocritical but because inconsistency is an appropriate response to contradiction.

So Coke and McDonald's are not trends, or symbolic of trends. Rather like whisky before them, they are particular images of globality that are held as a polarity against highly localized drinks such as sorrel and punch a creme, which unless you are West Indian you will probably not have heard of. Mattelart's (1991) *Advertising international* showed the commercially disastrous result when Saatchi & Saatchi believed its own hype about everything becoming global. The company nearly collapsed. In an English pub we would also find an extension of the range of potential spatial identifications from international or European lagers to ever more parochial "real ales". No doubt many aspiring anthropologists would choose one of the new "designer" beers which typically derive from some exotic location, such as Mexico or Malaysia where anthropologists have a distinct advantage in boring other people with claimed knowledge of the original homeland of the beer in question. The point this brings home is that semiotics without structuralism was never much use, as Coca-Cola found when it tried to change its formula and was humiliated by the consumer.

Finally we can turn back to the meta-context of this chapter, which asserts the scholarship of such contextualization against the common academic use of Coca-Cola as glib generality. There are many grounds for favouring theoretical and comparative approaches in anthropology against a tradition of ethnography as mere parochialism, which is hard to justify in and of itself. In this case, however, there are specific grounds for an ethnography of localism because here localism makes a particular point. Vanguard academics seem to view Coca-Cola as totalized, themselves as contextualized. This chapter shows, by example, how ordinary vulgar mass consumption is proficient in sublating the general form back into specificity. By contrast, in much of the academic discussion of post-modernism as also in political rhetoric we find the totalizing of Coca-Cola as a meta-symbol. This discourse when detached from its historical and localized context comes to stand for the kind of anti-enlightenment irrationalism and aestheticism that was once the main instrument used by fascism against the rationalist tradition of the enlightenment. The point is not dissimilar to Habermas's (1987) argument in *The philosophical discourse of modernity* against these same trends in modern academic thought.

The concept of meta-symbol certainly fits postmodern assertions about nothing referring to anything in particular any more. I do not accept at all that this is true for commodities such as Coke when investigated in production or consumption contexts, although this is what the academic asserts. But it might just be true of the way academics themselves use the image of Coke. First accepting its globality in a simple sense, Coke then becomes a general Capitalism, Imperialism, Americanization, etc. Then in discussions of postmodernism it may emerge as a kind of generalized symbol standing for the existence in commodities of a level of irrationalized meta-symbolic life (Featherstone 1991 provides a summary of these kinds of academic discussions). This parallels what Quinn (1994) sees happening to the swastika:

> Returning to the definition of the swastika as the "sign of non-signability", we can see that here the image comes to represent the symbolic realm or the symbolic process per se, as a meta-symbol or "symbol of symbolism", a status that Aryanism reflected by naming the image as the "symbol of symbols" set apart from all others and representable only by itself (Quinn 1994: 57).

Both the Coca-Cola corporation but even more a trend in academics and politics would wish to push Coca-Cola onto this kind of plateau. In collusion with the drinkers that consume it and often the local companies that bottle it, this chapter is intended to form part of a counter movement that would push Coca-Cola downwards back into the muddy dispersed regions of black sweet drinks.

Notes

1. The material for this chapter is taken in part from a larger study of business in Trindad called *Capitalism: an ethnographic aproach* (Miller 1997), which contains a wider discussion of the industry, while this chapter draws out the specific implications of Coca-Cola. A full acknowledgement of those who assisted in this project is contained in that volume. A version of this chapter has also been published in Danish in the journal *Tendens*.
2. At the time the exchange rate was approximately TT$4.25 to US$1.
3. This particular marketing ploy of calling fizzy drinks champagne is found in Britain in the nineteenth century, when drinks were made from a syrup called twaddle. This may well be the origin of the expression 'a load of twaddle', a fact entirely unrelated to the rest of this chapter!
4. Roti is the traditional Indian unleavened bread, sold in Trinidad wrapped around some other food to make a meal.

References

Barthes, R. 1973. *Mythologies*. London: Paladin.

de Boissiere, R. 1984. *Rum and Coca-Cola*. London: Alison & Busby.

Featherstone, M. 1991. *Consumer culture and postmodernism*. London: Sage.

Felstead, A. 1993. *The corporate paradox*. London: Routledge.

Fine, B. & E. Leopold 1993. *The world of consumption*. London: Routledge.

Gillespie, M. 1995. *Television, ethnicity and cultural change*. London: Routledge.

Habermas, J. 1987. *The philosophical discourse of modernity*. Cambridge, MA: MIT Press.

Lévi-Strauss, C. 1966. *The savage mind*. London: Weidenfeld & Nicolson.

Macmillan, A. 1922. *The red book of the West Indies*. London: Collingridge.

Marchand, R. 1985. *Advertising the American dream*. Berkeley: University of California Press.

Mattelart, A. 1991. *Advertising international*. London: Routledge.

Miller, D. 1994. *Modernity: an ethnographic approach*. Oxford: Berg.

Miller, D. 1997. *Capitalism: an ethnographic approach*. Oxford: Berg.

Morley, D. 1992. *Television audiences and cultural studies*. London: Routledge.

Naipaul, V.S. 1967. *The mimic men*. Harmondsworth: Penguin.

O'Barr, W. 1989. The airbrushing of culture. *Public Culture* **2**(1), 1–19.

Oliver, T. 1986. *The Real Coke: the real story*. London: Elm Tree.

Pendergrast, M. 1993. *For God, country and Coca-Cola*. London: Weidenfeld & Nicolson.

Quinn, M. 1994. *The swastika*. London: Routledge.

Tollison, R., D. Kaplan, R. Higgins (eds.) 1986. *Competition and concentration: the economics of the carbonated soft drink industry*. Lexington, MA: Lexington Books.

Yelvington, K. (ed.) 1993. *Trinidad ethnicity*. London: Macmillan.

CHAPTER 9

Signs of the new nation: gift exchange, consumption and aid on a former collective farm in north-west Estonia

Sigrid Rausing

The transformation of the former Soviet Union is to a large extent defined by changes in material culture, or in other words by changes in the culturally constituted relationships to objects. The desire for consumption tends to be taken for granted in the West, albeit often with the added assumption that the increased availability of goods constitutes a kind of banalization, or vulgarization, of culture.[i] This chapter, focusing on a local and specific context, constitutes an investigation of the appropriation of Western objects on a former collective farm on a remote peninsula in Estonia. I shall argue that the present transformations of the notions of exchange, material success and national identity are to an important extent articulated in terms of the relationships to Western objects, within the wider context of the move towards independence and a market economy.

While local discourses about the changes were essentially ambivalent during the time of my fieldwork, since they were associated with an increase in poverty and unemployment as well as with national independence, the change in material culture was primarily characterized by a move towards a Western and particularly a Scandinavian and Finnish style. These changes were experienced differently by me and my informants. What to me looked increasingly familiar, powerfully speeding up my own sense of getting used to living in the community, to them was fairly recent, representing a foreign and deliberate style, accessible primarily through aid from Sweden. Virtually everybody in the community, for example, wore Swedish clothes, donated by charitable organizations. To me, these clothes looked so ordinary – jeans and T-shirts, with the non-committal patina of everyday life – that it took some time to understand their local context. Photographs of just a few years ago, however, revealed a style that was radically different: boys in caps and blue uniforms, girls in white shirts and pinafores; men in flared gabardine trousers, women in tight skirts. For the people in the community, then, the Swedish clothes were still situated on the cusp between the foreign and the normal, whereas for me their "ordinariness" acted as a somewhat deceptive sign situating the people and the culture in the western/ northern European rather than the Soviet sphere.

Given, however, the nominal "Western-ness" of Estonians within the Soviet context, the appropriation of the new style is complex. It represents the "normal" as a normative referent defined in terms of north-west Europe. To extend the example of the clothes, although a pair of jeans has acquired the status of "normal" very recently, the knowledge that such clothes are "normal" in the West, combined with their present easy availability through aid shipments, means that they are genuinely not regarded as special any more. "Normality" as a term, however, still does not tend to represent the "normal" as in the everyday, but rather a state of what should have been had Estonia not been incorporated into the Soviet Union, and what must now be worked for. Appropriately, then, the dissolution of the Soviet Union means that the national discourse of future goals has shifted from a Utopian social state, to a Western-identified "normality". The confines of being defined as Western within the Soviet context, however, means that the changes in material culture are greeted with less of the surprise, enthusiasm, or confusion, than might be expected: the "normal"/optimal reaction to the new things is a silent appropriation, redefining the objets as already taken for granted.

Western objects in Estonia, then, are contextualized within a series of historical trajectories and ideologies. Following Nicholas Thomas (1991), the assumption throughout this chapter is that objects have no essential meaning, but rather are understood through various appropriations and recontextualizations. Global economies do not control the meaning of commodities: they provide entanglements (Thomas 1991: 123). Similarly, the appropriation of Western objects in Estonia cannot be understood simply as part of a wider process of globalization: local meanings, and particularly the notion of "normality", frame and modify the appropriations of the global. In the context of doing fieldwork in an area undergoing drastic change, the theoretical preference of context over essence seems particularly appropriate.

In this chapter, then, I shall look at the local contextualizations of a number of different Western objects, ranging from locally avaliable consumer goods, products like corn flakes or washing powder, to objects donated from Sweden, which themselves range widely from agricultural machinery to clothes and various household objects. I shall consider the contexts and appropriation of these objects in relation to the transitional and ambivalent position of Estonia, which historically and geographically is located between east and west, as well as at local constructions of wealth and success. Both the concepts of national identity and success were highly objectified in the Soviet Union. Nationality was predominantly seen as an ethnic identification, usually associated with particular republics or areas of land, encompassed by the concept of citizenship in the USSR (Smith 1990; Haida & Beissinger 1990; Bremmer & Taras 1993; Lieven 1993: xxiii). Material success in the Soviet context was generally perceived as entangled in a nexus of underhand dealings and speculation, where to some extent it still lingers (cf. Humphrey 1995: 61). The association between commerce and criminality is also of course emphasized by the spectacular post-Soviet expansion of Mafia-type organizations.[2] The particular Estonian objectification of success also includes a process of differentiation from the Russians, as well as other Soviet peoples referred to by the term "Caucasians", including the Georgians and the Armenians, who are commonly regarded as both more "mercenary" and less "civilized" than the Estonians. This process of distinction acts to further underline the negative aspects of material success.

After briefly describing the setting of the collective farm, this chapter consists of three related sections. It begins with a section on local concepts of gift exchange and trade, which includes a consideration of the ambivalence surrounding material aspirations and success. Following on from this, I look at the local consumption of Western objects, focusing on the question of how the concept of being in some sense "already Western" frames the appropriation of the new objects. The last, and longest, section is concerned with the aid coming from Sweden, looking in particular at the effects of the twin town agreement made with Åtvidaberg, a small town in the middle of Sweden. This relationship is framed by the fact that about half of the population in the area before the Second World War was Swedish. The Estonian Swedes, about 8,000 people, had inhabited the islands and coastal areas of north-west Estonia since at least the thirteenth century. Before the war, a wave of Swedish ethnographic and media investigations of these people, whose isolation and poverty were supposed to have protected their culture from industrial modernity, was paralleled by a nation-wide campaign to help to alleviate the poverty of the Estonian Swedes.[3] The peninsula where I worked was one of the main centres of this revival, adding to the privatization of the collective farm the transformation of the area from the Soviet Estonian to the Estonian Swedish.

In this section the focus will be on how the giving and the receiving of the aid is framed by two separate cultures, both of which have certain claims to kinship with each other, which are at least partially differently defined, with equally tenuous roots and expectations. The aid project, then, forms the focus of this part of the chapter, which also builds on the data of the previous two sections. The focus remains on the material culture, exploring the complex relationship between the Estonians and the Swedes through an analysis of the various relationships to the aid objects. It would be wrong, however, to regard these objects simply as mediums of exchange. Like all the objects considered in this chapter, they embody particular memories, aspirations and ideologies, which means that there is nothing accidental about what is given: in this sense, the objects given incorporate, as well as constitute, the project of aid.

The collective farm

In February 1993 the collective farm, named, like hundreds of farms throughout the Soviet empire, after Lenin, ended.[4]

In 1949, collectivization was carried out throughout Estonia, establishing a high number of small collective farms, most of which were created on the basis of existing villages. The peninsula where the farm was located was defined as a border protection zone, and was therefore isolated from casual visitors. There was a checkpoint on the only road out, where papers were checked, and there were troops stationed in some barracks at the site of a ruined manor house outside one of the villages. In November 1993 the relatively new sign for the collective farm, renamed the *Noarootsi Kolhoos* was finally replaced by a sign for a new bank that had opened a branch in the village. Illustrating much of the contemporary process of change, although the new sign remained, the branch itself closed down within a few weeks.

Pürksi, with a population of 323, was the only village on the peninsula that had increased its population since the war. It formed the centre of the collective farm, housing certain standardized functions, including the administrative office, the culture house, the crèche and the school, as well as eight blocks of flats built between the early 1960s and 1990. Spatially, the village was organized around a dusty unpaved square, formed by the school and the culture house. Also, there was an old manor house, which during Soviet times had fallen into a state of dilapidation and which was under renovation during the time of my fieldwork, in order to be turned into an annexe for the school.[5] In addition to this, the old village of Pürksi included some ten old farms, spread out in the surrounding area. In the Soviet era there was also a dairy, defunct since the 1970s, and a small shop placed next to it. This shop, the old co-operative, now had to compete with the new, private, farm shop, housed in one of the old workshops. While the new one concentrated on food and a small café operation, the old one also sold household stuff, pots and pans, exercise books, shoes if they got an assignment. It was altogether a more Soviet space, with Russian jars of jam and pickles with rusty lids and falling-off labels and a dusty shelf by the big glass window where the alcoholic old men sat and drank. The distinction between the two, however, tended not to be expressed in terms of one being "private" and the other "Soviet". Both were described as "co-operatives", the old one belonging to a county-wide chain, or system, of collective farm shops, while for the new one the term was strictly nominal, stemming from the interim period between 1989 and 1991 when free enterprise was allowed in the Soviet Union under the label of "co-operatives". Both, also, were predominantly seen as communal services and were supposed to be acting in the interests of the community as a whole.

Exchange

Western objects in Estonia are contextualized within a number of historical trajectories and ideologies encompassing a particular cultural system of gift exchange. Local conceptions of gift exchange are deeply entangled in notions of egalitarianism and balance, embedded both in Soviet socialism, and in notions of "the north", and Scandinavian egalitarianism. The emphasis on equality and balance, as well as the fact that the Soviet economic system was dependent on extensive informal barter, means that the requirement of reciprocity is important. Ideally, as in all systems of gift exchange, there should always be a balance between giving and receiving (Mauss 1990). An imbalance in gift exchange, including the gift of inappropriate objects, marking hierarchy by giving too much or escaping obligations by giving too little, is perceived as embarrassing both to the giver and the receiver. It should be emphasized that, on my field site, the obligation to reciprocate was a powerful social rule. Invitations to coffee, for example, which constituted the most common form of formal social events, were reciprocated with small presents, for example of packets of biscuits or, in spring and summer, flowers. Bringing gifts to informants on the farm, for example of imported fruit bought in Tallinn, or biscuits from the shop, was always a delicate matter, since they usually felt compelled to give me something of equal worth back. Since the fruit was expensive I was sometimes overwhelmed with boxes of Estonian sweets or chocolate, or even crocheted table mats or decorations, objects which, to a Western way of reckoning, were far more valuable than a few oranges or kiwi fruit. This was a complex gift exchange, formed by the evolving dictates of two different economies, so that the value of the reciprocation was always approximate and uncertain.

Partly the emphasis on reciprocation was due to the detrimental effects of the Soviet system on the economy. In many ways the gift exchanges I observed had more in common with systems of barter, primarily because there was no in-built inflation of the system: my informants expected returns of equivalent rather than of higher value (Mauss 1990: 28, 42). In this context, the categories of barter and gift exchange were merged, linking culturally constituted relationships with economic rationality, supporting recent arguments concerning the nature of barter as a social form mixing the economic with the cultural (Humphrey & Hugh-Jones 1992). One of the most striking differences between the Soviet and Western economic systems concerns the role of friendship and kinship networks. The importance of economic reciprocity and balance within those networks was linked to economic necessity, and constitutes one of the many unforeseen side effect of the economic system. Du Plessix Gray (1991) in her book on Soviet women quotes from an interview with a writer, who states that

> Friendship is a most important and dangerous thing in our country. Of course it's far more valuable in our culture than in yours – Russians have little else, even if we have money there is nothing to buy with it, only friends can help you locate decent food, clothes, basic comforts, friendship is a central aid to survival. (du Plessix Gray 1991: 177)

The Soviet economic system, then, of the so-called "second world", was industrialized but not fully monetary in the sense that barter, bribes and gift exchange played more important, less separable, roles than in the West.

In Estonia, after the relative prosperity from the late 1960s to the middle of the 1970s, a period of economic stagnation followed that meant real shortages, long queues, commonplace bribes to shop assistants and, consequently, an increasing reliance on family and friends (Taagepera 1993: 98–101). The pre-war economy, which was primarily based on agriculture mixed with light industry, meant that most urban native Estonians still had relatives with private plots on the collective farms. The produce, typically apples, potatoes and cabbage, supplemented with onions and perhaps berries and mushrooms from the forests, was brought to the towns within those family networks, usually in return for shop products or other favours. A substantial part of the economy, then, operated on informal barter and gift exchange systems within kinship and friendship networks, as well as an illegal but normalized system of bribes outside of these networks.

Some of my informants complained that whereas "before",[6] if you asked somebody for a favour, say a lift to the next village, they would do it in the expectation of a deferred return favour, whereas "now" people wanted immediate payment in the form of money. Parts of the barter/gift exchange, then, which was an important form of exchange in the Soviet system, are now becoming monetarized. The at least potential acceleration in the speed of transactions which comes with monetarization was generally perceived as involving a loss of communal affection: in the previous system reciprocity was delayed enough to at least sometimes be viewed as disinterested kindness. In a parallell process, the long periods of waiting in various queues that were an intrinsic part of the Soviet system – housing queues, hour-long lines for the shops, year-long waiting lists for the purchase of furniture or cars – were also disappearing. During the time of my fieldwork the housing waiting list was the only queue that was, at least partially, still in force. The abolition of waiting as a daily form of social activity mirrors, then, the less positive decrease in the delayed form of reciprocity in favour of a cash-based, more immediate, form.

One of the consequences of the economic changes was a visible process of wealth polarization. The most noticeable aspect of this was not that certain people were ascending – the people who were going up were always people who had done well during the collective farm as well, and who were generally considered capable – but that other people were descending. In particular, there was a category of people who were regarded as eccentrics, usually alcoholic men who were seen as interesting characters, whose implicit and anarchic evasion of the power of the state in the Soviet context gave them a certain, if ambivalent, status. This status was now rapidly diminishing. The fall of the Soviet Union had ended what association there was between alcoholism and resistance, and the end of the subsidies of the collective farm meant that they had to be supported by direct taxation on their neighbours rather than by a state that most people were at least to some extent resisting.[7]

If the question of the previous system was inherently controversial, the notion of the cultural proximity to Sweden and Finland represented the opposite: a unifying discourse of national identity. It was frequently mentioned as a factor that differentiated the Estonians not only from the Russians, but also from other Soviet peoples such as the Georgians or the Azerbaidzhanis. The notions of balance, tranquillity and egalitarianism were central to the concepts of Scandinavia and "the North". The balance indicates equality and harmony, important features both in the Estonian, and also to a large extent the Soviet *mentalités*. People must be in harmony with themselves, both in terms of body and mind. In Estonia, the conception of what the national characteristics of the Estonians are, is to a large extent defined by what the Russians supposedly are not. While the Russians, then, are regarded as overly dramatic, given to flattery and falsehood, the Estonians tend to see themselves as quiet, honest and hard-working. Essentially romantic notions of "the North", contemplation of nature, and a mistrust of commerciality are also prevalent. The care with which everything is fairly calculated, and the ambivalence regarding entrepreneurship, are also indicative of the centrality of balance. Estonians are both wary of being ripped off (by non-Estonians, probably), and careful not to charge too much, and to do a proper job for the money.

Despite the government's commitment to the free market, the people who have made good, the *tõusik*, are often seen as somehow less "Estonian" in people's imagination; very smart and with dangerous connections. Even the people who are generally positive towards them tend to see them as a special type with certain inherited characteristics; the "have a nose for it", the *"Fingerspitzengefühl"* . They seem already to belong to another imaginary entity that is only partially contained by the entity of Estonia, and peopled, otherwise, by Russians and the so-called Caucasians.[8] For example, during the time of my fieldwork, there was a new Estonian series following the adventures of a newly rich family, followed largely because of its provocative nature. It displayed people who were clearly modelled on TV series such as *Dallas*, being at the same time rich, glamorous and bad. While these categories are not perhaps entirely fused in the American context, in Estonia the wealth firmly implies both badness and glamour, in that order. Arguably the family represented the antithesis of what was generally seen as "good": rich and flamboyant, with frequent dealings with

195

the criminal world, they represented the ambivalent nature of success expressed in the identity of the *tõusik,* or the newly rich.

Consumption

Before the currency reform in 1992, when the Kroon was introduced as the only legal tender in Estonia, the economy was divided into an eastern and a western zone. The hard currency stores, which during the Soviet times had been limited to a few, had multiplied, and still carried almost only Western goods, whereas the old shops tended to sell only Eastern bloc produce. Even though this strict division does not exist any more, the price differential between formerly Soviet and Western goods was still considerable during the time of my fieldwork, and of course the packaging acted a sign of origins. In September 1993, for instance, the average monthly wage was 800 Kroons (about £40); a local purchase of 2 kilos potatoes, 1 loaf of bread, 1 cabbage and 0.5 litre of milk cost 9 Kroons, or 45 pence. In comparison, a bottle of poor French wine from the supermarket in the nearest town cost 65–90 Kroons, while a tin of cheap instant coffee cost at least 30 Kroons and Nescafé about 50. Despite the considerable price difference, however, some of my informants were willing to consume, for example, corn flakes, the cost of which represented about six hours of average work, while at the same time expressing concern about their shortage of money. In that context, Western products effectively represented markers for the return to (national) "normality", where individual consumption also represented collective change.

The term "normality" connoted a powerful means of situating Estonia in the West. It tended to be used by people who were relatively successful in the new state, usually had contacts abroad, and who strongly identified with the new nation. "Not normal" for those people was the usual definition of life in the Soviet Union, the statement of collective, or national, abnormality often juxtaposed with a statement about the meaninglessness of Soviet work, immersed in symbolism rather than "normal" rationality. Without wishing to minimize the difficulties and frustrations of the Soviet system, this was also a way for people to situate themselves on the West within Western-ness; a way of acknowledging that although Estonia was by nature Western there were also degrees of Western-ness within Estonia itself. It was part of a system of distinction where the notion of Western-ness was associated with success, which in itself was entangled in a nexus of difficulties and ambivalence.

The world of goods in this region, as in any other, was bound up with questions of identity, and particularly, perhaps, with questions of national and class identity. One would therefore expect a considerable difference between the Russian and the Estonian experience of the new goods, and that indeed seems to be the case. Humphrey (1995) describes how in 1993 Western goods in Moscow, although initially desirable, were also inherently suspect, less clean, organic and trustworthy than Russian goods. In a consumer mirage of the contingent ideology of the land and nationalism, she describes how her middle-class Moscow host family preferred "our fatherland butter" over a US brand, how Western salami was assumed to be spiced with unhealthy chemicals, and how, generally, Western products at the time tended to be seen as unassimilable and contaminated (Humphrey 1995: 54, 58).

These perceptions were noticeably different in Estonia, where Western goods tended to be categorized as "normal", while products made in the former Soviet Union were often suspected of being polluted by chemicals or Chernobyl radiation. Although the display of "Western-ness" was problematic, as will be discussed, it also signified important contacts abroad. Hence Western objects, which had been given by relatives or visitors, were common features of the home. They tended to be utilitarian in nature, such as books, bottles of vitamins, or toothpaste, and to be recontextualized as essentially decorative items. Foreign books, for example, often occupied prime positions in the ubiquitous wall units, and collections of empty bottles of Western shampoo decorated the bathroom shelves. As with the Western clothes, the objects occupied a shifting and ambivalent position somewhere in the middle between the low-grade Soviet and the special and hand-made Estonian, which, importantly, was still regarded with a high degree of national pride.

Informants sometimes stated that there was no difference between Western and Estonian products – any more, they sometimes added, acknowledging the Soviet past. What this meant was that the few recent Estonian products that could successfully pass as "normal" were enlisted as representative for the newly independent republic. On the whole, however, the difference between Western and Estonian goods was actually striking, particularly in terms of the packaging. Like the gifts from abroad, Western consumer goods were references to another world, but while the status of gifts could remove an object from a primarily functional to a decorative context, Western objects bought locally tended to remain functional, emphasizing their nominal "normality". The relatively high degree of knowledge about the West meant that people were aware of the original contextualization, and how people "normally" used the products. Within the complex and ambivalent system of distinction that was currently operating, in order to fully, genuinely, come across as "Western", people therefore had to treat mass-produced Western objects bought locally with the same degree of nonchalance with which they would be treated in the West, despite the fact that the relative cost of the products was fantastical. The private shop in the village, for example, started stocking Ariel washing-powder, at a cost of about 35 Kroons, or six times as much as the local powder, which itself had increased so much in price that it represented nearly an hour's average work. Inflation, then, operated on two levels: indigenous products were rapidly becoming more expensive as subsidies were removed, at the same time as foreign products took some part of the market share at far higher prices. The high cost did not, however, mean that Ariel was treated like an exclusive designer product. People knew that it was "normal" to use such powders, and it tended, therefore, to be appropriated in the Estonian context as equally "normal", its superiority defined in strictly functional terms.

There was also a category of products that had been bought on journeys to Sweden or, more likely, Finland, at a time when the availability of the goods in question was doubtful in Estonia. Consequently, people who had been abroad regularly (53 per cent of the population of the village had been abroad at least once) tended to keep obsolete stockpiles at home of flour, pasta, rice or soap, all things that were now available at a lower price in Estonia than in Finland. These stockpiles represented the Soviet economic rule that (outside the black market) objects were usually worth more than the money you paid for them. In 1993–4, the monetary policies in Estonia meant that on the whole the opposite tended to be true; there was a shortage of money, and an abundance of goods.[9] The fact that each shop could now set its own prices meant that people moved from shop to shop following much the same pattern as they did when there was a shortage of goods: instead of trying to locate the goods themselves, people were now trying to locate the cheapest goods. This tended to be true for all the countries of the former Soviet bloc. Eva Hoffman, for example, reported a Polish friend stating, "And the shopping takes longer because I have to go from place to place to compare prices. It used to be, you bought an egg, you paid for an egg. Now they all think they can charge whatever they want!" (Hoffman 1993: 7)

Aid: the relationship to Sweden

The local relationship to Sweden is built on two historical trajectories, the first being Sweden's territorial conquests in the Baltics which culminated in the seventeenth century, and ended, outside of Finland, with the Peace of Narva in 1721. The second trajectory started towards the end of the nineteenth century, and intensified during the 1920s and 1930s, when the celebration of modernism led to a related concern that what was essentially Swedish was being submerged under a wave of industrial modernity. The Swedish minority in Estonia, who mostly inhabited the poor coastal areas in the north-west, were then identified, in Sweden and to some extent in Estonia as well, as what would later be called "culture carriers", embodying a traditional national culture that was disappearing in Sweden itself (cf.

Frykman & Löfgren 1979, 1985). Also, charitable organizations were set up in Sweden in order to help to alleviate the poverty of the Estonian Swedes, who were regarded, within the discourse of aid, as part of the so-called *förskingringen,* the dissemination of Swedes abroad.

Since the majority of the Swedish Estonians (*c.* 7,000 out of a total of 8,000, in an Estonian population of about 1 million) left for Sweden during the Second World War, there are few Swedish-speaking people left in the area. Indeed, on the peninsula of Noarootsi, which before the war had a population that was about 50 per cent Swedish speaking, many of the people were descendants of Estonians resettled by the German army from the front on the farms and cottages left by the Swedes. However, in the post-Soviet context, the notion of a Swedish heritage is being revived through various means, not least through the world of material culture, and more specifically the aid, which predominantly takes the form of shipments of various donated objects, received through the twin town agreement with the Swedish town of Åtvidaberg. The revival, which is taking place primarily in Noarootsi and on the nearby island of Wormsi (Swedish Ormsö), is encouraged and promoted through a number of organizations in Sweden, notably the organization for the Estonian Swedes. The prospect of aid and the desire to leave the Soviet identity behind means that it is also promoted locally. Thus, for example, all of the people who are in positions of power in the village have learnt Swedish. The two most powerful people, the village mayor and the head of the village council, speak Swedish fluently. There is a Swedish teacher in the village, sent out by the Swedish Council, who runs well-attended adult classes as well as the classes for the school children. Nevertheless, the promotion of Swedish-ness also to some extent conforms to Soviet notions of representations, constructing a Potemkin façade behind which there is a different reality.

According to my survey, 73 per cent of the people in the village had relatives abroad, usually in Sweden, Canada, Britain or Australia. These relatives were almost all refugees from the Second World War, and many kept in touch during the Soviet years, sending food and clothes. Of the people with contacts in the West, 80 per cent also received gifts from their contacts. Needless to say, perhaps, having relatives abroad, and particularly relatives who kept in touch, tended to be treated with some suspicion in the Soviet Union. Despite the multiplicity of real connections with the West, the local discourse on Western-ness still tended to be reserved, or even left unarticulated. For people who aspired to it, it was felt to be a body of knowledge that they should already know by virtue of the "Western-ness" of Soviet Estonia. For these people there was often a sense of familiarity being enacted and displayed; a recognized strategy with uncertain limits, easily straying into what was seen by others as a form of pretentiousness. Ironically, of course, the fall of the Soviet bloc had the effect of transforming the elegant if nominal Western-ness of Estonia in the context of the Soviet

Union into the poor and under-nourished Eastern-ness of a former Soviet state in the context of the West.[10]

There was also a certain amount of pride in having no connections with the West, which was true also for the people who had relatives abroad but who had no contact with them. The pride was situated within the increasingly apparent polarization within the village, dividing those who were going up from those who were going down. Going down might be a source for despair but at least for the older generation it was also still infused with an ideological pride in poverty, in having "workers' hands", in having been a worker all one's life. For these people there was still a sense that connections with the West may threaten a person's integrity, tempting them to stoop to ingratiation or corruption. They would answer the questions in the section of the survey that had to do with contacts abroad with visible pride if they had no contacts, and with evasion and reserve if they did have contacts, particularly in regard to the question about whether they had received gifts, including money and medicine, from their contacts. For this group Hann's contention that people's perception of the failure of socialism was caused not so much by the failure of socialist ideology itself, so much as by the failure of the leaders to adhere to the ideology, rings very true (Hann 1993: xi).

The gifts from the West, for this group, tended to be received within a context of humiliation, of being a poor relation, unable to keep up the injunctions regarding the balance of gift exchange. The threat to integrity was particularly important in relation to officials from the twin town, since it was obvious that the material gain that might result from those connections went far beyond what individual Western relatives might give you, into the realm of refrigerators and washing machines, or even a new bathroom. There was one family in particular that had worked itself into the position of special hosts for the various visiting officials who would come over practically every month. Like many people in the area they were part Swedish, but completely assimilated as Estonians during the Soviet times. In a process that mirrored the process of the community as a whole, they harnessed their nominal Swedish-ness in the project of becoming hosts. This took various forms, from learning Swedish (the mother and the daughter) to enacting a kind of learnt "Swedish-ness" with the Swedes, an informal heartiness, hugging relative (Swedish) strangers, which was very far removed from the formality and irony of respectable Estonians.[11] Indeed, the fact that this family was not seen as particularly respectable – the father was a heavy drinker – was what made it a viable strategy for them to take on Swedish-ness as an identity.

In contrast, the two most respectable people in the village, the history teacher, who was also the head of the village council, and the village mayor, had next to no social contacts with the visiting officials in spite of the fact that they were more or less constantly in touch regarding the aid programme for the village. The Swedish visitors, despite being initially somewhat taken aback, tended to see this in terms of the long hours they worked, and the necessity for that important Scandinavian concept of "peace and quiet" (Gullestad 1990). In fact, however, socializing with the powerful representatives from Sweden was on the whole done only by people who were outside the mandated balance of gift exchange, since there was no way that the Swedes could ever be realistically paid back. That meant that socializing tended only to happen with people whose social status was low enough to in any case preclude them from reciprocity and hence the world of the respectable.

The head of the local school, who was married to the former director of the collective farm (now a businessman), and had also been on the collective farm board, had a lot to do with visiting Swedish groups. They always came to the school, which was transformed under her direction to a "Swedish school". The visiting Swedes were usually informally dressed, not least since the visit for them tended to be conceived in terms of a field-trip to a remote and primitive area where practical clothing was seen as the appropriate style. Informal dress in Sweden, however, has many other meanings, encompassing the sense of "ordinary Swedish-ness" that to some extent is still perceived in terms of a representation of the nation.[12] The headmistress, sensing the ideological implications of the Swedish dress-code, tended to mimic the informality, often wearing clothes during these meetings which she would never wear in a normal school day: jeans and warm sweaters, flat shoes, little or no make-up, Soviet bleached hair (which was normally elaborately puffed up) flattened and naturalized, all to the effect of enacting, or enhancing, kinship through style.

On my field site the main relationship to the West was mediated by the twin town agreement with Åtvidaberg in Sweden. Inevitably the contract was more of an adoption than a genuinely reciprocal relationship, although the actual contract, signed in March 1990, was worded in terms of careful reciprocity; aiming to further the common interests of the two localities, to create connections within culture, sports, and on the economic plane, to develop co-operation on the technical and agricultural level, and to arrange exchanges and mutual family holidays. In practice, cultural exchanges were limited to the question of the revival of the Swedish cultural heritage, and sports exchanges were non-existent. The main part of the work had developed into an extensive aid and training programme for the village. On a comparative note, there was also a genuine twin agreement originating in the Soviet times, when all the Estonian collective farms named after Lenin organized revolving sport tournaments , taking it in turn to act as hosts and putting on big parties to celebrate the event. This was one of the few ongoing traditions from that time. Unlike the Swedish events, it was barely advertised, and took place in an atmosphere that was both more festive and more relaxed.

The impulse behind the twin town agreement was the widely felt notion in Sweden that "one should do something for Estonia". One of the members of the town council, who was born in Estonia, was asked, therefore, to find a suitable town. Since his father had been the Swedish head of the agricultural college which was housed in the manor house of Birkas (Est. Pürksi) before the Second World War, and had been an instrumental figure in forging a sense of Swedish-ness among the Estonian Swedes, he went back to the same village. During the 1930s, the college had come under increasing pressure as the liberal minorities policies of the 1920s were gradually revoked in favour of widespread Estonianization. It is important to remember that the programme of aid which seems now to be at least partly enacted within a spirit of gaining some influence for Sweden in the area is also entangled in the history of the (mild) repression of the Swedish minority by the Estonian authorities. When, for example, the representatives from Åtvidaberg use the Swedish rather than the Estonian names for villages in the area, they do so in the knowledge that these names were officially banned in the 1930s. The twin town agreement therefore encompasses a rather poignant historical continuity, coincidentally illustrating the restorationist spirit of the post-Soviet republic.

There is, however, an important sense in the projects of both aid and trade of taking Estonia from the Russian to the Swedish sphere of influence, and of reclaiming a neighbour, which, like Finland and Norway, also constitutes former Swedish territories. The dominating discourse in Sweden tends to see Estonia both as poor and backwards, enmeshed in and damaged by Soviet irrationality, but, at least partially, "one of us". The concept of irrational, symbolic and low-productive working practices tends to dominate any Swedish discussion about specific post-Soviet Estonian features, although people also speak in terms of an unexpected level of suspicion, dishonesty and reserve. The discourse of aid consequently encompasses a notion that what should be given is not only objects but also rationality, including efficiency and good working practices. For example, in an early report from the Åtvidaberg committee, it is stated:

> The very varied and somewhat unpractical clothing of the workers gave birth to the thought that we should present how a Swedish employer keeps his employees with work clothes: three standard overalls, where a clean one is used on Monday, a second one goes to the laundry, and a third one is an extra hanging in the cupboard. From the Estonian side there was a great deal of interest in the thought of acquiring some fabric and information about how to make overalls, and then building a local enterprise. Help to self-help, in other words! (Report December 1990)

These concepts, as Orvar Löfgren (1991) argues, have been incorporated as part of the modernist project into the national identity of Sweden to the extent that, to Swedes, "Swedish-ness" is largely constituted by the notion of rationality (Löfgren 1991: 104).[13] Swedish business people who are investing in Estonia invariably comment on the impossibility of working with anybody over a certain age, usually somewhere between 20 and 35: they are seen as hopelessly indoctrinated by Soviet ideas and, literally, beyond hope of ever productively participating in the new economy. For example in a commercial report on Estonia written (in English) for business people thinking of investing in the country, the following is stated regarding the labour situation:

> Blue collar labour is fairly well trained and likely to do well provided led by exiled Estonians or other westerners. The hourly wages are one tenth of the German or Swedish ones. As the Estonians today (i.e. without western leadership) take double the time the net present advantage is one fifth – still considerable. Some Swedish companies are quite pleased with the hire work performed by Estonian factories. White collar labour, accommodated to years of plan and commando economy [sic], show little or no creativity, and have to be instructed in detail by westerners. Financial management is unknown. There is a lot of unnecessary in-house production (excessive vertical integration). Strong western leadership, advice and education is required. The implication of the market economy is vaguely understood – to most people it means "high living standards". The mental reorientation required is colossal. Many, sorry to say, have to be considered lost cases. One Swedish businessman went as far as to say that "don't waste your time on anyone older than 20 years – they are beyond correction." (Wachtmeister 1992: 4)

While the majority view in Sweden is that helping Estonia is an act of solidarity with a neighbour, there is also a minority view, which associates Estonia, and the other Baltic states, with war crimes and Nazi Germany. The view of Estonia as inherently suspect[14] merges into a view of it as also, simultaneously, inherently boring, and the Estonian Swedes as the epitome of the quaint traditional folk culture which combines dullness with the Heimat aesthetic redolent of the Nazis (cf. Motyl 1994). The view of Estonians as essentially unfortunate, however, is far more widespread, particularly among members of various organizations such as choirs, church groups and social clubs. The question of kinship and neighbour-hood is of central importance in the aid movement. The idea of same-ness rather than the constructed other-ness that is the basis for the large-scale state development aid encourages people to give objects from their own homes. The idea is that the objects would be appropriately recontextualized within an Estonian home, which tends to be thought of as a Swedish home with fewer objects and a lower standard. The sense of kinship, then, is a central concept in the aid movement. For example, in a letter to the village mayor from the head of the Åtvidaberg committee for Noarootsi (Swedish Nuckö), he writes about the visit of a group of students from the local school to Åtvidaberg:

> Your five students and two leaders have made excellent propaganda for Nuckö and our twin town relationship. The most important event occurred on the Eve of the First of May (Walpurgis night), when they presented themselves one by one in front of 4000–5000 people. The reaction was interesting when people discovered that they spoke Swedish, and good Swedish at that – suddenly these children were seen not as strangers but as young people who really belonged to us and our northern community. (Letter from Olle Söderbäck, 6 May 1991)[15]

The Åtvidaberg twin town agreement is by no means unique: many of the small towns and village councils in Estonia now have an agreement like the Noarootsi one. Few, however, are as active, and are so tied in with the question of the revival of the Swedish heritage. There are also frequent *ad-hoc* collections, such as the collection by a group of shift workers at a factory in the north of Sweden for a hospital in Tallinn, inspired by the high national figure for the 1991 Christmas shopping (internal report, TPPM Forshaga 1993). The group collected about £5,000, which they used for food and medicine. They were then able to collect about one and a half tons of clothes and toys from the small town where the factory is based, as well as a number of second-hand wheelchairs and other equipment from several hospitals. The high response, which surprised the organizers, is symptomatic for the movement of aid to Estonia.

One of the meanings inherent in the high level of response is the satisfaction taken in the imagined recontextualization of the objects. The journey of the objects from affluence to need symbolically enhances their value, reflecting and increasing the imagined wealth of the donor. Again, the sense of kinship, and the imagined appropriateness of the recontextualizations from the Swedish to the Estonian home must be emphasized: this is a form of kinship that is closely related to the nation and the concept of northern-ness, which partially and with some ambivalence incorporates Estonia. Any object from a Swedish home is regarded as intrinsically appropriate for an Estonian home, in a way that it would not be for, say, an Armenian or, even, Lithuanian, home. In real terms the similarity is largely imaginary. Estonian homes, particularly in the blocks of flats, are predominantly steeped in Soviet normativity which is rather different from Swedish styles. The important point for the purposes of this chapter, however, is that the Swedish donors imagine their donated objects being recontextualized appropriately, clinching the deal of the symbolically offered kinship.

As the donor is paradoxically enriched, so the recipients are symbolically impoverished. The contrast is magnified by the difference in perception of the aid: the Swedes involved in *ad-hoc* aid efforts often complained about the lack of gratitude or even co-operation from the Estonian side. For the Estonians, having to deal with the aid reflects a paradoxical transformation from being relatively well-off "Westerners" within the Soviet Union, to being impoverished "Easterners" in the context of the West. Receiving charity, disturbing the cultural injunction of balance, was essentially perceived as humiliating. There was a widespread feeling that, if anything, the Estonians should be sending charity to other countries, like Armenia or Georgia. The drive to collect clothes and blankets for the victims of the earthquake catastrophe in Armenia some years ago was often mentioned to me, sometimes with the addition that Estonia sent more blankets per head than any other Soviet nation. Being on the receiving end of a similar effort was difficult. The older students in the school where I taught, for example, were scathing about a shipment of second-hand clothes that had arrived from Sweden which they thought was of inferior quality, and therefore reflexive of the view of the Estonians in Sweden. "They must think that we run around naked here," one of them said. There was, then, a perceived insult in the gift of something so bad, things the Swedes obviously did not want themselves, but thought were good enough for the Estonians. By contrast, during the sale of a shipment of clothes and furniture in June, a local woman showed me the baby coat she had been able to buy cheaply,[16] and asked me whether I thought it would be appropriate for her to write and thank the person who had donated the coat – the baby's name and address was inside the jacket. This was clearly an impulse of gratitude, but it was also, I would argue, an attempt to redress the balance and give some-thing back, and hence to shift the context of the object from charity, which by definition is impossible to reciprocate since it paradoxically functions to institutionalize inequality, to a gift.

The programme of aid is comprehensive, including not only a large amount of agricultural and utilitarian objects, but also training programmes in Sweden for selected trainees, and a whole new central heating system that runs on wood chips, and includes a wood-chipping machine. The thinking behind the heating system self-consciously reflects the idea of Swedish social awareness, taking into account a multiplicity of factors, including the availability of badly managed woods, the environmental advantages of wood chips as compared to coal, the jobs created in the process of felling and trans-porting the trees, and the training of two local people in Sweden in how to actually build heating centres of this kind, the idea being both that it would become a model for other collective farms in Estonia, and that a local industry constructing them might be created. Also, two unemployed people from Åtvidaberg were sent over on a job creation scheme to clean up after the installation, proper and thorough cleaning and painting not being entrusted to the Estonians. They were not a success, however, doing a cursory job, and spending most of the evenings in the bar complaining of boredom and isolation. It was clear that they fell in between two categories; not powerful enough to be interesting to the people who were cultivating contacts with the Swedes, and not eccentric enough to be interesting to the intellectual elite. The complaints of isolation, therefore, were not exaggerated.

In another large-scale effort a communal freezer house was built, with 64 compartments rented out to individuals in the blocks of flats. The administration of the freezer was assigned to a group of locals, who set the rent at running cost, to the dismay of the Swedes, who would have set it higher to cover the cost of future repairs: it was another much talked-about piece of evidence of the hopelessly Soviet lack of common sense and rationality of the community. The freezer house stands at a right angle to two of the apartment blocks, and faces a third one, in effect creating a square. It is, deliberately, painted a traditional Swedish red, which is a reference and a claim, just as it was in the 1920s and 1930s when the Estonian Swedish farmers were encouraged to paint their traditionally grey houses red. In an article about the twin town work for *Hembygsbladet*, a Swedish rural news journal, the head of the committee mentions the redness of the freezer house: "Both agriculture and individual households should benefit from the freezer house, constituting 64 compartments, which was installed by 10 unemployed young people from Åtvidaberg – it is the only building painted red with white corners in the whole of Nuckö!" (letter from Olle Söderback 11 November 1993). Unfortunately, the Swedes left before it was quite finished, leaving the door unpainted and the steps uncovered. Instead of completing the job, the state of unfinish was allowed to continue, secretly regarded by the Swedes as another Soviet sign, showing the same characteristic lack of care and responsibility.

There are only two exclamation marks in the article quoted above, and both function as signs of Swedish-ness for the Swedish audience. In terms of material culture, Swedish red with white corners constitutes a symbol for Swedish-ness, with connotations of rural peace and quiet (cf. Frykman & Löfgren 1979: 68; Gaunt & Löfgren 1983: 9, 41). The other exclamation mark is equally significant in terms of the Swedish view of themselves, and of the post-Soviet Estonians: "On the agricultural side we have had a number of trainees over in Sweden, who were able to follow the farm work on some local farms in Åtvidaberg for 4–5 weeks, and thereby gain some experience of how an efficient agriculture can, and perhaps should, be run. Regarding the question of efficiency there is as you know much to be desired in Estonia!" The gift of efficiency and rationality, then, is therefore seen as the other side of the aid programme, the invisible inculcation of what is regarded as real work practices, in contrast to Soviet symbolic work.[17] Thus for example the head of the committee tried to enlist support from other organizations, notably from the Swedish International Development Agency (SIDA). The grant from

SIDA would cover a three- or four-day course for agricultural workers on training with local Swedish farmers, where the trainees would be taught the fundamentals of Swedish democracy, constitution, local authority organization and tax laws. The training, then, would cover not only Swedish farming methods but also the "Swedish model", including both a model of government, and a wider concept of co-operative and consensual efficiency (letter from Olle Söderbäck 20 October 1991).[18]

In addition to the business people and the aid officials, the third group in this context is of course the Estonian Swedes. The majority of the Swedish-speaking Estonians fled to Sweden during the war, and many are now coming back to visit relatives left behind, or to see their old homes. As former owners, they are legally entitled to reclaim their confiscated property, and nearly all of them are doing that. Initially this law led to a deep sense of unease among the new inhabitants, often descendants of Russian Estonian refugees from the Front during the Second World War, who feared that their houses might be taken away from them. The inhabitants of one small island, which was 100 per cent Swedish speaking before the war, were even debating whether they should collectively defect to Latvia, in order to bypass the whole problem. The present occupiers, however, were finally given a lifetime assured occupancy right which has improved the relationship.

The Estonian Swedes in a sense inhabit a symbolic bridge between Estonia and Sweden: having real kinship ties in Estonia, they are also deeply assimilated in Sweden, indistinguishable as a group from other Swedes. In spring and summer many of them come over regularly, often staying with the people who are now living in their old homes. They bring practical presents – aspirin, coffee, vitamins, paint for the dilapidated old farmhouses. Like the aid, the objects are utilitarian rather than frivolous, representing, again, the core concept of rationality in relation to Swedish-ness. In their cases, however, cycles of gift exchange do develop, and what they are given back tends to be representations of the nation or the region: craft objects, berries, smoked flat-fish, mushrooms. Hence the relationship to Sweden is also framed by objects moving from Estonia to Sweden: objects that the older people remember from their childhoods and that are unavailable in Sweden. These are not only gifts. One man who comes back regularly told me that the first time he came back, in 1989, he brought with him a barrel of drinking water from Stockholm because he was afraid of Soviet pollution. Now, he said, every time he goes back to Stockholm he brings with him a barrel of water from his old well in Estonia: the Stockholm water, he says, is not anything like as good.

Conclusion

The process whereby Estonia is moving from the Soviet Union to the West is, then, articulated in terms of the appropriation of Western objects. The objects constitute powerful signs of three separate but overlapping categories, "Western-ness", "Swedish-ness" and "normality". There is, as we have seen, a marked sense of ambivalence surrounding the objects, stemming from a number of different historical trajectories and cultural imperatives. I have tried to analyze some of these, focusing on the centrality of balance and the ambivalence of material success, connected both to Soviet egalitarianism and to the Estonian self-identity, which is constructed largely in opposition to the projected extravagance and imbalance of the Russian character.

As we have seen, the importance of balance has particular implications for the cultural system of gift–exchange, emphasizing the obligation to reciprocate. The lack of balance and the economically unequal relationship between Sweden and Estonia which the aid highlights has the effect of making the reception and appropriation of the objects at least to some extent problematic. Furthermore, it has a marked influence on the manner of socializing between the (almost exclusively male) aid officials from the twin town of Åtvidaberg and the local population. The meeting between the two groups is complex, and, from the Estonian side, perceived in relation to the question of gift exchange and balance, and respectability or lack of respectability. The inability to reciprocate on equal terms means that the more respectable members of the community avoid social contact with the Swedes, leaving the less respectable people to develop sociable relationships with them. That particular constellation is further emphasized by the way in which the Swedes, as outsiders with a certain amount of power, are slotted into the role of authority, echoing the authority of the Soviet rulers. This, in the world turned upside down, still carries a taint of disrespect. The fact that they associate exclusively with people who are not regarded as educated, sophisticated, or particularly respectable, clinches, so to speak, the social identity of the Swedes.

The consumption of Western goods available in the shops indicates both success in the post-Soviet state, and a process of differentiation from the Soviet system, which also includes a distinction from the people who are not successful in the new system, and who are more likely to regret the loss of the Soviet system. Material success, as we have seen, is viewed with some ambivalence, both because it is seen as essentially unbalanced, and because it is associated with various degrees of corruption. The history teacher, for example, who represented the epitome of intellectualism locally, avoided the new shop and Western products. There is a powerful incentive, therefore, to normalize material success, incorporating the new objects into a discourse of normality that is measured by the standards of the West rather than of the former Soviet Union. The notion that Western-ness represents normality, moreover, is strongly backed up by the essentially Western self-identity of the Estonians during the Soviet era, in contrast to other Soviet peoples. Using the teacher as an example, again, his dislike of the new shop was never articulated in terms that would have distinguished Western and indigenous products: the idea that there was a distinction was avoided even by people like him.

It is also clear that the community leaders have a real interest in presenting the village and area as "Swedish". The actual lack of Swedish roots for the majority of the population was not initially known to the Swedish aid officials, just as they did not know that the majority of the students in the high school, some of whom got invited to Sweden for extended periods of study, are neither local nor with any Swedish ancestry. In an unconscious illustration of the importance of kinship, I was told by an aid official that they had discovered that one girl who had been invited to Sweden was not local, and, therefore, not in any sense Swedish. She had also, unfortunately, stolen a number of things from her host family. Significantly, the two stories intermingled to the point where the theft was seemingly rationalized in terms of the girl not being Swedish; her suddenly discovered status as "foreigner" was unconsciously connected to her identity as a thief. The revival of Swedish-ness, then, represents the assumption of yet another identity for the area: an identity that has some relevance for the place, but much less so for most of the people. In terms of the Russian and Soviet past, it is another Potemkin façade, the public presentation of a false reality named after the interior minister of Catherine the Great, who ordered attractive façades of prosperous villages to be erected along the banks of the Volga, in order to hide the destitution of the real villages from the imperial gaze.

It is important to remember, also, that this is essentially a society in transformation, where the appropriation of Western goods is going through a particular and fleeting phase. This has ramifications also for the older objects, which are increasingly contextualized as "old" and "Soviet". Amitav Ghosh (1992) describes the relationship of the fellaheens of Egypt to the concept of "development" as follows:

> I had an inkling then of the real and desperate seriousness of their engagement with modernism, because I realized that the fellaheen saw the material circumstances of their lives in exactly the same way that a university economist would: as a situation that was shamefully anachronistic, a warp upon time; I understood that their relationships with the objects of their everyday lives was never innocent of the knowledge that there were other places, other countries that did not have mud-walled houses and cattle-drawn ploughs, so that those objects, those houses and ploughs, were insubstantial things, ghosts displaced in time, waiting to be exorcized and laid to rest. (Ghosh 1992: 201)

Similarly, the inhabitants of the former collective farm knew that not only was the farm itself rendered obsolete by the "changes", but so was the greater part of their material culture; the dusty and dilapidated "culture house", the agricultural machinery slowly rusting in a backyard, the Russian kettles and the polyester clothes.

This chapter has attempted to demonstrate the significance of material culture in the current process of transformation in Estonia. The consumption of Western objects constitutes an appropriation of Western-ness which defines the transformation to the West, at the same time as it reveals and emphasizes the Soviet rather than the Western aspects of Estonia itself. Furthermore, focusing on the specific setting of a collective farm, it has explored the ways in which the relationships to the new objects articulate particular social and historical trajectories, entangling the Soviet past and the relationship to Russia with the relationship to Sweden and the restoration of the Swedish cultural heritage on the peninsula.

Notes

1. This view is part of the Western tradition summed up by Graham Greene in his statement that "I would rather end my days in the Gulag than in – than in California" (Amis 1993: 6). Alternatively, the view that global systems are appropriated locally, and therefore are not oppressive, has been aptly described by Richard Wilk as the "It's All Right, They've Appropriated It" school of thought (Wilk in Cohen et al. 1995: 115).
2. I deliberately use the word "expansion" since criminal organizations existed within the Soviet system too. One of the reasons for Yeltsin's initial popularity on becoming first secretary of the Moscow city committee in 1985, for example, was his efforts to deal with the Moscow mafia as well as with the widespread level of corruption (Yeltsin 1990: 95–7).
3. The projected isolation and consequent cultural authenticity of the Estonian Swedes nicely conforms to Hobsbawm and Ranger's (1983) concept of the invention of tradition, not least because a large portion of the Estonian Swedes were in fact traders and seamen, mingling in different cultures to a far greater extent than their Swedish counterparts, frequently emigrating, and usually speaking a smattering of Estonian, Finnish, Russian and German, as well as Swedish. Furthermore, their Swedish dialects contained many words and expressions taken from Estonian and German, and do not, therefore, as was frequently assumed, constitute an isolated and ancient form of Swedish (Hobsbawm & Ranger 1983).
4. The formal, Estonian name of the collective farm was "V.I. Lenini Nimeline Kolhoosi".
5. The current renovation of the manor house closely follows its renovation after the First World War, when the first Estonian Republic was created (Peace of Tartu 1920). Then, as now, the renovation was largely financed from Sweden, with the aim of setting up a Swedish school. Then, the school was agricultural, bringing modern agricultural techniques to the Estonian Swedish farming

population. Now, the "Swedish-ness" is more tenuous, based on the Soviet system of specialized high schools. It is, however, central, in the discourse of the revival of Swedish-ness in the area, the analyis of which forms the main part of my doctoral dissertation.

6. The concepts of "before" and "now" were pivotal in the discourses about the changes.

7. Cf. Eva Hoffman (1994: 3), who quotes from an interview with a Polish film-maker: "Oh, I'm more pessimistic all the time," he briskly informs me. "Things are falling apart." "But are they falling apart more than before?" "It doesn't matter whether they're falling apart more. Before it gave me pleasure when they fell apart; they were falling apart for Them."

8. Clearly, also, this is a discourse that is related to the European discourse of anti-semitism.

9. Despite the strict monetary policies implemented by the then minister of finance Madis Üürike, the level of inflation was about 50 per cent. In an interview with the minister, I was told that the level of inflation was caused by heavy foreign investments in Estonia, which brought significant amounts of capital into the country. This particular form of inflation, combined as it was with strict curbs on all forms of social welfare, had a particularly adverse effect on the poorer sections of the population.

10. Emil Tode's (1995) novel *Piiririik*, translated into Swedish as *Gränsland* (border country), about a young Estonian man living in Paris, documents the process of coming from a land on the edges of Europe, which, like Carlo Levi's Lucania (Levi 1982: 12), is only partially incorporated by Western civilization, to Paris, the symbolic centre not only of civilization, but also of everything that is stylish and hedonistic, represented as the opposite of Estonia. He describes seeing a group of Estonians by a shop window:

> I recognised them from afar, before I heard them speak, standing in front of the window display of Samaritaine, reviewing what was displayed, but actually desiring it, desiring all these products and all the wealth which their poor eyes saw for the first time. To tell the truth it was myself standing there. You see, if once you have stood in front of those windows you might assume a superior expression, but you will still remain standing there forever. Oh, it's too miserable, too pathetic to write about! One can only write about tolerably literary, tolerably noble sufferings, not about eastern Europeans stopping in front of the glittering shop-windows of this city, dressed in tracksuits and trainers. (Tode 1995: 115; my translation from Swedish)

11. This particular form of informality is of course relatively recent in Sweden itself.

12. That is, since the decline of the Social-Democratic project of "Folkhemmet", the nation as the home of the people, where the "ordinary" and the utilitarian were promoted as national virtues.

13. Within the logic of structuralism, the binary opposite to (modernist) rationality might be defined as the essentially romantic feeling for nature, equally powerful in making up the Swedish national identity.

14. The suspect nature of the non-Russians is of course reinforced by the fact that

all the war trials of recent years have been of non-Germans, since the German war criminals were largely de-Nazified by the Allied Forces after the war. The non-Germans, on the other hand, often escaped to the West through the displaced persons camps and false papers. I am indebted to Ken Roth of Human Rights Watch for this comment.

15. Walpurgis night, Valborgsmässoafton, is an important event in the Swedish calendar, when large bonfires are lit at night, which popularly are supposed to constitute a celebration of spring and the return of light. The festivities explain the size of the audience.

16. The money raised from these sales went to a local fund aiming to help the people in the area. Although the woman had bought the coat, therefore, she was well aware of the fact that it had been given as charity.

17. The notion of the symbolic nature of Soviet work was of course widely shared by Soviet people too, encapsulated in the joke that "they pretend to pay us and we pretend to work."

18. Cf. Löfgren's (1991) "Att nationalisera moderniteten" (nationalizing modernity) where he concludes that even the government's project of encouraging cultural diversity, and giving grants to immigrant groups for various cultural activities, involves a powerful "Swedification apparatus", operating through the requirements of successful grant applications: a democratically elected board, proper accountancy, childcare and gender-awareness training (Löfgren 1991: 114).

References

Amis, M. 1993. *Visiting Mrs Nabokov and other excursions*. Harmondsworth: Penguin.

Bremmer, I. & R. Taras (eds) 1993. *Nations and politics in the Soviet successor states*. Cambridge: Cambridge University Press.

Cohen, C.B., R. Wilk, B. Stveltje (eds) 1995. *Beauty queens on the global stage: gender, contests and power*. London: Routledge.

Frykman, J. & O. Löfgren 1979. *Den kultiverade människan*. Stockholm: Liber Förlag.

Frykman, J. & O. Löfgren 1985. *Modärna tider*. Stockholm: Liber Förlag.

Du Plessix Gray, F. 1991. *Soviet women walking the tightrope*. London: Virago.

Gaunt, D. & O. Löfgren 1983. *Myter om Svensken*. Stockholm: Liber.

Ghosh, A. 1992. *In an antique land*. London: Granta.

Gullestad, M. 1990. Peace and quiet. *Social Analysis* **29**, 38–61.

Haida, L. & M. Beissinger (eds) 1990. *The nationalities factor in Soviet politics and society*. Boulder, CO: Westview.

Hann, C. (ed.) 1993. *Socialism: ideals, ideologies and local practice*. ASA Monograph 31. London: Routledge.

Hobsbawm, E. & T. Ranger (eds) 1983. *The invention of tradition*. Cambridge: Cambridge University Press.

Hoffman, E. 1994. *Exit into history*. London: Minerva.

Humphrey, C. 1995. Creating a culture of disillusionment. In *Worlds apart: modernity through the prism of the local*, D. Miller (ed.), 43–69. London: Routledge.

Humphrey, C. & S. Hugh-Jones 1992. *Barter, exchange and value: an anthropological approach*. Cambridge: Cambridge University Press.

Letters and reports made available from the files of the Åtvidaberg committee.

Levi, C. 1982 [1947]. *Christ stopped at Eboli*. Harmondsworth: Penguin.

Lieven, A. 1993. *The Baltic revolution*. New Haven, CT: Yale University Press.

Löfgren, O. 1991. Att nationalisera moderniteten. In *Nationella identiteter i norden – ett fullbordat projekt?*, A. Linde-Laursen & J.O. Nilsson (eds). Nordiska Rådet.

Mauss, M. 1990. *The gift: form and reason for exchange in archaic societies*. New York/London: Norton.

Motyl, A. 1994. Negating the negation: Russia, not-Russia, and the West. *Nationalities Papers* **22**(1), 263–75.

Park, A. 1994. Ethnicity and independence: the case of Estonia in comparative perspective. *Europe-Asia Studies* **46**(1), 69–87.

Smith, G. (ed.) 1990. *The nationalities question in the Soviet Union*. London: Longman.

Taagepera, R. 1993. *Estonia: return to independence*. Boulder, CO: Westview.

Thomas, N. 1991. *Entangled objects: exchange, material culture and colonialism in the Pacific*. Cambridge, MA: Harvard University Press.

Tode, E. 1995. *Gränsland*. Stockholm: Wahlström och Widstrand.

Trapans, J. (ed.) 1991. *Toward independence: the Baltic popular movements*. Boulder, CO: Westview.

Wachtmeister, A. 1992. *Estonia*. Wallåkra: Sweslo Housing AB.

Yeltsin, B. 1990. *Against the grain*. London: Jonathan Cape.

CHAPTER 10

At home and abroad: inalienable wealth, personal consumption and formulations of femininity in the southern Philippines

Mark Johnson

The starting point of this chapter derives from the arguments put forward by Annette Weiner (1976, 1985, 1992) in a series of books and papers concerning the relationship between women and inalienable possessions in Pacific Island societies. Inalienable wealth, according to Weiner, refers to things that objectify a group's cosmological authentication and through which their identity is reproduced: objects, such as sacred heirlooms, which may be temporarily alienated in exchange, but which are ultimately reclaimed, removed from, and/or kept out of, circulation. Weiner suggests, moreover, that it is not primarily men, but women who are involved in the processes through which inalienable wealth is created and maintained. Specifically, Weiner argues, the symbolic association of women with bio-logical reproduction cannot simply be viewed as a way of circumscribing them according to the nature/culture, female/male, private/public divides, but rather must be seen as metaphors for describing women's involvement in the production of *cultural* value and social identity, that is, the repro-duction of cosmological authentication. One example of this is women's involvement in the production, exchange and display of cloth and clothing, which in the Pacific, as in many other parts of the world, is not only symbolically linked with reproduction but also an important form of inalienable wealth (see e.g. Weiner & Schneider 1989).

This chapter serves both to extend and critique Weiner's arguments, drawing on ethnographic research conducted over an 18-month period during 1991–2 in two Muslim Sama and Tausug communities in the southern Philippines. The first part of my research was concentrated in Paniran, a small minority Muslim community in the port area of Zamboanga, a city with a population of approximately 500,000, just over 76 per cent of which is Christian Filipino. The majority of my research, how-ever, was conducted in the town of Jolo, Sulu, which has a population of just under 55,000, of whom 90 per cent identify themselves as Muslim. Not only is Jolo a major trading and population centre for the Muslim Tausug and Sama, but also together with Islam it is an important symbolic point of identification. It was also the site of some of the fiercest fighting between armed Muslim separatists and Philippine government forces in the 1970s.

I have highlighted ethnicity and recent social conflict because one of the problems with transposing Weiner's account of social identity and cosmo-logical authenticity onto the situation in the southern Philippines is that it elides the wider historical context of colonial and post-colonial state and nation building within which the discourses of ethnicity, "cultural traditions" and "cultural authenticity" or "Kastom" are located and have taken shape (cf. Keesing & Tonkinson 1982; Jolly 1994). As I shall suggest, while women's association and involvement with "traditional" clothing and gold jewellery is a clear demonstration of Weiner's general thesis about women and inalienable wealth, their valorization as keepers of cultural tradition is also part of the present-day discourse of ethnic nationalism, among both Muslim separatists and State functionaries alike (cf. Blanc-Szanton 1990; Siapno 1994). Another problem with transposing Weiner's account onto the local situation is that while women in Sulu are both com-mitted and active participants in the creation and augmentation of things considered inalienable (whether these are regarded as cultural traditions or specific objects, such as gold heirlooms), they also express an interest (not recognized or articulated as such by Weiner) in possessing things whose value resides not in their endowment as vehicles for shared social memory and collective identification but precisely in their perceived distance from the world of cultural traditions and familial identity, things that are con-sumed, following Miller (1991), as objects of absolute freedom, fantasy and desire.

The contrast drawn by women between investment in forms of inalien-able wealth and investment in objects of fantasy and desire is not only associated with different images of femininity, but also increasingly articu-lated in terms of the contrast drawn (both materially and verbally) between the variously imagined worlds of *adat* (roughly custom and tradition) and *istyle* (style); the former an important touchstone of local Muslim identity, the latter associated primarily with an imagined American otherness. Elsewhere (Johnson 1995a, 1995b, 1997) I have examined the ideological and historical background of the entanglement of these imaginary worlds, an entanglement that began in the early part of the twentieth century with the colonization of Sulu by the Americans, and which continues to inform, even as it is informed by, the more recent experiences of state and separatist violence. In particular, I have focused on the way in which Islam and the USA have been inscribed onto the bodies of local gay-transvestite men, who (I argue) have been constructed as mediatory figures between them: those who are considered to have lost their masculinity, which is defined by the defence of Islam, and to have been "overexposed" to and transformed by a potent otherness into culturally unrecognized/unrecognizable women.

Here I expand this argument to demonstrate more generally how the various oppositions and transformations of *adat* and *istyle*, the traditional and the modern, the local and the foreign, Islam and the USA, the world at home and the world abroad, are part of the ongoing makings and markings of ethnic and gendered identifications in the southern Philippines. In the extreme and as a totalizing set of aesthetics, each is associated with a particular kind of sociality, *adat* with the production of remembrances – shared social memories – and the possession of inalienable wealth, and *istyle* with personal freedom and/or "doing one's own thing – *kanya-kanya in istyle*". While *istyle* may become incorporated within, and transformed by, *adat* – the reworking of Western-style wedding receptions into such things as native modern *istyle* weddings being just one example of the incorporation of new material objects into pre-existing structural forms – it may also become a repudiation of *adat*, an objectification of absolute freedom that lies outside the terrain of *adat*. This is particularly significant for women for whom, I shall argue, *istyle* and the possibility of work and consumption abroad has become an important means for transcending and reformulating the dominant version of femininity as repository of cultural value and keeper of tradition.

Between *adat* and *istyle* : women and the making of tradition

Traditional and modern attire

I begin with a description of the contrast drawn between traditional and modern dress and the meaning and significance of the occasions where each is considered appropriate attire. Traditional, native or, as it is sometimes called in parody of the divisions between tradition and modernity, *istyle kamaasan* (the style of the elders or forebears), designates two main design patterns in women's clothing. The most prevalent is a variety of loose-fitting blouses, including the *sambra*, a waist-length, short-sleeved, lace-trimmed blouse, and the *sablay*, a long, flowing, long-sleeved blouse traditionally clasped together with a *dubluun*, a gold coin pin, or alternately a semi-precious stone mounted in gold. Less prevalent, but considered even more refined, is the *bitawi*, a tight-fitting, long-sleeved blouse with a plunging neckline, decorated with gold buttons, especially associated with weddings. All three of these are worn in conjunction with either loose light trousers, *sawwal*, or a sarong, *habul*, tied at the waist. Additional sarongs or embroidered cloth may also be worn draped across the shoulder (see Bruno 1973: 12–17 for a complete description).

The defining characteristics of traditional, native attire, however, lie not simply in the design but also in the texture and colour of the fabric, which for special occasions consists mainly of rich and glossy silks, satins and velvet (imported from Malaysia) in bright but generally single colours, most especially yellows, oranges, reds, greens and purples or metallic golds and

217

silvers. This sets it apart, on the one hand, from the everyday *pyjamas* worn around the house which, though similar in style to the loose-fitting *sablay* and *sawwal,* are often made out of brightly printed but much less opulent and cheaper cotton fabric. On the other hand, it also sets it apart from formal (skirt and blouse and whole dress) and rugged modern *istyle* (*maong* or denim and T-shirt). These, while obviously encompassing a variety of colours, designs and patterns, tend towards what might be regarded as a more conservative taste regime that juxtaposes whites and other light pastel colours with earth tones and various shades of darker blues, greys, etc.

In addition to differences in design pattern and fabric, there are two other features that distinguish traditional and modern dress. Traditional attire is almost without exception accessorized by gold, pearls and shell jewellery and, to a lesser extent, silver and other precious stones, whereas modern *istyle* may include pieces of costume jewellery in addition to gold. However, the defining aspect of *modern istyle* is some kind of beauty treatment, i.e. manicure/pedicure, hair style or "make-up/hair-do", from gay-transvestite beauticians. The latter is particularly true of more affluent, educated professional women, some of whom make weekly visits to the beauty parlour.[1]

There is a fairly straightforward, and perhaps not unexpected, division of occasions where each, the traditional and the modern, are considered most appropriate if not *de rigueur*. Modern *istyle* predominates on an everyday basis outside the home: at work, school and shopping, and for special occasions at secular calendrical events (including birthdays, school-related events such as acquaintance parties and graduation, and Christmas which, while not devoid of religious significance for Muslims, is by contrast to other Islamic celebrations primarily regarded as a secular event). In contrast, traditional attire is a focal point not only for major life-course events, such as first hair cuttings, weighings, weddings and death celebrations, but also for religious and ritual calendrical events, such as *Mawlud al Nabi,* the Birth of the Prophet Muhammad, and most especially *Hari Raya Id El Fitri'* , the feast day marking the end of *Ramadan,* the month of fasting.

These temporal, spatial and sartorial delineations of tradition and modernity are part of a wider conceptual framework that hierarchically contrasts the eternal, enduring and encompassing cosmological significance of Islam and Muslim traditions (*adat* and *agama*) with the purely transient and terrestrial significance of things associated with *istyle,* which are primarily thought about in terms of an imagined American otherness (cf. Kiefer 1972; Johnson 1995a). They also constitute a significant part of the redressing of local history, the rich textures and bright colours of traditional clothing evoking for some persons the splendour and regalia of the formerly independent Sultanate. More specifically, traditional clothing is seen to recall a world ordered according to a strict hierarchy of signs, place and persons – the dressing up of bride and groom for weddings customarily referred to as, "borrowing the characteristics of the nobility" (Bruno 1973: 127). The traditional order of things – in which persons knew their place in the hierarchy and fulfilled their respective duties and obligations – is in turn contrasted with the present-day situation in which people increasingly do their own thing (which is said to be characteristic of the American *istyle* of doing things). At the same time, traditional distinctions based on wealth, power and status tend to be flattened out in reiterating a history of resistance to colonialism in which everyone is said to have, or be able to have, an equal share, the overriding emphasis at religious occasions and calenderical celebrations, being both on the authority of elders (*kamaasan*) and on community solidarity in the face of forced assimilation by the Christian Philippine State. What is not flattened out, but if anything further defined in these productions of tradition, is the position of women as the embodiment of cultural purity and authenticity, as the careful debate surrounding weddings illustrates.

Two weddings and a faux pas

One of the interesting developments since the 1960s with respect to weddings has been the increasing trend to follow the traditional wedding ceremony (*pahalal kawin*) and the three-day celebration that follows (*paglingkud tu*) with a modern reception. Both events are marked by (among other things) the clothing appropriate to each.[2] The traditional part of the wedding ceremony requires that the bride wear the *sambra* or *bitawi* (described previously) and ideally for the groom as well, the tight-fitting *kuput kamaasan* (trousers of the men of old), in addition to a short, tight jacket, similar in appearance to the *bitawi* worn by women. The modern reception, on the other hand, necessitates that the bride should wear a white Western-style wedding dress (or some variation), while for the groom, this means either Western, "American-style" coat and tie, or the *Barong Tagalog*, the "national" Filipino dress shirt made from *pina* (woven pineapple fibre). Where families cannot afford to host two events, however, *istyle*, as it were, gives way to *adat*, although not, as might be expected, because of the comparative expense of modern as opposed to traditional clothing, since the latter if anything can be more expensive. Rather, where a family is on a very tight budget, the expectation is that even if – as is often the case – the groom wears modern *istyle* for the marriage ceremony, the bride will be dressed in traditional attire. On only one occasion during 18 months of fieldwork did I observe a marriage celebration in which the bride wore a modern, Western-style wedding dress for the initial marriage rituals.

The wedding was, in fact, the second of two weddings I attended which took place during the first few weeks of research in the mainly Muslim Tausug and Sama community of Paniran. Both weddings were among comparatively poor families, and both weddings were described as having been elopements, which among other things reduces the amount and expense of the formal marriage negotiations, exchange and celebrations. In the first wedding ritual, the bride was dressed in traditional *sablay* and *sawwal* while the groom was dressed in long-sleeved shirt and slacks. The wedding, I was told, was a modest, simple affair, reflecting the exigencies of modern life among poor Muslim families. While the celebrants apologized that the wedding was nothing like the splendour of weddings among the wealthy or former aristocracy, it was made clear that what I had observed was true to Islamic religion and local Muslim cultural traditions (Fig. 10.1).

In the second wedding, which followed about two weeks later, the groom was dressed in a long Arabic-style gown complete with headdress, while the bride was dressed in a white Western-style wedding gown. At first I thought that I had stumbled upon my first example of cultural innovation, since I knew, both from the previous wedding I had attended and from previous pictures of weddings I had seen, that it was usually men who wore Western-style clothing for their weddings. I was slightly disappointed, therefore, when the groom's mother (actually his mother's sister) who, because the bride's family objected to the wedding, had taken charge of the marriage arrangements, told me somewhat apologetically that they had rented the wedding dress at a discount from a gay-transvestite beautician friend (who also did the make-up/hair-do for the bride). Apparently they had not been able to afford to buy the cloth and pay to have a traditional outfit made for the bride. Moreover, I soon discovered that the dress had become the subject of

Figure 10.1   This wedding was described as a simple but authentic Muslim wedding since the bride wore traditional attire.

widespread gossip in the community; some people expressed the opinion that it was scandalous and disgraceful for a Muslim woman to have worn a "Christian" wedding dress for Islamic wedding rites (Figs 10.2 and 10.3).

Whatever the reason for the choice in the first place, the groom's mother suggested that it was better to wear a Western-style wedding dress than risk the humiliation of either having to ask the bride's parents to provide a suitable outfit, or borrowing a suitable outfit from friends.[3] As it was, she told me, she and her husband had borrowed so much money from friends they were "unable to hold their shame". Their inability to purchase a new traditional outfit for the bride was considered by her not only to be another indicator of her poverty but also and more importantly an indicator of the fact that she did not receive any support from her family – particularly her stepfather who, although able to help, observed the proceedings from an apparently well-removed distance.

Among those who criticized the marriage ceremony, however, the wedding dress had become a focal point for raising questions and making statements about ethnic–religious identifications. Specifically, the flouting of traditional Muslim conventions was said, by people who identified themselves primarily as Muslim Tausug (who constituted an outspoken majority in the community), to be typical of the Samal, the group with which the second family was identified.[4] The most outspoken critics of the wedding dress were in fact family members and people related to the families of those who were involved in the first wedding. What is interesting about this is that the groom's family were themselves recent converts from Christianity to Islam while the bride's family network consisted of people who, although they traced their ancestry back to Sama forebears, generally identified themselves as being Muslim Tausug.[5] Indeed, one suspects that their criticism was in large part a product of the instability of, and the need to reaffirm for themselves and others, their own identification as Muslim Tausug in opposition to both the majority Christian population outside the immediate community, and the smaller and politically weaker group of Sama within the community.

What this example demonstrates, therefore, is not simply the way in which forms of traditional material culture, such as dress styles, are developed and deployed in processes of social exclusion and affiliation, but also the way in which women and the things associated with women have become foregrounded in struggles over various national and ethnic identities and claims to cultural superiority and authenticity.[6] Traditional clothing is, of course, not absent as a sartorial discourse among men - traditional attire for men consisting of a variety of loose and tight-fitting trousers and jackets (similar to those worn by women), in addition to a special "Muslim" money belt and the *pis siyabbit*, a square handkerchief worn either as a turban or carried as a handkerchief.[7] Nevertheless, not only are women more likely than men to wear traditional clothing, but also they

Figures 10.2 and 10.3 Bride and groom from a wedding which some people in the community regarded as inappropriate since the bride wore a

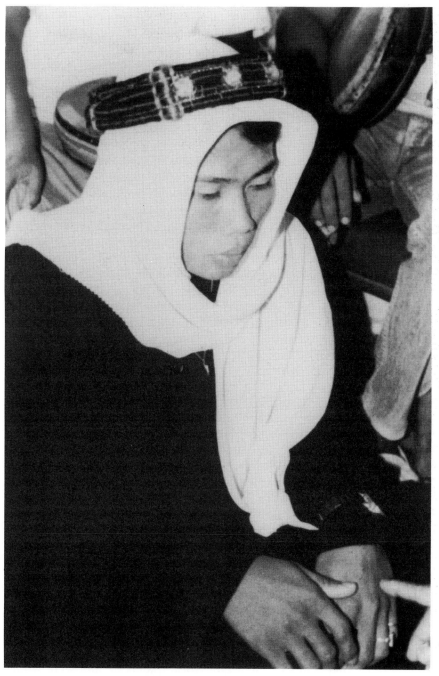

'Christian' wedding dress for a Muslim ritual.

are more likely to invest in it financially. Some women buy the requisite cloth and pay to have a new *sambra* and *sawwal* made each year during Hari Raya. Moreover, greater care is usually taken by women to articulate a complete clothing ensemble, particularly during special occasions, whereas men, if they do wear traditional clothing, will often include only one article of traditional clothing, i.e. wearing the loose cotton *sawal* trousers with T-shirts, or wearing the *pis siyabbit* either tied around their head or thrown over their shoulder as a handkerchief. While the contrast between traditional clothing and modern *istyle* was made and sustained as much by men as by women, as a mark of, and a political statement about, their identification as Muslims, in practice, it is women more so than men who are actually expected to wear traditional clothing.[8]

Native modern style: women and reformulations of tradition

While it is women, more so than men, who are expected to embody *adat*, this does not mean that they are not, any less than men, also expected to embody *istyle*. Just as there has been an increasing emphasis on modern receptions following traditional marriage rituals, there has also been an increasing emphasis placed by parents on their daughters' education (with which *istyle* is associated). One can chart since the 1960s a dramatic increase in the number of women pursuing and obtaining higher academic qualifications and entering *professional* occupations as seen in Table 10.1.

The question is, how to understand such changes? Lacar (1991), who provides substantial documentation of the trends towards professional employment and education among Muslim women, contends that they are indicative of the positive transformations taking place in Philippine Muslim society as a whole and for women in particular whom he characterizes as having been in a "desperate" state with no "significant role" in traditional society. However, his characterizations both of women in traditional society and of the effects of increasing education and professionalization on changing gender roles are oversimplified and overstated.

In the first place, women often had a very active public life in "traditional" society, although this is not, as Errington (1990) points out, in itself a sign of being held in high regard or public esteem. Although unmarried women of virginal status (*budjang*) were, up until the early part of the twentieth century, isolated under the careful protection of their families (Bruno 1973) they emerged, upon marriage, from this lengthy liminal phase as respected and relatively independent persons who were extremely active in community life (see also Blanc-Szanton 1990 on women in the Visayas). Warren (1981: 220) notes, for instance, that by the mid-nineteenth century, some of the leading local traders in Sulu were women who owned and managed their own slaves, quoting a nineteenth-century observer as saying:

Table 10.1 Relative numbers of men and women as a percentage of overall population pursuing higher education from 1960 until 1990 (data compiled from Table 8 of the 1990 Sulu Provincial Profile and Table U4 of 1990 Housing and Population Statistics, Central Statistical Office, Manila)

	Men	Women
1960	76%	24%
	(2,512)	(809)
1970*	60%	40%
	(6,191)	(4,171)
1980*	54%	46%
	(4,727)	(4,066)
1990	49%	51%
	(12,057)	(12,404)

*The apparent decrease in total numbers of men and women pursuing education between 1970 and 1980 is due to the fact that the 1970 figures include the province of Tawi-Tawi which at that time was still a part of the province of Sulu.

> In Sulu, the wives of chiefs are entrusted with the principal management of accounts, and carry on much the trade, it is said that they have considerable knowledge from the Manila captives, who are of a superior class.

At the other end of the social spectrum, captive women slaves (usually, although not always, people identified as Christians taken in raiding expeditions mainly along coastal dwellings on Luzon, the Visayas and the northern coast of Mindanao) were a prime commodity in the traditional polity. While many ended up working alongside captive men in forced agricultural labour, others were taken, and/or given away, by powerful men as concubines or secondary wives. In the latter case, they were able to secure their manumission through, and commoner status for, their children – most of whom were fully incorporated as Muslim Tausugs – and were given some opportunity to work to increase both their own and their husband's status.

While this brief account cannot begin to do justice both to the wide variety of women's experiences in the past or to the various historical workings and reworkings of femininity, at the very least it provides a necessary corrective to the stereotyped portrayal, in the Philippines as elsewhere, of oppressed Muslim women (Fawzi El-Solh & Mabro 1994). Indeed, a more realistic appraisal is to see women in Sulu as having been (both historically and in the more recent past) constrained and enabled by a structural configuration similar to that of women in many other Pacific and Insular Southeast Asian groups as repositories of status–honour and ancestral identity (Ortner 1981; Errington 1989, 1990; Blanc-Szanton 1990; Weiner 1992). Not only was there (and still is) a much higher expectation on women to uphold the prestige of their families by publicly preserving their virginal status as sisters, but also a greater expectation that they, and not their brothers, would, prior to formal courtship and marriage, complete a course of instruction in Qur'anic reading, which among other things would increase the amount of bride-wealth that could be demanded.[9] Moreover, not only were/are women sacralized as mothers in the growing up of their kindred's remembrances (children and grandchildren referred to as *panumtuman umbul satu*, the number one or best remembrances), but also they are entrusted as caretakers or guardians (*tagdapuh*) over a family's inalienable wealth, such as ancestral heirlooms (*pusaka'*), usually gold, but also traditional cloth and clothing of the kind described previously. Indeed, women are spoken about as being sacred passageways between heaven and earth, their bodies, the vagina in particular, at times likened to the sacred *Ka'aba* (the black stone in Mecca and *axis mundi* of Islam). Women are, in sum, the very picture of cosmological authentication and encompassment.

Viewed in this light, it is possible to suggest an alternate reading of cultural change. It is less an expression of radical transformation than, in what is often said to be a characteristically Southeast Asian example of cultural entanglement and transformation (Anderson 1972; Wolters 1982), a demonstration made, through and by women, both of the superiority of older traditions and their ability to encompass, absorb and create new traditions. Thus, for example, education is now not only considered to be *'pusaka'* (an inheritance), but also is often related to the inflationary amounts of bride-wealth now being demanded for women. Doctors draw bride-wealth in excess of 200,000 pesos, nurses 100,000+ and teachers 50,000 to 100,000. Moreover, just as the ritual celebrating the completion of Qur'anic reading instruction (*pagtammat*) foreshadowed traditional nuptial ceremonies, so too high school and college graduation ceremonies foreshadow the modern wedding reception, with families splashing out not only on the celebratory meal, but also on make-up/hair-do, new dresses, fancy shoes, etc.

The most dramatic example of the reformulation of *istyle* in terms of *adat*, however, can be seen in the newly emerging trend among the wealthy educated elite to hold native modern *istyle* weddings. The whole point of native modern *istyle* weddings, as described to me by a local tailor, was to collapse the distinctions between the traditional and the modern. This was accomplished, among other things, by condensing the spatial and temporal separation of the marriage ritual (usually held in the home) and reception (usually held in a banquet hall) into one major event and by refashioning traditional cloth and clothing in terms of modern *istyle* (and vice versa). In one of the most elaborate ceremonies, which resembled more of a stage/ theatre production than it did a wedding, the bride (a medical professional), who was dressed in the latest version of a native modern *istyle* wedding dress, was carried into a packed auditorium in a palanquin accompanied by a fully uniformed choir. The ceremony itself took place on a revolving dias-like platform, imitating mechanically the traditional turning round of bride and groom that marks the end of wedding rituals.

All of this might be seen as yet another example of localization (Wolters 1982), a retranslation of global forms in terms of local sensibilities. However, while accurate in its own terms, one of the problems with this reading is that it tends to obscure the specific social and historical processes that have produced the discourse of "tradition" and its transformations (see Pemberton 1992 for a thorough critique of culture in Java). This includes reifications of the feminine as embodiments of cultural authenticity. Moreover, to the extent that localization is used to describe a singular view of cultural development and transformation, it tends to obscure the multiple and varied identifications that women make with different and at times competing images of femininity. The point is that while women's opportunities are expanding in certain respects, as the contrast between *adat* and *istyle* and the transformation of the latter in terms of the former indicates, there has also been a further valorization of women as repositories and keepers of cultural tradition. This dual process has led to new forms of social and cultural constraints as well as new possibilities for contesting and reclaiming images of femininity. However, in order to get a glimpse of what these possibilities entail, and of some of the identifications women make, it is necessary to explore further the intentions that women express both as producers and guardians of tradition and as consumers of modern *istyle*.

Women and the spatialization of *adat* and *istyle*

Sacred heirlooms and personal jewellery

I suggested in the introduction that while women are both committed and active participants in the creation and augmentation of things considered inalienable (whether cultural traditions or material objects), they also express an interest in possessing things whose value resides not in their endowment as vehicles for shared social memories and collective identification but precisely in their perceived distance from the world of cultural traditions and familial identity. A primary example of this is women's involvement with gold jewellery (*bulawan/pamulawan*). Gold jewellery is said to be a primary indicator of a woman's social worth or value, a necessary part of any outfit worn outside the home and a constituting part of a woman's beauty. At a very early age girls have their ears pierced and are given a set of gold earrings as a remembrance from their parents. Women also receive gold jewellery as part of the gifting transactions surrounding marriage, and any gold within the household, apart from the small amounts of personal gold jewellery a woman's husband may own, is regarded as being a woman's portion (*suku' babai*).

According to customary law (*adat*), they have exclusive use rights over this. Much of a woman's gold jewellery is, in fact, considered to be sacred heirlooms (*pusaka'*): to lose or sell such gold is to bring a curse from one's forebears. Thus, while in practical terms women are considered to have day-to-day ownership and control over the gold, they are ultimately only guardians over what is ultimately seen as belonging to their kindred's forebears and ancestors. Like women themselves, gold jewellery is seen to be a repository for, and a marker of, cultural tradition and authenticity.

Paradoxically – in Weiner's (1992) sense of the apparent contradiction between keeping and giving – one of the most interesting things about gold jewellery as a form of inalienable wealth is the articulation between it being both a repository of social memory and identity and of economic value, an active capital resource (*puun*) for the family. Indeed, gold jewellery is, as often as not, in the pawnshop, part of an ongoing cycle of indebtedness and reclamation. As I have suggested elsewhere (Johnson n.d.), it is partly as a result of its temporary alienation and subsequent redemption (as well as the deployment of the money raised through its deposit), that gold jewellery accrues, and is invested as a vehicle of, social memories (remembrances). Thus, its overall value as an object of ancestral potency and cosmological authenticity is increased.[10] Moreover, although these transactional movements rely and directly draw on the involvement and investment of many persons, including husbands, brothers and sons, they are primarily orchestrated and managed by women in the household. Here is a clear demonstration of Weiner's point about the central role that women play in the complex interchange between capital, social identity and inalienable possessions.

A certain tension emerges, however, and is articulated by women, between, on the one hand, gold which through its circulation in and out of pawnshops is invested with familial identity, status and honour and, on the other hand, gold which they acquire on their own and attempt to keep out of the circulation of debts and remembrances (shared social memories). This is particularly the case among more affluent women. Many of these women own, and/or are involved in the buying and selling of, gold jewellery as items of personal consumption (see also Moore 1981: 266–9). As one working professional woman put it, one of the reasons she bought gold jewellery was to have "a memento for myself, a symbol (literally a visible item of *remembrance*), of my work/labour". This illustrates Miller's (1987; see also Thomas 1991) point that things of even the seemingly most fixed kind, such as gold jewellery, often thought about in terms of sacred heirlooms and remembrances, have the potential to mean different things for different people in different contexts.

The struggle to redefine the value and meaning of gold jewellery as an object invested with one's own and not someone else's memories, is only one way in which an image of femininity is expressed by women separate

228

from that as being the embodiments and guardians of familial or ancestral identity. A less subtle approach is the consumption of things unambiguously associated with American *istyle*, defined as "doing things one's own way" or "everyone following their own style" (*kanya-kanya in istyle*). This includes, for instance, smoking Philip-Morris cigarettes and wearing what is locally considered to be excessive quantities of bright make-up and costume jewellery, particularly at occasions that are otherwise associated with *adat*. These practices are seen to controvert the normatively inscribed notion of "the simple" and are otherwise stereotypically associated with "overexposed", gay-transvestite beauticians. Most women in fact eschew this kind of overt stylistic posturing, quietly pursuing and negotiating these sometimes competing interests and intentions in the mundane encounters and transactions that characterize everyday life. As I suggest below, however, not only has the advent and possibility of work abroad created a new space for consumption defined in terms of personal satisfaction and identity, but also it has increasingly spatialized the contrast between personal consumption and inalienable possessions and further crystallized the image of femininity with which each is associated.

Working and spending abroad

One of the most important sociological developments in the Philippines, as elsewhere in the developing world, since the mid-1970s, has been the increasing numbers of persons (both professional and unskilled) working abroad as international contract labour. The overall scale of this development can be seen in the fact that in 1995, remittances from overseas workers accounted for 25 per cent of all Philippine exports (Markillie 1996: 7), while some sense of the significance of overseas workers at the local level can be seen in data compiled from a survey-questionnaire conducted in the town of Jolo, a comparative backwater removed from larger metropolitan recruiting centres. Although only 2 per cent (6 of 244) of survey respondents interviewed had worked abroad, well over one-third (39 per cent) of all respondents claimed to have one or more relatives working abroad. Significantly, women not only account for some 70 per cent of those reported to be working abroad but also appear to account for a comparatively higher proportion of professional or skilled workers abroad as shown in Table 10.2.[11]

Previous literature on working abroad has had two main foci. The first has been on exploring the scale and local economic impact of remittances sent back by migrant workers. It suggests that very little of overseas remittances are actually spent on local investment in productive enterprises, creating a new system of dependency based around overseas earnings (see Arcinas 1986; Jackson 1990). A second focus has been on the conditions of persons working abroad, in which case what has been emphasized is the comparative lack of legal rights that workers have in host countries and

Table 10.2 Number of relatives working abroad by gender, occupational status and place of work

| | Occupational division | | Locale abroad | | |
	Professional (medical and engineering)	Non-professional (domestic and labourer)	Middle East	Other	
Women	38	35	66	7	(73)
Men	10	22	26	6	(32)

their dependence on the benevolence of individual employers (Catholic Institute for International Relations 1987). This can be seen in the much-publicized case of two Filipina maids who were sentenced to death in Singapore and the United Arab Emirates (*Philippine News* 11 October 1995; Markillie 1996). What has tended to be overlooked and neglected in this research, however, is the actual intentions of persons working abroad and in particular of the importance of consumption in their desire for, and experience of, work abroad. While for many persons (particularly women who work aüêdomestic helpers), life abroad can be a frightening and alienating experience, for others (women more so than men), it may also be an extremely liberating and pleasurable experience. Both of these extremes emerged in women's narratives of time spent abroad, but it was the latter in particular that emerged in the desire that many women expressed to work abroad.

In order to illustrate the kind of potential that working abroad has for women, I present the case of three women, who had either shortly returned from working abroad and/or were talking about and planning to go abroad. The first of these was a woman,whom I shall call Piang, who had, at the time of fieldwork in 1991–2, only recently returned with her younger sister from working in Kuwait, following the Iraqi invasion. Relating their story, Piang began by telling me about the experience of her youngest unmarried sister who, as a college dropout, was told by her father (a relatively wealthy and powerful leader outside the town of Jolo) that as she had no qualifications she ought to stay at home until she should be married. Her sister refused, however, and said that she wanted to go abroad, to find her own way in life and provide for herself. Their father was quite angry with her and told her that if she left, then, "To hell with you!" Nevertheless, she decided to leave and with the help of her father, who eventually relented (since apart from anything else, having a son or daughter working abroad is prestigious), later joined Piang in Kuwait where the two sisters worked together as domestic helpers in the same house until the invasion.

Piang (who herself was married and at that time had two young children) went on to discuss the way in which parents cultivated an attitude of dependence among their children by giving them everything they needed, only to turn around and consume any money that they were able to earn abroad. People did not just work abroad for themselves (*baran-baran nila*), she told me, but for their family, for their parents. The only way to avoid having one's earnings used up in this way, she said, was to invest it in gold. After returning home from abroad, the gold could be worn until one ran out of money, at which time it could be either sold or pawned to raise the necessary cash.

What was especially poignant about Piang's story, however, was not simply the expressed tension between discharging her obligation to her parents and saving money by investing in gold. More interesting was the tension between the need to invest in gold for her immediate family – i.e. her children and husband – and the intense desire and immense pleasure of buying and consuming things for and by herself in Kuwait. Framing her comments in terms of regret, she said that since returning home she had undergone a change of thinking with respect to making a living. "It is very true," she said, "making a living is very difficult. If you have money, you should be careful, save money. If I have another chance to work abroad I will try and save money." As she explained:

> *Piang* : At the time when I was abroad I was spoiled. Whatever I saw that I needed I would buy it. My employer asked me, "Why do you throw away your money, is it very easy for you to work, to come to the Arab country? You're not saving. Look at your attitude towards this, like the other Filipinos who come to work here. Look here you are all working as housemaids in Arab countries – you're spoiled with all the money." Calling from Kuwait to Manila, one *Dinar*, one minute. The boss got angry, "Money is nothing to you, that's why you cannot find money. Spoiled with money, or sending money back to relatives. Is it easy for you to work here?"
> *MJ* : What would you buy?
> *Piang* : Things to eat – hamburger. *Masarap in hamburger*, "Hamburgers are very delicious." I looked at magazines with food. Hungry Bunny [fast food restaurant in Kuwait] I said, I want that. Very delicious, lots of meat, that's why it's delicious. That's why my money went. Even when my boss said, "Hulma', I'll buy for you." I would say I want to buy it with my own money. *Mabaiya' aku magkaun bang sin ku.* "I wanted to eat when I paid for it with my own money." My sister and I worked in the same house. In one year she was able to buy gold. She did not spend her money like me. In two years I was only able to buy a little gold.

The emphasis on eating with one's own money, and buying things for oneself, obviously subverts the common protocol (which persists despite everyday evidence to the contrary) of parents (especially fathers) and husbands as being the providers and provisioners. More importantly, I would argue, it is an extension of the desire that women sometimes express to possess and consume things that are kept out of the circulation of shared remembrances. Thus, quite apart from the fact that beef hamburgers are by virtue of their meat content a high status food, it is perhaps not too much to suggest that the Hungry Bunny hamburger was especially delicious precisely because, unlike gold jewellery, there was no possibility that it would become ensnared in the exchanges through which objects are transformed into the embodiments of a social identity in which other persons have a symbolic share. To put it otherwise, the very impermanence and immediacy of consuming the hamburger, as contrasted with the enduring quality of gold jewellery as an objectification of shared remembrances, meant that it was, and would remain, a very personal memory and experience.

This aspect of working abroad, not surprisingly, articulates with the discourse of *istyle*. A good example of this comes from discussions that I had with two married women (sisters-in-law), one who had previously been abroad, another who was planning to go abroad, for whom a constant topic of conversation when we met was their desire to work abroad. At first they told me, in common with many others, that they wanted to go abroad because their children were getting older and they needed to have an increased income in order to support them through private educational institutions so that they would be sure of getting good professional qualifications. They also mentioned wanting to buy some land, start a business and build a cement house.

However, the discussions would usually come around to their expressed desire to visit other places, to see the world and to escape the drudgery of watching the children. They wanted to go "walk-about" and to "have a look at the style *(istyle)* of persons in other lands", saying they would even be willing to "pick apples" if they had to. In particular, the freedom that they saw as implicit in work abroad was contrasted to a situation in which, according to local protocols, they were supposed to stay at home, to mind the children, not to dress up or wear make-up outside the home or go out of the house without the permission of their husbands, although, on certain occasions, they did smoke Philip-Morris, wore bright make-up and made pretences at being *maarte* (ostentatiously glamourous), as an assertion of their independence.

The point, however, is that the trip abroad has further accentuated and increasingly spatialized the intentions that women express. On the one hand, the actual experience of women working abroad (as at home) continues to be characterized by the tensions expressed, for instance, by Hulma' with regards to investing in gold for her family and buying things by and for herself. On the other hand, however, the world abroad, which is conceptualized in terms of its proximity to the USA, increasingly comes to be identified (both by men and women) with that aspect of *istyle* articulated in the notion of doing one's own thing. Thus, the Middle East, which draws the most migrant workers from the Philippines and which is in certain respects conceptually considered closer to US *istyle*, simultaneously becomes, for Muslim women in particular, both an important site for consolidating their Muslim identity and acquiring cultural capital for deployment at home (achieved mainly through the completion of the *hadj* and bringing back various visible markers of their affiliation with global Islam, including prayer rugs, plaques and clocks with Qur'anic inscriptions, Arabic-style clothing, etc.) but also a site for participating in the dream and freedom of personal consumption with which *istyle* is associated. At the same time and largely in contrast to the world abroad, the world at home has increasingly become reified as a locus of *adat* (custom and tradition), of reproductive femininity, and of inalienable possessions: things that are considered morally more worthy of self-investment but also, at times, more burdensome.

Conclusion: on alienation and inalienability

I began this chapter by demonstrating the usefulness and validity of Weiner's (1992) arguments in thinking about the centrality of women, both as locus for, and as active agents in, the production of inalienable wealth and the objectification of familial and local identity. However, I have also suggested that it would be mistaken to overemphasize questions of cosmological authentication and social reproduction while ignoring both the historical processes that have given rise to the discourse of "tradition" and "cultural authenticity" and the other kinds of social intentions that women articulate, among other places, through consumption abroad. In this case women working abroad exemplify Miller's (1987) more general point about the positive and negative potentialities of alienation (used here in the Hegelian sense to refer to the separability of subject and object and subject from subject) in commodity exchange, which (following Simmel) he describes as one of the fundamental and ultimately unresolvable contradictions of modernity. As Miller (1987: 74) points out, it is easy enough to demonstrate the ways in which individual people are reduced through monetization and commoditization to a "quantitative mass of wage labourers, who are appraised only in terms of their contribution to capital." Certainly this is what has tended to happen to overseas contract workers who are often spoken about in terms of remittances and capital flows back into their countries of origin. What is overlooked, however, is that it is often only through personal consumption that individuals are able to overcome, if only ever partially and incompletely, the reifications of social relationships premised on inalienability, and be or become something or someone else. That is to say, while inalienability tends towards relationships

233

in which self-identity is subsumed within or by larger collective identifications, such as ethnicity, personal consumption presupposes and allows for
relationships with objects, as with other subjects, that are "always potentially
alienable", and therefore mutable.

To push the point further, the spatialization of inalienable wealth and
personal consumption in terms of *adat* and *istyle*, the world at home and the
world abroad, can be related to Simmel's (1978: 63, cited in Miller 1987: 70)
space of desire, a deliberate and literal distancing, as much between subjects
as between subject and object, which makes possible and allows for multiple
kinds of identifications. As Gell (1992) argues in a not unrelated context,
one of the primary reasons that men in "old Melanesia" went abroad to
engage in inter-tribal barter or commodity exchange was not for economic
or political reasons but precisely because of the immense pleasure and sense
of freedom experienced in transactions constructed in opposition to the
moral obligations and cosmologically weighted transactions of the
domestic economy within local communities. Gell's article suggests in fact
that the potentialities of commodity exchange, including personal consumption, for articulating the different kinds of persons one might be, were
recognized long before the advent and transformations of colonial capitalism. Thus, the tension between these two processes (of inalienability and
alienation) are neither entirely new, nor gender exclusive.

Nevertheless, not only has there been an exponential expansion in the
scale and pace of commoditization and a corresponding increase in the
feminization of labour, particularly in developing and newly industrializing
countries, but also a seemingly exponential increase in the concern (among
anthropologists as much as anyone else) with questions of inalienability and
cosmological authenticity (cf. Spencer 1990). It is this dual process and
experience of increasing alienation, on the one hand, and the resurgence of
the inalienable in the discourses of ethnicity and the nation, on the other,
that in Sulu has placed women at the nexus of the oppositions and
transformations of *adat* and *istyle*.

In summary, I have suggested that *adat* and *istyle* may represent several
things in relation to women and present-day formulations of femininity. As
a marker of things modern, fashionable and foreign, *istyle* is a foil for
creating and reinvigorating a sense of the cosmological superiority of local
Muslim customs and traditions, i.e. *adat*, part of the making and remaking
of ethnic and gendered identifications between people and things, such as
gold jewellery and traditional/native attire, which valorize women as
keepers of cultural purity and inalienable wealth. Moreover, to the extent
that the temporal and spiritual primacy of *adat* is reaffirmed through its
juxtaposition with *istyle*, it sets the stage for and makes possible the
translation of foreign *istyle* in terms of the aesthetic sensibilities and
structural forms of local *adat*. To put it otherwise, the contrast drawn
between *adat* and *istyle* is not about defining an insuperable boundary

between tradition and modernity, but an attempt to set the preconditions for and delimit the possibilities of what local culture, particularly as embodied by women, might be or become in relation to the modern.

The alternative, however, expressed in women's desire to work and travel abroad, is that *istyle* may be or become not just a foil for, or transformation of, *adat*, but rather a way of imagining and articulating an altogether different set of relations between people and things: *istyle* as objectification of freedom, a repudiation of collectively fixed or inalienable identities, in favour of the alien as a possibility space for making multiple identifications. This is not to say that *istyle* is the sole medium for expressions of freedom. On the contrary, even the seemingly most fixed objectifications of *adat*, such as gold jewellery, may be used by women to express the contrary ideals of personal freedom and individuality. In this respect, the careful debate over modern *istyle* weddings and the insistence on the reformulation of *istyle* in terms of *adat* may be seen less as an attempt to maintain the integrity of local culture in the face of an external threat, than it is an attempt to regulate and constrain the otherwise unspoken challenge and potentiality of formulations of femininity based around an ideal of freedom that are already latent within *adat*. Yet as I have argued in this chapter, it is precisely the continual regulation and valorization of the feminine as repository of cultural value and keeper of tradition that explains why women sometimes define themselves in terms of *istyle* and the world "abroad" rather than in terms of *adat* and the world "at home".

Notes

1. Women were traditionally made up for weddings and for the ritual celebration upon completion of Qur'anic reading instruction (*pagtammat*) with white powdered faces and stylized jet-black eyebrows similar to that in other parts of Indonesia.
2. The development of dual wedding celebrations is not unique to the Philippines. It is a part of urban traditions in Indonesia, and in ethnic communities in other parts of the world (e.g. Indians in Trinidad: D. Miller, personal communication).
3. I was not able to talk to the bride about how she felt about wearing a Western-style wedding dress during the ceremony itself and the couple left the following day to return to her parents' community.
4. Samal or Siyamal is a derogatory term having connotations of the uncultured and religiously ignorant used by the Tausug in reference to the Sama, people who speak Sinama and who, like the Tausug, also consider themselves to be Muslim.
5. Conversion to Islam is sometimes referred to as *balik Islam*, people, particularly Christian Filipinos, who are said to return to their "original" or "true" identity as Muslims.
6. This is a common feature in many ethnic–nationalist movements and

mobilizations, see for instance Shukrallah (1994) and Yeganeh (1993) on women and the objectification of cultural traditions in nationalist movements in Egypt and Iran respectively.

7. Out of all local clothing the *pis siyabbit* is, in fact, the most authentically "traditional" inasmuch as unlike women's clothing, the cloth is woven locally. Most of the traditional weaving centres for the *pis siyabbit* on the island of Jolo have all but disappeared (Szanton 1973). Ironically, the exception to this are Muslim weavers sponsored and supported by the Catholic Notre Dame de Jolo community development project, who not only sell the cloth as turbans/handkerchiefs, but also use the cloth to produce document folders, "bum bags" and backpacks for the tourist market.

8. Age and marital status are, to a certain extent, a factor in whether or not women choose to dress in "traditional" clothing, with older married women more likely than younger married and unmarried women to wear traditional clothing consistently, particularly if they are not themselves the celebrants or members of the celebrants' immediate family. However, at the major annual religious festivals such as Hari Raya women of all ages, with the possible exception of young girls, will wear traditional attire, while men will often still be wearing jeans and T-shirts.

9. Kiefer (1972b: 126) notes the difference in completion rates between men and women undertaking traditional Qur'anic reading instruction, but puts this down to the fact that young men are unable to put up with the discipline required of them.

10. Weiner (1992), I think, in her attempt to move attention away from exchange and reciprocity underemphasizes the point that it is only in and through circulation, through gifting, that objects obtain a social history, and become an objectification of ancestral identity and potency.

11. The data presented here are not precise inasmuch as they are not drawn from a random sampling and do not meet strict statistical criteria. The only other data available, however, come from the 1990 Census, which suggests there are just over 800 overseas from the province of Sulu, although it does not give a breakdown by sex. Jackson (1990: 78) reports between 0.7 and 5.2 per cent of families in Sulu are dependent on overseas remittances. If the figures I have are in any way indicative of general trends, then it appears that Sulu is (compared to other parts of the Philippines) unique in the number of women and comparative number of professionals working abroad, mainly in the Middle East. Arcinas (1986) notes that in 1983 75 per cent of workers in the Middle East were men, but in 1983 only 10.4 per cent were employed in professional occupations.

References

Anderson, B. 1972. The idea of power in Javanese culture. In *Culture and politics in Indonesia*, C. Holt (ed.), 1–70. Ithaca, NY: Cornell University Press.

Arcinas, F.R. 1986. The Philippines. In *Migration of Asian workers to the Arab world*, G. Gunatilleke (ed.). Tokyo: United Nations University.

Blanc-Szanton, C. 1990. Collision of cultures: rhetorical reformulations of gender in the lowland Visayas, Philippines. In *Power and difference: gender in Southeast Asia,* S. Errington and J. Atkinson (eds), 345–83. Stanford, CA: Stanford University Press.

Bruno, J. 1973. *The social world of the Tausug.* Manila: Centro Escolar University.

Catholic Institute for International Relations (CIIR) 1987. *The labour trade: Filipino migrant workers around the world.* London: CIIR.

Errington, S. 1989. *Meaning and power in a Southeast Asian realm.* Princeton, NJ: Princeton University Press.

Errington, S. 1990. Recasting sex, gender and power: theoretical introduction and regional overview. In *Power and difference: gender in island Southeast Asia,* S. Errington and J. Atkinson (eds), 1–57. Stanford, CA: Stanford University Press.

Fawzi el-Solh, C. & J. Mabro 1994. Introduction: Islam and Muslim women. In *Muslim women's choices: religious belief and social reality.* Oxford: Berg.

Gell, a. 1992. Inter-tribal commodity barter and reproductive gift-exchange in old Melanesia. In *Barter, exchange and value,* C. Humphrey & S. Hugh-Jones (eds). Cambridge: Cambridge University Press.

Jackson, R.T. 1990. The cheque's in the mail: the distribution of dependence on overseas sources of income in the Philippines. *Singapore Journal of Tropical Geography* II(2), 75–86.

Johnson, M. 1995a. Transgender men and homosexuality in the southern Philippines: ethnicity, political violence and the protocols of engendered sexuality. *South East Asia Research* 3: 46–66.

Johnson, M. 1995b. Negotiating style and mediating beauty: transvestite (gay/ Bantut) beauty contest in the southern Philippines. In *Beauty queens on the global stage: gender, contests and power,* C.B. Cohen, R. Wilk, B. Stoeltje (eds). London: Routledge.

Johnson, M. (1997) *Beauty and power: transgendering and cultural transformation in the southern Philippines.* Oxford: Berg.

Johnson, M. (n.d.) On golden remembrances: exchange transformations in the southern Philippines. Submitted to *Journal of Material Culture.*

Jolly, M. 1994. *Women of the place: Kastom, colonialism and gender in Vanuatu.* Camberwell: Harwood.

Keesing, R. & R. Tonkinson (eds) 1982. Reinventing traditional culture: the politics of Kastom in island Melanesia. *Mankind* 13(4) (special issue).

Kiefer, T. 1972. *The Tausug: violence and law in a Philippine Moslem society.* New York: Holt, Reinhart & Winston.

Lacar, L.Q. 1991. The emerging role of Muslim women. *Philippine Studies* 39(1), 3–22.

Markillie, P. 1996. Back on the road: a survey of the Philippines. *The Economist* 6 May, 1–22.

Miller, D. 1987. *Material culture and mass consumption.* Oxford: Basil Blackwell.

Miller, D. 1991. Absolute freedom in Trinidad. *Man* 26, 323–41.

Moore, E.R. 1981. *Women and warriors: defending Islam in the southern Philippines.* Ann Arbor, MI: University Microfilms International.

Ortner, S. 1981. Gender and sexuality in hierarchical societies: the case of Polynesia and some comparative implications. In *Sexual meanings: the cultural construction of gender and sexuality,* S. Ortner & H. Whitehead (eds), 359–409. Cambridge University Press.

237

Pemberton, J. 1992. *On the subject of "Java"*. Ithaca, NY: Cornell University Press.

Shukrallah, H. 1994. The impact of the Islamic movement in Egypt. *Feminist Review* 47: 15–22.

Siapno, J. 1994. Gender relations and Islamic resurgence in Mindanao, southern Philippines. In *Muslim women's choices: religious belief and social reality*, C. Fawzi el-Solh & J. Mabro (eds). Oxford: Berg.

Simmel, G. 1978 [1900]. *The philosophy of money*. London: Routledge.

Spencer, J. 1990. Writing within: anthropology, nationalism, and culture in Sri Lanka. *Current Anthropology* 31(3), 283–300.

Szanton, D. 1973. Art in Sulu: a survey. *Sulu Studies* 2, 3–69.

Thomas, N. 1991. *Entangled objects*. Cambridge, MA: Harvard University Press.

Warren, J.F. 1981. *The Sulu Zone 1768–1898*. Singapore University Press.

Weiner, A. 1976. *Women of value, men of renown: new perspectives in Trobriand exchange*. Austin: University of Texas Press.

Weiner, A. 1985. Inalienable wealth. *American Ethnologist* 12, 52–65.

Weiner, A. 1989. Why cloth? Wealth, gender and power in Oceania. In *Cloth and human experience*, A. Weiner & J. Schneider (eds), 33–72. Washington, DC: Smithsonian Institution Press.

Weiner, A. 1992. *Inalienable possessions: the paradox of keeping while giving*. Oxford: University of California Press.

Weiner, A. & J. Schneider (eds) 1989. *Cloth and human experience*. Washington, DC: Smithsonian Institution Press.

Wolters, O.W. 1982. *History, culture and region in Southeast Asian perspective*. Singapore: Institute of Southeast Asian Studies.

Yeganeh, N. 1993. Women, nationalism and Islam in contemporary political discourse in Iran. *Feminist Review* 44, 3–17.

Index